27 FOUR LEAF CLOVERS

Andrea Sissons

CONTENTS

INTRODUCTION

If you're expecting the words that follow to be the finely polished prose of a seasoned novelist, let me set the record straight: I have absolutely no idea what I'm doing writing a book. Yet, here it is in your hands-this collection of thoughts, experiences, and spiritual wanderings that somehow assembled itself into the pages of "27 Four Leaf Clovers." I'm crazy like that; I felt a compelling urge to write it, and so I did.

This book is not crafted by a skilled author trained in the artful dance of language and plot. Rather, it's penned by someone who's just taking life as it comes, doing their best to never miss an opportunity to do the right thing. It's just my story, the one I felt I was supposed to tell. If you've decided to pick it up and give it a chance, I hope it serves its purpose in your life in some small, perhaps unexpected way.

Writing this was an act of faith as much as it was an exercise in storytelling. Each word and each chapter were steps on a path I walked, often without a map, guided by something or Someone much larger than myself. I've stumbled through both the writing and the living of it, and if there's any wisdom here, it's that which we gain by simply continuing to move forward, trusting the path will appear beneath our feet.

Thank you for joining me on this journey. I hope that within these pages, you find laughter, tears, and maybe a little inspiration. Most of all, I hope you see the possibility of light and renewal, no matter the darkness you might face. Here's to finding our four-leaf clovers, wherever they may be.

CHAPTER 1
DEFINITELY NOT
THE BEGINNING

The alarm system, that electronic harbinger of doom, began its relentless serenade at dawn, pinging away with the enthusiasm of a salesman who knows he's already made the sale. "Battery low," it chirped, a metaphor so on the nose that Annie couldn't help but wince. Here was life, insisting on participation, one annoying ping at a time.

She reached for her AirPods, those tiny instruments of auditory escape, as a knight might reach for his sword, ready to do battle with the day's dragons—namely, silence, solitude, and the incessant demands of a household teetering on the edge of pastoral chaos. The small scabs inside her ears, a mark of her valiant efforts, barely registered anymore. After all, what's a little physical discomfort compared to the Herculean task of drowning out the relentless internal monologue that came with being Annie?

"Listen to God in the Silence of your heart and you will know His Perfect Plans for you," so the scripture went, Psalm 37:4, etched in the back of her mind like a forgotten grocery list. Annie knew it well, knew it like she knew the back of her own hand—wrinkles, veins, and all. Yet, the silence of her own heart was a room she'd rather not enter, thank you very much, because God's plans, while undoubtedly perfect, were also notoriously inscrutable and, more often than not, inconveniently timed.

Stepping into the backyard at the crack of dawn, Annie found herself unwittingly cast in the latest episode of what could be dubbed "Farmyard Follies," a daily dramedy where the goats were the main characters, and the set was an ever-evolving testament to Annie's eclectic life choices. The crisp air slapped her cheeks awake, a natural remedy against the impending caffeine dependency that loomed on the horizon.

Off to her left, the fire pit sat silent, its charred remnants not just a beacon of past revelries under a starlit canvas but a graveyard of memories where laughter once mingled with the crackle of flames and the pulsating beat from the speakers set the night alight.

Amid this country setting, a crane, momentarily mistaken for a feathered guest of honor, hastily reconsidered its visit as Gracie, ever the guardian of the realm, chased it off into the azure. A hare, too, made a cameo, darting toward safety, presumably critiquing the morning's script as overly dramatic.

The calm was shattered as the goats, upon sighting Annie, launched into a chorus of bleats that might have rivaled the decibels at a rock concert, albeit with significantly less musical talent. The deck, a veritable outdoor oasis equipped with furnishings that whispered of lazy summer evenings and quieter times, stood in stark contrast to the goat pen's chaotic charm.

This pen, a marvel of improvisational architecture, stood as a flagrant symbol of Annie's whimsical decision to play farmyard queen—a role she embraced with a mix of enthusiasm and what-the-hell-did-I-get-myself-into. The shelter, a Frankenstein-esque creation born from the carcass of a family pool, stood as a testament to her resourcefulness, if not her aesthetic sensibilities.

Looming over this comedic tableau was the larger narrative

of Annie's life: the small fruit trees bravely dotting the yard, striving towards life, juxtaposed against the stark figure of a dead tree near the deck, its half-removed carcass a somber reminder of tasks unfinished, of nature's relentless cycle of growth and decay.

Among this beautifully disjointed scene, Baby the chicken, perched regally upon Huck's back, surveyed her kingdom with the serene detachment of royalty. As Annie made her way towards the pen, bracing herself against the morning's serenade and the hopeful integrity of her makeshift barriers, she couldn't help but laugh at the absurdity of her life.

This daily ritual of chaos and care, framed by the backdrop of her half-wild, half-tamed domain, was a poignant reminder of the balancing act that was her existence. With every step, a silent prayer, hoping against hope that her jerry-rigged world would hold together for another day.

Each day promised change, a vague notion in the distance, like a storm seen from afar, its arrival certain but its impact unknown. And amidst this, her faith—a beacon, a guide, a sometimes-annoying reminder that there was, indeed, a plan. Not that she'd heard it over the pings, the barks, the bleats, and her playlist, which now included a song about someone leaving someone else, which, under the circumstances, seemed a bit on the nose.

In the orchestrated chaos that is Annie's morning ritual, one could find a semblance of structure, a desperate grasp at change—one cold shower, one biblical verse, and one strength training rep at a time. She delved into her Bible and a smattering of non-fiction books with the zeal of a scholar seeking the secrets of the universe, or at least the secrets to not feeling quite so adrift in her own life. Her cold showers, an exercise in self-flagellation disguised as mood enhancement and brain growth, were as much a part of her routine as her morning coffee. She'd seen a video discussing the wonders of the anterior mid cingulate cortex and thought, "Why not? Could be fun."

Then came the strength training, an hour or two of lifting weights as if she could physically hoist the weight of her existential questions off her shoulders with each rep. The 30-minute run that followed was less about fitness and more about outrunning her doubts, or at least trying to. But life, much like her children, demanded attention at the most inopportune moments. Questions about algebra, the sudden need for a Band-Aid, and the mystery of the disappearing left sock often punctuated her workouts, leaving her to start and stop her routine with the patience of a saint and the frustration of a woman on the edge of reason.

Between the squats and the Scripture, the protein shakes and the prayers, Annie worked tirelessly, a model of diligence in the face of stagnation. Yet, for all her efforts, the big picture remained as elusive as ever, a jigsaw puzzle with half the pieces missing. She wondered, not for the first time, what all this work amounted to. Was there a cumulative effect to these daily battles, a point at which everything clicked into place, or was she merely treading water in a sea of her own making?

The irony was not lost on her that in her quest for change, her days had become a series of well-worn paths, routines carved so deeply into the fabric of her life that they seemed to lead her in circles. And yet, in the silence that followed her exertions, when the last page of the morning's reading was turned and the sweat from her run had dried, she found a moment of peace in the trust that she was, indeed, moving forward. Maybe not with the grand strides she imagined, but with the small, determined steps of someone who believes that doing their best is all they can do, and that somehow, it would be enough to get her where she was supposed to be.

Annie's life, woven through with trials and tribulations, could easily be mistaken for a tapestry of misfortune, if not for the golden thread of her faith that turned it into something far more profound. Blessed with a steadfast belief in God's guiding hand, she navigated each twist and turn with a grace that belied the depth of the darkness she sometimes faced.

Her journey through love had been less a stroll through a park and more a trek across a battlefield, albeit one where the mines were hidden under flowers and the sniper shots came disguised as kisses. Married once to a man whose love was as tempestuous as his moods, she had weathered storms of passion and fury, finding herself often in the eye of the hurricane, praying for the strength to endure. The end of this saga came as abruptly as a curtain drop, leaving her and her daughters in a silence that was both a relief and a profound echo of loss.

The subsequent romance, if one could call a descent into neglect and violence romantic, further tested her resolve, leaving her with physical and emotional scars. Yet, Annie's mother, with the grim foresight of a Greek oracle, had warned her of the perils of future loves, suggesting that the path of romance might only lead her to harsher shores.

Despite the darkness, Annie's faith remained her beacon. She understood that life's challenges were not merely obstacles but lessons in disguise, opportunities for growth and understanding bestowed by a God who saw the bigger picture. This belief, that even in the darkest moments, there was a purpose and a lesson to be learned, shaped her approach to life.

Annie's faith taught her to focus on the moment, to do what was right in the here and now, and to trust that God would take care of the overarching narrative of her life. It was a faith not just in outcomes but in the process, a trust that the journey, with all its pitfalls and pinnacles, was as important as the destination.

Even when life seemed to spiral, when love brought more pain than joy, and the future seemed shrouded in uncertainty, Annie held onto the belief that hindsight would bring clarity, that one day, she might see her life through a lens closer to God's. A perspective where every heartbreak had its reason, every challenge its purpose, and every tear sowed the seeds for future joy.

This belief did not make her immune to doubt or fear; Annie was human, after all. But it did imbue her with a resilience that was nothing short of miraculous, a capacity to face life with a heart wide open, ready to embrace whatever came her way. It was this gift of faith, this trust in a divine plan, that carried her forward, a guiding light in the ever-unfolding story of her life.

Annie's existence, marked by the divine dance of faith and fate, was a testament to the power of belief, the strength found in surrender, and the profound peace that comes from trusting in a path laid out by hands far wiser than our own. Every moment of darkness was counterbalanced by the promise of dawn, every tear by the potential for laughter, and every ending by the hope of a new beginning.

In an afternoon that cascaded into evening with all the subtlety of a circus parade making its way through the quietest part of town, Annie found herself transformed from the maternal figurehead of morning routines into the illustrious chauffeur of adolescent pursuits. The transition was seamless, in the way that walking into a spider web is seamless—unexpected and with a lingering sense of having acquired unwanted baggage.

As the sun began its leisurely descent, painting the Oklahoma sky with strokes of orange and pink, Annie's vehicle became less a car and more a vessel navigating the choppy waters of extracurricular activities. Bella, her martial arts maestro, needed to be at tae kwon do, where she honed her skills in the ancient art of kicking and sarcasm. Eliana, the family's sunbeam, was off to dazzle the world of dance, her movements a blend of grace and unbridled enthusiasm that left audiences in awe and occasionally, due to her exuberant spins, in mild danger. Sophia, the burgeoning adult of the trio, had a schedule that was a mystery wrapped in an enigma, her comings and goings punctuated by the kind of confident exits usually reserved for stage actors.

In this whirlwind of activity, Annie's day stretched before her, each moment a countdown to the next drop-off, the next pickup, the next, "Mom, I forgot my [insert crucial item here]." It was a symphony of chaos, the kind only a family could orchestrate, with Annie as the reluctant conductor, her baton a set of car keys, her orchestra a trio of strong-willed daughters with schedules as complex as quantum physics theories.

Yet, amidst the hustle, a longing simmered within her—a yearning for the quiet that came with nightfall, when she could finally say goodnight to her charges, tucking away the day's adventures with a kiss and a whisper of "I love you." It was the promise of solace, a brief respite in the eye of the familial storm where her responsibilities eased, and she could bask in the glow of a day well spent, or at least survived.

As the clock ticked on, Annie reminded herself to savor these moments, to live in the present and embrace the madness with the grace of one who knew this circus wouldn't be in town forever. But as the shadows lengthened and her duties piled up like cars in a rush-hour jam, the fantasy of fast-forwarding through the chaos to that moment of peace became ever more tempting.

And yet, she soldiered on, her love for her daughters a beacon guiding her through the fray, her faith a shield against the slings and arrows of outrageous scheduling. Annie knew that this whirlwind of activity, this seemingly endless cycle of chauffeuring and caregiving, was not just a series of tasks to be endured but a mosaic of moments to be cherished. So, with a sigh and a smile, she navigated the transition from afternoon to evening, from chaos to quiet, ever yearning for the silence that followed the storm, when the world stood still, and she could, at last, catch her breath.

And as the night finally closed in, enveloping her world in a blanket of stars, Annie embraced the peace that came with completion, the sweet surrender to the night's embrace, where her duties were done, and she could simply be.

CHAPTER 2
NIGHTTIME

The last "goodnight" barely escaped the threshold of my mouth before I was practically sprinting down the hall, hurdling over a forgotten backpack and narrowly avoiding a faceplant into the living room couch. The silence of the house post-bedtime was supposed to be my reward, the pot of gold at the end of the rainbow, if the rainbow was made of laundry, dishes, and teenage drama.

But as the dust settled and the echoes of the day's chaos faded, I found myself not basking in the glow of solitude but pacing the cage of my own restlessness. It's funny how you spend all day yearning for a moment of peace, only to realize that peace feels a lot like being stood up on a date with yourself.

So, in the grand tradition of seeking comfort, I turned to my faithful companion: vodka and soda. Not just any drink, mind you, but the magical elixir that promised to erase the lines of worry etched into my forehead and replace them with a slightly unfocused gaze of contentment. "I deserve this," I told myself, pouring the first of what would be several rounds. "I've earned the right to unwind."

The irony, of course, is that while each sip was supposed to usher me into a state of blissful relaxation, what I got instead was the kind of buzz that makes you believe you're suddenly interesting and, more dangerously, that other people might find you interesting too.

It was around the second drink that my phone, that little rectangle of infinite possibility, started to wink at me from across the room. "Come hither," it seemed to say, a modern-day siren luring sailors to their doom. And like any good ship captain with a slightly tipsy sense of judgment, I heeded its call.

But the night, with all its silent hours, belonged to the version of me that wasn't just "Mom," but Annie—still a catch, at least in certain low-light conditions. It's a peculiar thing, to feel alone in a house full of people, to seek out strangers when you've just spent an entire day surrounded by the most familiar of faces.

This nightly ritual, part escapism, part genuine quest for connection, was my guilty pleasure. Not the kind you brag about, like a secret affinity for reality TV or an encyclopedic knowledge of European cheeses, but the kind that sits in your stomach, a reminder of the complexities of human desire and the lengths we'll go to fulfill it.

In the sober light of day, I'd undoubtedly question my choices, vow to stick to herbal tea, and delete my browsing history with the fervor of a spy covering their tracks. But tonight, in the warm embrace of my drink and the glow of my phone screen, I allowed myself the luxury of believing that somewhere out there, amid the digital ether, was an adventure waiting just for me.

There I was, opening a new dating app with the kind of optimism usually reserved for lottery ticket holders. "This time," I muttered, uploading my carefully selected photos, "it's going to be different." The photos were flattering, yes, but I'd wielded the filter with the precision of a Michelin-starred chef applying truffle oil—just enough to enhance, not overpower. "I'm not unphotogenic," I reassured myself, "I'm just... hard to capture." Like a ghost, if the ghost cared deeply about its cheekbones.

To be entirely honest, I've never quite managed to picture myself in my own mind. Body and face dysmorphia? Perhaps. People have always been quick to assure me of my beauty, but I've treated their compliments with the same skepticism I reserve for emails from exiled princes offering me vast fortunes.

However, as the evening wore on and my glass found itself inexplicably empty time and again, a marvelous transformation occurred. With each drink, my confidence bloomed like a flower in fast-forward, a time-lapse of self-assurance. "Is it possible to have beer goggles for yourself?" I wondered, chuckling at the thought. It seemed not only possible but probable, as the alcohol painted a rosier picture of my own attractiveness with each sip.

The drinks, like liquid courage, made it remarkably easy to not care—to post without hesitation. "Who needs reality," I thought, "when you've got Tito's?" I imagined my profile floating in the sea of digital courtship, a message in a bottle cast into the vast ocean of the internet. Maybe someone would find it, someone who could see past the filters, both literal and metaphorical, to the person I was still trying to picture clearly.

The irony of seeking validation from strangers while simultaneously doubting their sincerity wasn't lost on me. It was a peculiar kind of doublethink, a mental gymnastics routine I performed with the grace of a toddler in a tutu. Yet, there was a thrill to it, a sense of adventure in the act of putting oneself out there, of potentially discovering someone who could finally snap a photo that I didn't feel the need to edit.

So, as the night deepened and the line between confidence and delusion blurred, I found myself swiping, posting, and hoping with the reckless abandon of someone who had forgotten that tomorrow was a day that existed. In that moment, I was fearless, a digital age explorer charting unknown territories with a buzz and a smartphone.   With the dexterity of a seasoned tech user—or perhaps just someone who's had one too many— I set up my dating profile with the enthusiasm of a squirrel on its third espresso. "Cute," I thought, swiping right. "Cute," again, my thumb flicking across the screen with the precision of a maestro conducting an orchestra of potential suitors. As the vodka soda worked its magic, liberally diluting my usual skepticism, I found myself swiping on profiles that, in the harsh light of sobriety, I'd probably pass by without a second glance.

There's something about my optimism—it's like a superpower, albeit one that occasionally backfires, transforming glaring red flags into charming eccentricities. It's as if my eyes are equipped with a filter, much like the ones I debated using on my profile photos, designed to spotlight only the most redeeming of qualities and blur out the rest. "Who needs reality when you've got selective vision?" I mused, swiping away with abandon.

No sooner had my profile gone live than my inbox began to resemble a bustling marketplace, each message a pitch vying for my attention. "You're beautiful," they'd say, or something far less eloquent and exponentially more lewd, prompting a mix of laughter and a slight, unexpected flush of flattery. As insubstantial as I knew this whole endeavor to be, it was undeniably entertaining, a welcome distraction from the creeping loneliness of the evening.

Was it all somewhat empty? Sure. Meaningless, even? Probably. But amidst the solitude of my bedroom, phone aglow with the promise of human interaction, however superficial, I found a certain charm. Each message, each awkward attempt at connection, was like a lifeline thrown into the quiet of my night, pulling me into a sea of shared solitude, laughter, and the occasional cringe.

Navigating this digital sea, I couldn't help but chuckle at the absurdity of it all. Here I was, seeking some semblance of connection in perhaps the most disconnected manner imaginable, fishing for compliments and laughter in a virtual sea teeming with fish, some decidedly odder than others. And yet, there was a strange comfort in it—a reminder that even in the vast wilderness of the internet, there was room for genuine interaction, shared smiles, and maybe, just maybe, a spark of something real amidst the emojis and pickup lines.

This late-night foray into online dating, I realized, was less about finding "The One" and more about the thrill of the hunt, the joy of discovery, and the bittersweet cocktail of hope and skepticism with which I approached each swipe. It was a curious dance, one I performed with a mix of irony and hope, fully aware of the farce but secretly, foolishly, hoping for an encore that might just break the mold.

As the evening trudged on, stubbornly unfurling its hours like a red carpet leading directly to bedtime, I abandoned the solitary whisper of AirPods for the more encompassing embrace of a Bluetooth speaker. The music filled my bedroom, casting spells that momentarily lifted the weight of the world, until the vodka, ever the persuasive conspirator, suggested with a liquid whisper that it was time to bid adieu to the day.

It's amusing, really, how one can teeter between the edge of nocturnal abandon and the stringent discipline of self-care. Despite how freely the spirits flowed, my adherence to the nightly ritual of skincare and dental hygiene stood unwavering. Each application of cleanser, each pat of cream was a testament to a stubborn adherence to routine amidst chaos. And then, the retainer, my nightly nemesis since sixteen, snugly fitted as a reminder of past orthodontic victories and ongoing battles against the chaos of teeth shifting silently in the night.

Navigating this odd dichotomy of carelessness and care, of sinking into the depths of online flirtations while surfacing for the breath of self-preservation, I found a strange harmony. There's a curious grace in maintaining these islands of order in the swirling sea of my evenings, a grace that says, "I might dance with strangers in the digital dark, but I'll wake with moisturized skin and straight teeth."

With the precision of a well-rehearsed routine, I nestled the retainer into place, a nightly ritual that felt like closing the last page of an evening's adventure book. Each action, from the turn of the faucet to the final click of the retainer case, was a step toward reclaiming myself from the night's escapades.

And so, with my nightly rites completed, I approached the final act: surrendering to sleep. But here, in this sacred transition from wakefulness to dreams, I required a different kind of ritual. The lights were extinguished, the music silenced, leaving my room a sanctum of darkness and stillness. Yet, the world outside refused to be completely hushed—the chorus of tree frogs sang their night songs, and the distant rumble of a passing train whispered of journeys not taken, of paths that wound into the darkness beyond.

It was in this perfect balance of quiet and the soft, ambient symphony of the night that I found my peace. The darkness was a blanket, the silence a balm, save for nature's lullaby and the occasional reminder of the world moving without me. There, on the edge of consciousness, I drifted, buoyed by the serenade of frogs and the echo of distant travels, into the arms of sleep.

CHAPTER 3 LETS DO IT AGAIN

In an absurd repeat performance, the morning greeted Annie not with the gentle kiss of sunlight or the tender chirp of birds, but with the relentless, electronic ping of the security system—a sound now inextricably linked in her mind with the echoing ping of last night's vodka indulgences. The alcohol, once a river of forgetfulness and fleeting connections, had receded into a foggy delta in her brain, leaving behind the silt of guilt and a headache pounding out a rhythm of self-inflicted retribution.

With the solemnity of a penitent approaching the altar, Annie propped herself up and embraced the 32 ounces of salvation she had foreseen the need for, placing it on her nightstand the night before. The water, chugged in a display of morning devotion, was both a baptism and a purge, an attempt to wash away the sins of the night with the fervor of the newly converted.

Then, lying back down, she took a deep breath and began the countdown ritual she had adopted from some forgotten source, a digital-age incantation meant to propel her out of bed with the promise of a fresh start. "Five, four, three…" she intoned, reaching the final numbers with a mix of reluctance and resolve, "two, one." With that, she cast aside her covers like a chrysalis and planted her feet on the ground, a symbolic gesture of readiness to face the day's absurdities.

The temptation to dive back into the digital sea of messages and potential suitors from the night before tugged at her, an insidious siren call from her phone. Yet, recalling another piece of wisdom—"never pick up your phone first thing in the morning"—she resisted. Instead, she opted for the ritual of greeting the sun, an act less about vitamin D absorption and more about asserting some semblance of control over her day. She flung open the drapes and blinds, an act met with Gracie's stretch and a smile that might have been interpreted as canine optimism for breakfast's imminent arrival.

With the morning sun casting a hopeful glow on the remnants of last night's decisions, Annie moved, somewhat mechanically, towards the task of brewing coffee. It was a small act, but one laden with the promise of normalcy, a tether to the world of the living where headaches were temporary and guilt could be assuaged with action.

Thus began another day in the life of Annie, a woman caught in the cyclical farce of modern existence, where each morning's awakening was a reminder of the previous night's escapades, and the quest for redemption was as perennial as the setting and rising of the sun. And as the coffee machine gurgled to life, Annie braced herself for the day ahead, fortified by water, sunlight, and the ever-present, maddening pings of life's demands.

Clutching her coffee like the final shred of reason in an increasingly unreasonable world, Annie faced the dawn with a resolve usually reserved for those embarking on a quest of epic proportions. The morning conundrum of whether to wake the kids or luxuriate in the silence for just a moment longer presented a choice akin to deciding between sneaking a flask into a dance recital or enduring it sober: a no-win scenario. Sure, the appeal of quiet was intoxicating, but succumbing to it only promised a later descent into educational chaos and the kind of frantic day that no amount of planning could salvage.

Thirteen years into the homeschooling marathon, Annie sometimes wondered if she was less educator and more glutton for punishment. Each morning's awakening felt like rolling the dice on a board game where the rules changed daily. She summoned her daughters from their slumber with a blend of affection and the kind of efficiency that suggested she might, in another life, have been a military commander.

After serving breakfast with the swift precision of a line cook facing a rush, Annie dove into the dual role of mom and teacher, and, surprisingly, fitness fanatic. Indeed, amid the academic debates and cries of "Mom" that filled the air like a mantra, she carved out time for her sacred cold shower and a workout routine rigorous enough to make a Navy SEAL think twice. These moments of physical exertion weren't just about health; they were anchors in the tumultuous sea of her day, small assertions of control in a world that often felt like it was spiraling.

The day's journey through education was peppered with surreptitious glances at her phone, checking messages from potential suitors that promised adult conversation and the tantalizing possibility of romance. Each message opened was a brief escape, a reminder that beyond the confines of homeschooling and domesticity, a world of intrigue and adult interactions awaited.

As the day waned, marked by its victories and defeats, emotional outbursts, and the odd moment of genuine learning, Annie steered the ship with a mix of dark humor and dogged perseverance. Survival was the name of the game. If they could all end the day slightly more enlightened (or at least not noticeably dimmer) and in one piece, it was a victory.

CHAPTER 4 THE BATH IS THE BEST

If there's one thing I've always loved, it's water. Give me an ocean to gaze upon, a lake to dip my toes into, or even a puddle to splash around in, and I'm content. I've tried my hand at everything from swimming to surfing, always seeking that perfect communion with the waves, that moment when you're both part of the water and yet distinctly apart from it. But let's be honest, the grand aquatic adventures of my dreams often get traded in for something a bit more...domestic. A soak in the tub. It's not quite the wild surf of
Hawaii or the mysterious depths of the Mediterranean, but it's mine, and in those moments, I cherish it like a secret treasure.

The moment I sink into the bath each night, it's as if I've stepped into a witness protection program designed for overworked moms. Suddenly, I'm not the woman who can recite the multiplication table backward while making pancakes. No, I'm Annie: Unbound, Unbothered, and Unbelievably Relaxed. The woman who, for years, navigated the choppy waters of parenthood and homeschooling, now navigates a sea of bubbles, accompanied by the dulcet tones of my chosen playlist and the ambient croak of tree frogs who've got their life figured out more than I do.

With a strong cold drink clutched in one hand and my phone in the other, I marvel at how the universe's sense of humor has come full circle. Gone are the incessant calls of "Mom!" that punctuated my day. Now, in their place, the dings and vibrations of my phone provide a soundtrack of adult attention-seeking. It appears I've swapped one needy demographic for another. Each message, a beacon of grown-up whims and inquiries, fills the void left by my children's bedtime. It seems, after seventeen years of being the go-to for every crisis, from scraped knees to algebraic breakdowns, solitude feels like a shirt I've forgotten how to wear comfortably.

This nightly ritual, steeped in the irony of swapping one set of demanding voices for another, is my haven. Here, in the steamy embrace of my bath, I'm temporarily freed from the responsibilities that tether me to daylight reality. Yet, the comedy of it all isn't lost on me. In my quest for peace, I've simply traded one audience for another. The messages that light up my phone, seeking Annie the Confidante, the Flirt, the Friend, echo the daytime demands of Annie the Mom, the Teacher, the Everything.

And so, as I lay back, sipping my drink and surveying the latest volley of texts and notifications, I can't help but laugh. Maybe, after years of being perpetually needed, the idea of true solitude is as foreign to me as a quiet house. These evening messages, with their questions and musings, are just another form of care I dispense, albeit with a little more sarcasm and a lot less clothing.

As the night wears on and the water cools, I ponder the peculiar comfort I find in this new routine. Perhaps it's not the quiet I crave but the constant reminder that I'm part of a world that extends beyond my front door—a world that, like my bathwater, is sometimes warm, sometimes cooling, but always surrounding me, filled with voices that seek me out, not for band-aids or bedtime stories, but for the sheer pleasure of my company.

CHAPTER 5 FRIDAY

On this particular Friday morning, as if the universe had finally remembered Annie's address and decided to throw her a bone, she found herself facing a night of unprecedented freedom. Her daughters had plans that conveniently removed them from the equation, leaving Annie with something as rare as a quiet house: options.

Now, the dating app, that digital catalog of the hopeful and the hopeless, dangled before her two distinct types of men, each appealing to different aspects of her currently under-stimulated adult life.

Option 1 was Mr. Reasonably Attractive and Age-Appropriate. He proposed what sounded like an actual date—a novel concept in these days of "u up?" texts. Dinner, maybe drinks, or a movie. It was all so...normal. This man seemed like the embodiment of sensible shoes: reliable, comfortable, but unlikely to cause any heart palpitations of excitement. A safe bet for sure, promising an evening of pleasant conversation and maybe, just maybe, a goodnight peck on the cheek if the stars aligned.

Then there was Option 2: the Young and the Restless. These were the men from a category Annie assumed must be some sort of cosmic joke, tailored specifically for women like her. Young, absurdly attractive fellows who, for reasons beyond her comprehension, seemed to find older, single women irresistible. Opting for a night with one of them promised a foray into an adventure so spicy it could make a jalapeño blush. Sure, it might just be a fleeting escapade, but oh, what a glorious escapade it would be—fulfilling certain... let's call them, "carnal desires" that Annie, very much alive and kicking, could not deny existed.

The complexity of choosing between a potentially serene evening with a man who probably enjoyed discussing mutual funds, and a wild ride with a chap who likely used "lit" unironically, was a hilarious conundrum. It wasn't just about companionship; it was about acknowledging her own desires, ones that went beyond the intellectual and ventured, quite enthusiastically, into the physical.

The thought of making such a choice amidst the chaos of her daily life was laughable. Sure, she could ponder the pros and cons while folding laundry or debating the merits of the Pythagorean theorem with her youngest. Still, the reality was that this decision required the kind of attention only the quiet of an empty house could afford.

So, Annie put the decision on the back burner, letting it simmer throughout the day. The prospect of diving back into the dating pool, choosing between the comfort of sensible companionship or the thrill of a more carnal adventure, was a delightful distraction. It was a reminder that beneath the layers of "mom" and "teacher," there was a woman with desires that a night free from parental responsibilities could perhaps, finally, satisfy.

The promise of Friday night loomed large, filled with potential and a touch of comedic absurdity. After all, who said that a woman couldn't have her cake and, depending on the choice, eat it too? In Annie's world, where humor found its way into every nook and cranny, the dilemma of how to spend her rare night of freedom was not just about seeking companionship but embracing the entirety of her desires, carnal and otherwise. The night was young, and so, she felt, was she.

CHAPTER 6
IMPULSIVITY

As the last car retreats from the driveway, whisking my daughters away into the night, I'm left in a curious state of suspended animation, not entirely sure whether to suck in the world or blow out the cobwebs. But one thing's certain: whatever breath I take next, it ought to be deep. With the house suddenly as empty as a politician's promises, my head spins—a cocktail of possibility, relief, and a dash of nerves.

So, naturally, I migrate to where all great evenings begin: the kitchen, for a drink as cold and effervescent as my suddenly buoyant spirits. I unleash my trusty speaker from its daily sentence of playing only the most family-friendly tunes. Today, its Bluetooth connection heralds a liberation anthem, shuffling through my playlist of songs that certainly wouldn't make the cut for a PTA meeting.

As the drinks slide down with the ease of skaters on ice, and the music thumps its approval, I find myself in a one-woman karaoke session, belting out lyrics with the kind of abandon that usually precedes regrettable decisions. Scrolling through my phone, I wade into the digital sea of potential encounters when, ping, a message cuts through the noise.

There he is, a man with thick wavy brown hair and eyes so deep you could lose your morals in them. "Hey beautiful," he ventures. A coy "Hi 😊" is my parry, followed by the obligatory "What are you doing tonight?" To which I confess, "Nothing that I know of... my kids just headed off for the evening." He's been trying to catch my attention for days, a claim as plausible as me running a marathon. "Well, you have it now," I assure him, setting the stage for what comes next.

"Let's hangout tonight," he suggests, a proposition loaded with all the subtlety of a freight train. But, let's be honest, with those rugged looks, I'm not exactly in the mood for subtlety. "Sounds good to me," I reply, but not without a disclaimer: "Just so you know, I'm 6 foot 1." It's only fair to warn him; I've seen the surprise on too many faces, a mix of awe and a silent prayer they brought their best climbing gear.

"REALLY?!?! That's so hot!! And don't worry about it, I'm 6'2," comes his enthusiastic response. Not that height is a deal-breaker for me—I've grown accustomed to towering over most of the room—but I'd be lying if I said the thought of looking up for a change wasn't thrilling.

Three vodka sodas deep, I'm riding the high of unexpected freedom. "I've already had a few drinks, but my house is empty. Why don't you come over here?" I offer, the words flowing as freely as the liquor.

"Perfect," he agrees, and just like that, we're exchanging numbers—because, in a turn both comical and slightly terrifying, I've just invited a man over whose number I didn't even have.

Safety first, though. "Send me a video of you saying hi and my name, so I know this is really what you look like," I request, half expecting him to balk. Instead, he sends a clip that's equal parts cheesy and charming, confirming he's as easy on the eyes as his profile promised.

With my address now in the hands of a virtual stranger who, for all his physical appeal, might as well have been a catfish, I can't help but laugh. It's the kind of absurd scenario you'd expect in a rom-com, not your average Friday night. But here we are, and if nothing else, I'm about to find out whether life imitates art or if I've just made a hilariously bad decision. Either way, I'm ready for the adventure.

Under the gentle persuasion of vodka sodas, which, I must confess, have a way of smoothing over the edges of better judgment, I had a moment of clarity—a rare pearl in the ocean of my impulsive decision-making. It dawned on me, as these revelations often do, somewhere between the fourth chorus of an embarrassingly explicit pop song and rehearsing what might pass for seductive banter in the modern age, that Misty should probably be apprised of the unfolding scenario.

Misty, my guardian angel, endowed with the sacred power of GPS tracking and a penchant for true crime that could likely earn her a badge and a gun, was more than just a friend. She was my lifeline, the one person who, equipped with enough murder documentaries under her belt, would know exactly how to avenge my untimely demise—or at least, give the police a really solid lead.

Our friendship had weathered rumors of a romantic nature, which, while entirely unfounded, did little to deter the speculation. We were close, unnervingly so, the kind of close that prompted sideways glances and hushed whispers in less understanding circles. But ours was a platonic bond, forged in the fires of shared secrets and mutual eccentricities, a relationship so intertwined that others often mistook our closeness for something it wasn't.

The comparison to E.T. and Elliott might not flatter either of us in terms of physical resemblance, but emotionally, it was spot-on. Despite the five hundred miles that separated us, we seemed to possess an uncanny ability to sense when the other was in distress, a telepathic connection that had come in handy more times than I could count.

So, with the reckless abandon that only a middle-aged woman entertaining the advances of a significantly younger suitor could muster, I grabbed my phone and shot off a message to Misty, the contents of which boiled down to: "So, doing something potentially foolish tonight. There's a man. He's coming over. Yes, he's from the internet. No, I haven't lost my mind (jury's still out on that one). Anyway, thought you should know, just in case I end up as a cautionary tale on one of those shows you love."

Her response was swift, a mixture of incredulity, concern, and that unwavering support that had come to define our friendship. "Send me his pic, his name, and if you haven't already, make sure there's nothing too incriminating in your search history. Also, I'm setting my alarm for three-hour intervals. Text me. Or so help me, I will call the National Guard."

And just like that, with Misty's blessing (or what passed for it in our world of mayhem and misadventure), I felt a little less like I was freewheeling into the abyss and more like I was embarking on a questionable, yet closely monitored, adventure. The kind of adventure that, whether it ended in romance or in making a sworn enemy of my liver, would undoubtedly make for an interesting chapter in the book of Annie.

As the realization dawns that Josh (or whatever his real name might be) is en route, and I'm lounging in attire that screams "I've given up on life," panic sets in. The state of my attire —a charming ensemble of torn shorts and an ancient tee— suddenly seems catastrophically inadequate. And the toilet! When was the last time it saw a brush? The thought of him encountering any... let's delicately say "artifacts" of my less glamorous moments sends me into a frenzy.

With no time to spare, I transform into a whirlwind of frantic energy, propelled by the pulsating beat of my not-so-kid-friendly playlist. My Tito's and soda becomes my hydration station, akin to those water tables set up during marathons, though considerably less wholesome.

The shower becomes my makeshift sanctuary, the speaker and my drink accompanying me because, let's face it, there's no pausing the party, not even for basic hygiene. I tackle leg shaving with the fervor of an Olympic fencer, a feat of dexterity and speed that, by some miracle, leaves me nick-free.

Emerging from the bathroom, I embark on a beauty blitzkrieg: lotions, potions, and a desperate attempt to make my eyebrows visible to the human eye. A dab of cream blush here, a stroke of mascara there—because if I've learned anything, it's that my long lashes and blue eyes are my secret weapons, capable of elevating my appearance from "homebody in crisis" to "potentially has her life together."

In the midst of this chaos, my phone buzzes. Josh. "I'm about 20 minutes away, stopping by the store to grab some beer. Do you need anything?" My heart does a somersault, both thrilled and terrified by his impending arrival. "Nope, I'm all set here, just come on," I reply, my attempt at nonchalance belied by the fact that I'm still half-dressed, with one eye comically more mascara-ed than the other.

"OK, baby," he says, and I can't help but smile at the absurdity of it all. A glance in the mirror confirms that I'm as ready as I'll ever be—eyebrows on fleek, lashes for days, and an outfit that says "I tried, but not too hard." The house may not pass a white-glove test, but at least the toilet won't horrify him.

Now, all that's left is to wait. And waiting, especially when tinged with excitement and nerves, is excruciating. I've never been good at it; patience is not a virtue I possess. So I pace, sip my drink, and wonder if inviting a near-stranger into my home is my most brilliant idea or if it's the vodka talking. Either way, Josh is coming, and I'm about to find out. The night promises to be interesting, if nothing else, and as I take another glance around my imperfectly perfect chaos, I think, "Well, here goes nothing."

CHAPTER 7
HE'S HERE

The pressure inside me was like a shaken soda bottle, and with the house finally empty, it felt like someone was tentatively unscrewing the cap. Not off, but close, and my pent-up excitement and nerves were fizzing out like I was some human soda stream.

Sweat gathered in my armpits, betraying my cool demeanor in the most traitorous way possible. I found myself fanning my shirt like someone trying to send smoke signals in a hurricane. Then, the headlights cut through the night, and my heart did a little salsa dance. I'm not one for making grand entrances (or standing awkwardly at the door like I'm waiting for a surprise party in my honor), so I waited until I heard footsteps before flinging the door open with all the casual elegance I could muster.

His jaw dropped—a reaction that could have been part of his nightly routine, for all I knew. "You are gorgeous. Your pictures do not do you justice!" he exclaimed, and despite my inner skeptic doing a full eye-roll, I found myself grinning like a fool. "Thank you, you look great too," I responded, straddling the line between bashful and downright suspicious of his polished charm. Tall, dark, and dangerously handsome, he claimed to be 32, but something about him screamed "I just discovered what taxes are" in the best way.

He came bearing a case of beer like some kind of modern-day peace offering. I showed him to the fridge in my room, reserved for the essentials: beer and sparkling water. He slotted his contribution in with the ease of someone well-versed in the social dance of modern dating.

Then, in a move as casual as it was predictable, he suggested we take our drinks outside so he could vape. The great outdoors suddenly seemed infinitely more appealing, a space where the night could wrap around my jittery nerves like a comforting shawl. With the speaker now an integral part of our ensemble, we made our way to the backyard, under the expansive, star-lit sky. Arriving at the deck, I nonchalantly placed the speaker down and, in a move that felt as natural as breathing but likely looked as graceful as a giraffe on ice, hopped onto my favorite corner of the railing. This was my spot, my domain, where I'd spent countless nights contemplating the universe or just enjoying the silence.
There, perched like a queen on her throne if that throne was made of wood and potentially splintery, I let the waves of anticipation wash over me. It was a strange cocktail of excitement, dread, and the kind of suspense that usually precedes making decisions that are best described as "what was I thinking?"

But as we settled under the stars, with the cool night air acting as a much-needed reality check, I felt a flicker of something that might just be optimism. Or insanity. The jury was still out. Maybe this rendezvous would be the beginning of a hilarious misadventure, or perhaps just another story for the books. But one thing was for sure: under the watchful eyes of the cosmos, with vape clouds swirling around us, I was ready to find out.

The air around us had become so charged with sexual tension, it was practically visible, like some sort of erotic mist you might expect to find in a particularly risqué fairy tale. It had been an embarrassingly long time since I'd been in a situation that could lead to anything more than a polite hug or an awkward pat on the back. Not that I'd been keeping track— some numbers are better left uncalculated.

Deep down, in a place I don't often let myself visit, I knew where this night was headed the moment I learned the kids would be elsewhere. It's not that I'm prophetic; I just understand the basic principles of cause and effect, especially when it involves an empty house and the absence of my usual chorus of "Mom!"

Josh, with those soulful brown eyes and a physique that screamed "I occasionally rescue kittens from trees for fun," turned to me. "I'm dying to kiss you," he said, his voice carrying the weight of every romantic lead from every movie I couldn't admit to watching.

I've never been known to shy away from an adventure, particularly not one so...inviting. "Do it," I said, my voice steady, though inside, I was a cocktail of anticipation and something akin to giddy panic.

He didn't need to be told twice. Closing the distance between us with a step that had him right there, between my legs still perched on the railing, he wrapped his arms around me. The world seemed to tilt slightly, or maybe that was just me, losing my equilibrium in the most delightful way. His kiss obliterated any remaining thoughts of decorum or restraint I might have been clinging to, leaving in their wake a desire so potent it felt as though it might consume me whole.

And just like that, the outside world ceased to exist. There were no more worries about kids, no thoughts of tomorrow's responsibilities, just the two of us, wrapped up in a moment so intense it bordered on transcendental.

Eventually, he broke away, presumably in need of oxygen or perhaps just another hit from his vape. I, on the other hand, was left somewhat dazed, my heart racing like I'd just run a marathon in record time.

So there we were, under the vast expanse of the night sky, the silence between us now filled with the echo of what just happened and the promise of what was still to come. It was a pause, a momentary lull in the storm of passion that had just swept through us, and as he took another drag and a sip, I couldn't help but marvel at the curious turns life can take when you're least expecting it.

Josh, in a display of conversational agility that would make a late-night talk show host envious, navigated from flattering appraisals of my home and eclectic yard to more personal compliments with the finesse of a diplomat. Between sips of our respective libations, he lobbed questions about my life with the precision of a marksman, though his aim seemed less about getting to know me and more about finding his way back into my personal space.

And find his way back he did, with the stealth of a cat that's heard the can opener. Suddenly, he was there again, the gap between us disappearing as if by magic. This time, he did more than just invade my personal bubble; he lifted me right off the deck, an act that sent a thrill through me reminiscent of a teenager sneaking out for a midnight rendezvous. I've always felt more akin to a sturdy oak than a delicate daisy, but in his arms, I was suddenly reclassified in the botanical hierarchy— something rare and to be handled with care.

Being hoisted into the air like this was unexpected. It wasn't just the physical act that fanned the flames of my interest but the implicit understanding that he saw me as someone worth picking up. It was the kind of move that could fuel fantasies for months, a gesture so laden with implication it was practically a novella in itself.

Led by the hand, we retreated indoors, where my hallway of photographs became the next exhibit in our unfolding drama. I regaled him with the tales behind each image, our laughter creating a soundtrack to the makeshift tour. He played the part of the enthralled visitor to perfection, though I suspected his accolades were more about performance art than genuine interest. Yet, as we navigated the corridor of my life in snapshots, the path inevitably, perhaps strategically, led us back to my bedroom.

The sequel to our earlier drink session was swift, a blend of mixology and anticipation as I played bartender to his beer aficionado. What followed was a symphony of seduction that lasted into the wee hours, a marathon of romance that left me both exhilarated and utterly spent.

When the clock tolled for the end of our encounter, my declaration of needing sleep was met with understanding and a promise to call. His departure was a series of kisses, each one a signature, ensuring his memory lingered long after he'd left. The man was a maestro of the exit, leaving me in a state of satisfied disarray.

Locking the door behind him, I stumbled into a sea of blankets, my bed now a sanctuary of fluff and fond recollections. As sleep tugged at my consciousness, I couldn't help but reflect on the night's escapades with a mixture of amusement and awe. Life, it seemed, had decided to remind me of its capacity for surprise, delivering an evening of unexpected delight and leaving me to wonder, with a grin, what other adventures might lie just a text away.

CHAPTER 8
SATURDAY MORNING

When Annie's eyes flickered open that morning, the memories from the night before pounced on her like a particularly cheeky cat armed with memories instead of claws. The onslaught of these recollections zapped her awake faster than an espresso shot from a cannon, stirring a cocktail of emotions that had no business being in the same glass—part horror movie, part rom-com, and a sprinkle of existential drama for flavor.

Guilt gnawed at her with the enthusiasm of a beaver on a particularly juicy log. The handbook for Model Mothers probably had a whole chapter titled "Not Like This," but if last night was wrong, a part of her whispered rebelliously, she wasn't entirely sure she wanted to be right. The allure of the night's escapades was intoxicating, lighting a fire in her that she hadn't known she'd been carrying a match for.

Confronting these swirling emotions—or, heaven forbid, having a chat with the Big Guy upstairs about them—seemed as appealing as a root canal without anesthesia. After all, God already had the play-by-play; why bore Him with a re-run? Instead, Annie opted for the age-old tradition of internal evasion, shoving that nagging voice in her head into a closet and barricading the door with mental images of her to-do list.

Panic fluttered in her chest, not unlike a moth trapped in a lampshade, at the thought that she might have inadvertently lost her children to the universe simply by not thinking about them for a few hours. A rapid scan of her phone dispelled this melodrama—no messages from the girls. Breathing a sigh of relief, she fired off a "Good morning, girls. I love you" into the digital ether of their group chat, receiving prompt reassurances that all was indeed well in the realm of motherhood.

A perusal of last night's digital breadcrumbs showed she'd managed to signal to Misty, her ever-vigilant friend and potential future FBI agent, that she was still among the living, thereby averting a premature deployment of the national guard. And then, there it was—a message from Josh that sparkled with the promise of future misdemeanors: "Good morning, baby. I had so much fun last night. I definitely want to do that again. Text me when you wake up."

His message sent her already whirling thoughts into a tailspin, a mental state that stabilized momentarily with the knowledge that her daughters were safe and content. But then, with the dexterity of a juggler adding another ball to the act, the realization that she was still alone in the house nudged her mental equilibrium once more.

In a world where strategic ambiguity and the delicate dance of seduction are often championed as the keys to romantic victory, Annie took a decidedly different approach. The art of playing hard to get, a game as nuanced and perplexing as chess but with higher stakes and no clear rules, was one she had no patience for. It wasn't just that she didn't know the rules; it was more that she suspected the rules were made up on the spot by people who enjoyed confusing texts and interpretive guessing games more than actual conversation.

So, in typical Annie fashion, she eschewed the conventional wisdom of waiting an arbitrary number of days before contacting someone of interest. Instead, she grabbed her phone the morning after and fired off a "good morning" text with the eagerness of a kid on Christmas morning. If her enthusiasm was palpable, that was because it was genuine. Why pretend to be aloof and uninterested when her reality was anything but?

If he found her eagerness off-putting, then, in Annie's mind, he was clearly not the right audience for her brand of unbridled optimism and zest for life. Annie was many things—practical, occasionally reckless, and prone to hangovers that felt like a personal vendetta—but above all, she was unabashedly enthusiastic and perpetually hopeful.

The notion of dampening her excitement to play a role that felt as comfortable as a pair of shoes two sizes too small was absurd to her. If romance, or whatever this was shaping up to be, required her to be anything less than her most authentic self, then it was a game she had no interest in winning.

In this chaotic symphony of human connection, where everyone seemed to be following a script she'd never been given, Annie chose to write her own music. It was a tune that might occasionally be out of step with the prevailing rhythms of the dating world, but it was uniquely hers—a melody of honesty, excitement, and the kind of optimism that could light up a room.

So, with the send button pressed and her intentions broadcast into the void, Annie awaited a response, not with bated breath and calculated indifference, but with the open-hearted anticipation of someone who knew no other way to be. Annie was gingerly navigating the aftermath of her wild night, her phone erupted with a buzz that jolted her like an electric shock. The text? A curveball from her daughters, declaring their plans to stay away for another night, effectively extending Annie's solo reign over the household kingdom. This was the adult equivalent of finding an extra fry at the bottom of the fast-food bag—a delightful surprise, albeit one that left her feeling slightly greasy with guilt and exhilaration.

The news landed with the subtlety of a marching band crashing through her hangover haze. Suddenly, the prospect of another 24 hours of freedom unfurled before her, waving its arms frantically to get her attention. Here she was again, standing on the edge of a diving board over the pool of potential debauchery, still dripping from her last plunge.

 Annie, embodying a mix of pragmatism and daredevilry as if she were auditioning for a role in the world's most paradoxical ballet, catapulted from her bed with the urgency of a cat on a hot tin roof. The hangover that greeted her was not so much a gentle reminder of the previous night's festivities as it was a full-blown brass band rehearsal in her skull, each throb a cymbal crash echoing in the caverns of her brain.

With the steadfast resolve of a soldier marching into battle, she launched into her morning routine.

CHAPTER 9 MOWING

With the echoes of last night's festivities still humming in the background of my consciousness, I launch into my morning routine with a vigor that's part defiance, part necessity. The workout acts as a sort of exorcism for the lingering spirits of my hangover, while my aggressive hydration strategy feels like I'm trying to drown the beast from within. The only specter that refuses to be banished is the hangxiety, a familiar yet unwelcome companion in the aftermath of any revelry.

Outside, the sun is putting on a show, dialing up the thermostat to a scorching 95 degrees. It's the kind of day that sings a siren song to souls like mine, who thrive under the relentless caress of summer rays. My relationship with the sun, however, is a tale as old as time, marked by love, betrayal, and a somewhat masochistic loyalty. My frequent pilgrimages to the dermatologist's office—where parts of me are regularly frozen, zapped, or sliced off in the name of health—serve as testament to our tumultuous affair.

Yet, each layer of sunscreen I apply feels like armor, a protective ritual that allows me to dance with the sun without getting burned... too badly. I've become a warrior of SPF, my skin a canvas for layers of protective potions, each application a defiance against the UV onslaught.

But today, amidst this backdrop of self-care and solar flirtation, my heart beats for a different kind of escapade. The task of mowing the lawn, a chore for some, is my sanctuary. There's something about the roar of the mower, the smell of freshly cut grass, and the rhythm of back-and-forth motion that transports me to a place of zen-like peace. It's my meditation, my escape from the complexities of life. The zero-turn mower, a vestige of a bygone era with my late husband, stands ready in the garage, a steel steed awaiting its rider.

With my earpods delivering the soundtrack to my sundrenched escapade, I charge into the garage, fueling up the mower with the same enthusiasm one might reserve for a cherished ritual. It occurs to me that the mower and I are not so different—we both run on fuel, though mine is admittedly more spirited. A concoction of vodka and soda awaits in a knockoff Yeti, a nod to the notion that hydration can come in many forms.

After anointing myself in a veritable suit of sunscreen armor, turning my skin a shade paler than a ghost at a snowstorm, I don my battle gear: a bikini under a long-sleeved sun shirt, an apparent contradiction that makes perfect sense to a sun-chaser like me, topped with sunglasses designed to repel not just UV rays but the gaze of mortals.
Drink in hand, I emerge onto the deck, where my chariot awaits.

The act of mowing transforms under my command from a mere chore into an act of pure joy. Each swath of grass conquered under my mower's blades is a victory, a harmonious blend of man, machine, and nature.

Today, the lawn is not just a patch of grass to be trimmed but a realm to be mastered, a kingdom where I reign supreme atop my roaring mount. The beverage in the cup holder, an innovation of pure genius, is my loyal companion in this endeavor, a reminder that even the most mundane of tasks can be elevated to an occasion with the right attitude—and the right drink.

As I navigate the lush expanse of my backyard, the world falls away, leaving only the simplicity of the task at hand. The zero-turn mower feels like an extension of my own body, its levers responding to my every impulse, gliding, turning, and speeding through the yard with a grace that belies its power. It's in these moments, under the commanding sun and with the symphony of nature buzzing around me, that I find a rare peace. Mowing isn't just a task; it's my personal ballet, a dance of steel and grass where I am both conductor and performer, orchestrating a masterpiece of lines and turns that sing of freedom and the simple, pure joy of being alive.

An hour into my duel with the great green sea beneath me, piloting my trusty zero-turn mower like a seasoned captain, my slightly vodka-imbued buzz was as steadfast as my course. Then, out of the serene blue, my phone decided to perform its best impression of an air raid siren. "Incoming call from Josh T," it proclaimed, his surname an enigma, reduced to a mere initial that stood for "Tinder" or perhaps "Temporary?".

I brought my verdant voyage to an abrupt halt, the mower coughing into silence, and answered with a "Hi" that I hoped sounded more 'cool summer breeze' and less 'I've been waiting by the phone like a teenager from the '90s.'

"Hey babe, what are you up to?" slid Josh's voice through the line, smoother than a politician at a fundraising gala.

"Just out here doing donuts on the mower, halfway through taming the wilds of my backyard. And you?" I replied, aiming for breezy but likely hitting somewhere in the realm of 'caffeine-addled songbird.'

Seeing an opportunity to weave a web of reconnection, I launched my bait. "I found your vape you left here last night," I said, my tone casual yet laden with the subtext of 'come hither and claim thy forgotten treasure.'

"Oh, I've been looking for that. I'll have to swing by soon," he responded, the words heavy
with the implication of a deliberate ploy to ensure a return visit.

"Yes, you should," I agreed, the corner of my mouth twitching into a knowing smile.

Then, as if on cue, Josh veered off-script into territory that was all too familiar to me. Declarations of possession, of wanting me to be "his and only his," gushed forth—a whirlwind of attachment that, by all rational accounts, should have sent me sprinting for the hills. Yet, here's the kicker: having previously been entangled with men who considered "controlling" and "possessive" as endearing personality traits, Josh's rapid-fire commitment spiel didn't scare me. It felt like slipping into a warm bath of nostalgia—comforting, familiar, and oddly reassuring.

The pragmatic part of my brain, the part that's supposed to learn from past mistakes, began frantically waving red flags, signaling a retreat. But then there was my indefatigable optimism, transforming those red flags into rose petals strewn along the path to potential love. "Perhaps this is it," it whispered seductively. "Why wouldn't it be? You, my dear, are a catch—even mid-mow."

"So, let's give it a whirl," I found myself saying, embarking on this new adventure with the
kind of gusto usually reserved for final scenes in rom-coms.

He lavished me with all the right words, sweet nothings that filled the airwaves before he bid adieu to return to the salt mines of his employment. And just like that, the call was over, leaving me in the silence of my half-mowed lawn, contemplating the pact I'd just made.

There I was, adrift in the suburban savannah, making life decisions aboard a piece of lawn equipment, fueled by vodka and a reckless disregard for my own dating history. This new chapter with Josh T., a man whose last name remained as much a mystery as his intentions, felt like the opening scene of a dark comedy—one where I was both the unwitting protagonist and the punchline.

As I resumed my mowing, the absurdity of the situation didn't escape me. Here I was, navigating the familiar waters of possessive affection with the same zeal with which I attacked my unruly lawn—because, apparently, I'm a woman who finds strange comfort in the known quantities of clinginess and

control. It's a peculiar place to find oneself,
sure, but if life's taught me anything, it's that sometimes, you
just have to roll with the punches... or in this case, mow with
them.

After conquering the lawnscape with a determination fueled
by vodka and defiance, I was a sight to behold: a mix of
sweat, grass clippings, and the kind of buzz you can only get
from combining vigorous physical activity with alcohol. The
weedeater and I had danced a ballet of destruction, leaving me
victorious but visibly worn—like a gladiator who'd mistakenly
wandered into a garden party.

Driving the mower and its companion back to their respective
homes in the garage felt like the final act of an opera, grandiose
and slightly tragic, especially considering my inebriated state.
The sun, ever the merciless overseer, had done its work,
draining me of any reserves I might have had left. By the
time I stumbled into the shower, I was ready to wash off the
battle scars of my yard work—each splash of water sluicing
away layers of dirt and fatigue, revealing the somewhat lesser-
known species of Annie: the Clean and Slightly Less Rebellious.

Emerging from my aquatic cocoon, I felt transformed, albeit
into a version of myself that was significantly more tired
and drunk than the one that had embarked on this suburban
odyssey. It was then, in this state of post-shower bliss and tipsy
reflection, that I remembered the promise I'd made to Josh.
With a sigh that carried the weight of a thousand unsolicited
"Hey, you up?" messages, I took out my phone and began the
digital purge.

Deleting my dating accounts felt like cutting off limbs, albeit
ones I didn't particularly need or want. Each confirmation
button I pressed released me from the chains of digital
courtship—a world where being polite often meant getting
trapped in a vortex of mind-numbing small talk with people
whose most interesting trait was their uncanny ability to look
nothing like their profile pictures.
As for the apps themselves, banishing them from my phone

was akin to cleaning out a closet filled with clothes I hadn't worn in years but kept "just in case." For a people pleaser like me, navigating the tightrope of being kind without leading someone on was a nerve-wracking circus act. "One lunatic at a time," I muttered to myself. After all, if I was going to juggle craziness, I might as well do it with someone who had already proven their ability to send me to the moon and back, albeit in a handbasket.

Josh, my designated lunatic, at least had the decency to be easy on the eyes and knew just how to light up my neurotransmitters with his particular brand of charm. "At least he's a cute lunatic," I conceded, a smile playing on my lips as I contemplated our fledgling whatever-it-was.

With my phone now as sanitized as my freshly showered self, I guzzled down water like a fish preparing for a desert crossing, popped in my retainer with the enthusiasm of a child putting on braces for the first time, and collapsed into bed. By 9 p.m., I was out cold, a blissful end to a day that had seen me reborn as a warrior, a gardener, and a woman on the cusp of something resembling a relationship. In the silent embrace of sleep, I was free from the noise of the world, the hum of the mower, and the ping of incoming messages. For a few precious hours, I was just Annie, serene and utterly content in my vodka-induced, lawn-trimmed, Josh-accepting bubble.

CHAPTER 10 SUNDAY

Sunday morning rolled around with all the subtlety of a brass band in a library, and there was Annie, blinking into the semi-darkness of her bedroom at the ungodly hour of 7 a.m. Her body felt like it had been through a cocktail shaker—part alcohol, part sunstroke, and part impromptu facial by Mother Nature herself, courtesy of being blasted in the face by the dirt and grass debris of yesterday's lawn mowing escapades.

Sleep, that capricious entity, had once again played its cruel game, luring her into a sense of security before abandoning her at the first hint of dawn. Alcohol, that treacherous friend, promised the sweet embrace of oblivion but delivered a sleep so shallow it wouldn't drown a gnat.

In another life, Sunday mornings were for church, a ritual performed with the kind of regularity that would make a Swiss watch envious. But that was before her world tilted on its axis with her husband's passing. Afterward, Annie did try to find solace in the pews, hoping to stitch together the fabric of her fractured spirit with hymns and prayers. But it turned out God had a penchant for interior design—specifically, for rearranging the furniture of her soul with all the finesse of a reality TV makeover show.

It seemed that every service was an exercise in divine excavation, as if God himself was determined to guide her through the shadowy recesses of her heart. But Annie, ever the reluctant spelunker, responded in the way any sane person confronted with their own labyrinthine psyche would: she ran for the hills, or more accurately, hid under the bed like a frightened kitten at the first rumble of thunder.

The prospect of publicly disintegrating into a sobbing mess, her grief laid bare for the congregation to see, held as much allure as a swim through shark-infested waters with a cut on her leg.

Thus, she began spinning excuses with the creativity of a master storyteller, constructing a complex narrative of avoidance aimed solely at convincing the toughest critic she knew: herself. Weeks of absence turned into months, and months into years, until the thought of returning to church was akin to considering a leisurely swim across the English Channel—wearing cement shoes.

Now, the very idea of walking back into that church felt like stepping onto a stage mid-performance, only to realize you've forgotten both your lines and your pants. Perhaps God had been ready to shepherd her through the valley of the shadow of death, but Annie, in her infinite wisdom, decided she'd much rather take the scenic route, thank you very much. The church, with its open doors and open arms, remained in her periphery, a monument to what might have been had she been brave enough to face her demons head-on. Instead, she chose the path of most resistance: outright denial, seasoned with a healthy dose of humor and the occasional vodka-infused lawn mowing session. After all, if you're going to navigate the wilderness of the soul, you might as well do it with a freshly manicured lawn.

Annie launched into her daily routine, a sequence as familiar to her as the back of her hand, yet performed with the precision of a ritual dance. It was the same old song and dance of any other day—cold shower to reading to exercise— a triptych of normalcy that both anchored and occasionally weighed her down.

As she moved through the motions, the weight of impending responsibilities began to press upon her. Her children's return was on the horizon, bringing with it the end of her brief interlude of solitude and the resurgence of her maternal duties. With their arrival would come the familiar cacophony of laughter, bickering, and the endless barrage of needs and wants that characterized her days.

In this cyclical existence, where the extraordinary often lay hidden within the folds of the mundane, Annie prepared herself for the transition. The constancy of her morning habits offered a semblance of stability, a quiet before the storm of activity and demands that her children's presence would unleash.

Annie was midway through her daily rigmarole, the kind of routine that had become as predictable as a sitcom rerun, when her phone did a little jig across the table. It was Josh. "When can I see you again?" the message pulsed on the screen, a digital heartbeat echoing through the quiet of her morning.

Instantly, Annie's heart did a somersault, catapulting her back to that electrifying moment on the deck—kisses that made time stand still, being lifted as if she weighed no more than a feather, an intoxicating cocktail of emotions swirling within her. And she couldn't help but break into a grin, the kind that spreads slowly until it takes over your whole face. "How about next weekend?" she typed back, her fingers dancing over the screen with an eagerness she hadn't felt in ages.

"Let's do it," he replied, and then came a barrage of compliments so grandiose, they teetered on the edge of lunacy. Each message from Josh was like a sprinkle of fairy dust on the drab canvas of her daily existence, injecting a shot of hope into the mundanity she'd been wading through. It was like suddenly finding a secret passage in a familiar room, leading to possibilities untold.

Annie reveled in this delightful detour from the monochrome of her life, feeling a surge of optimism that maybe, just maybe, change—or at the very least, some assistance in her quest for excitement—was just around the corner. Yet, deep down, where the whispers of realism dwelled, she knew she was likely engaging in a masterclass of self-deception. But in that moment, with Josh's effusive words lighting up her phone screen, Annie allowed herself the luxury of the fantasy, choosing to bask in the glow of potential happiness, however fleeting it might be.

CHAPTER 11 A LITTLE SPARK

Annie's week unfolded in its usual parade of predictability, each day a carbon copy of the last, with one significant alteration in the pattern: her thoughts increasingly meandered to her phone, to Josh, and the tantalizing possibility of what might be. Throughout the week, her phone became a beacon of hope, intermittently lighting up with messages that nourished her ever-hungry romantic optimism. Josh, it seemed, had become a master chef of communication, serving up just the right blend of compliments and hope, seasoned with a tantalizing hint of distance. Like a fish on a hook, Annie found herself caught in the delicate balance of anticipation and uncertainty, never quite sure when the next message or call would reel her in further. Each notification set her heart racing, a Pavlovian response to the digital breadcrumbs Josh scattered with what felt like strategic scarcity. His messages were like the sun on a cloudy day—brief glimpses of warmth and light, all too quickly obscured by the reality of waiting for the next break in the clouds.

Josh, it appeared, had cracked the code on how to keep Annie in a state of hopeful suspense. With every message, he painted strokes of joy and validation on the canvas of her day, yet always left the painting unfinished, ensuring she remained eager for the next brushstroke. This delicate dance of connection and withdrawal left Annie in a constant state of longing, her optimism fueled by his words, her desire for more stoked by his calculated distance.

Somehow, Josh had distilled the essence of hope and yearning into a potent concoction, serving it up in measured doses that kept Annie coming back for more. In this choreographed ballet of interaction, he was both choreographer and lead dancer, guiding Annie through a routine that was equal parts exhilarating and maddening. And Annie, for her part, followed his lead, her steps driven by the twin engines of hope and longing, always waiting for the music to swell, for the dance to reach its crescendo.

Annie's mind was like a vintage radio, occasionally picking up the sage, if somewhat static-laden, broadcasts from Grandpa in the great beyond. His favorite hit single, "Never set your eyes on ANY man completely, they will always let you down, they are after all only men, instead keep your eyes on Jesus," had a way of playing on loop whenever she found herself knee-deep in man-related muddles. It was as if Grandpa was DJing from heaven, dedicating his celestial playlist to guiding her love life.

Grandparents' love is its own genre of affection, distinct from the parental brand—it's like comparing classic rock to top 40; both have their merits, but only one comes with the wisdom of the ages. Annie had hit the familial jackpot with her maternal grandparents, who were to parenting what The Beatles were to music: undeniably the best. Losing her paternal grandparents early was like missing out on a couple of great albums, but her mom's parents played their greatest hits well into Annie's adulthood, with her grandmother only recently taking her final bow.

Their love was the kind that didn't need constant airplay to be felt; it was always there, a golden oldie hit that you never doubted. If anyone's advice could cut through the static of life, it was theirs. Their guidance had been a guiding light, a love song that never got old.

Yet, here she was, tuning into Josh FM, letting the smooth

jazz of his compliments and the rock anthem of his attention drown out Grandpa's wise old tracks. His texts were like catchy pop songs: instantly gratifying but potentially fleeting, the kind that stick in your head but might not stand the test of time.

As the countdown to Friday night commenced, Annie was catapulted into a frenzy of preparation, her anticipation bubbling over. The mission? To transform her home from a vibrant testament to family life into a pristine exhibit, flawless enough to pass the scrutinizing gaze of a man who, in Annie's mind, might very well judge her soul by the cleanliness of her baseboards.

Armed with an arsenal of cleaning supplies that would put a professional janitor to shame, Annie embarked on her domestic crusade with the intensity of a reality TV makeover show host. The challenges were formidable. Gracie, her lovable but mud-adoring dog, seemed to have a sixth sense for the worst possible timing, making aquatic escapades in the pond before attempting stealthy, mud-laden incursions back indoors.

Bella, in a moment of what can only be described as explosive creativity, decided the living room was the ideal venue for a hoverboard-meets-smoke-bomb performance art piece. The aftermath? A carpet adorned with a permanent, screaming testament to the folly of youth and pyrotechnics.

Then there was Eliana, the household's resident slime scientist, whose concoctions managed to defy both gravity and any known cleaning solution, leaving a gleeful trail of goo across every surface within reach. Her experiments, while undoubtedly pushing the boundaries of slimology, added layers of complexity to Annie's quest for cleanliness.

And Sophie's bathroom—oh, that no-man's-land of teenage

chaos and questionable hygiene choices—was promptly quarantined. Annie made a mental note: under no circumstances should Josh venture into that biohazard zone. Better to pretend that part of the house didn't exist than to risk the horrors within escaping.

Thus, Annie's week unfurled with the drama and intensity of an epic tale of valor against the forces of clutter and chaos. Each swipe of the rag, every pass of the vacuum, was a defiant act against the entropy that her family so effortlessly generated. In this grand narrative of cleanliness, Annie was the plucky protagonist, wielding her mop like a knight brandishes a sword, charging headlong into the fray with the hope that come Friday night, love—or at least the illusion of domestic perfection—would prevail.

CHAPTER 12
FRIDAY IS HERE

It's Friday evening, and the moment I've been circling on my calendar with a mix of dread and anticipation is finally here. The kids, bless their hearts, have just zoomed off down the driveway, leaving me in a peculiar state of solo anticipation. Josh, with his unique blend of being emotionally distant yet somehow possessively needy, has left me floating in a limbo of uncertainty about his arrival time. But here I am, practically vibrating with excitement for our evening together.

So, I fire off a text into the void, "Hey, the kids are gone. What time do you think you will be over?" His reply comes sauntering back, dripping with a casualness that somehow manages to out-casual everything else he's said all week: "Oh, it's still hot out there. I'm gonna wait a lil while and then I'll head that way."

Now, under normal circumstances, I possess the patience of a toddler on a sugar high at a birthday party—essentially, none whatsoever.

The thought of being left to marinate in my own anticipation, not even knowing the duration of the wait, sends my frustration levels skyrocketing. I've been on tenterhooks all week, buoyed by the thought of this night. Wasn't he the least bit eager to see me too?

Attempting to decipher Josh's thought process is like trying to read War and Peace through a kaleidoscope: disorienting, slightly nauseating, and ultimately futile. Diving into that rabbit hole might just shatter the cozy bubble of denial I've been snuggled up in, forcing me to confront the stark reality that Josh might just be as disingenuous as a politician's promise.

But, rather than unleashing the full spectrum of my impatience and risking coming off as a few sandwiches short of a picnic, I decide to play it cool. "OK, sounds good. Just let me know when you head this way," I type, my fingers betraying none of the inner turmoil churning inside me.

"Sure thing, babe," comes his reply, a response so devoid of urgency it might as well have been a postcard sent by snail mail.

So there I am, left to stew in my own concoction of excitement and irritation, a cocktail that's becoming all too familiar. Yet, as the minutes tick by, I can't help but cling to the hope that, despite the waiting game, the night ahead might still unfold into something magical—or at the very least, marginally less chaotic than my usual Friday fare.

As the minutes morphed into hours and the sun relinquished its hold on the sky, my companions were my trusty Bluetooth speaker and the steady presence of my usual drink. The alcohol, a consummate magician, began to dissolve the mental filters I'd painstakingly maintained, leaving me in a state of impatient vulnerability. "Hey, are you still coming?" I texted again after a seemingly interminable wait, my patience worn thinner than the plot of a daytime soap opera.

But this time, something odd happened. The bubble that carried my text into the ether wasn't its usual confident blue but a hesitant green. "Huh, that's odd," I mused, concocting scenarios that ranged from technical glitches to sudden cross-country relocations. Shrugging it off, I returned to my drink and the endless scroll of my phone, hoping for distraction.

Thirty minutes ticked by—thirty long, Josh-less minutes—and still no response. With a sense of foreboding, I fired off a simple, poignant "?", watching as it too embarked on its journey tinted with the green of uncertainty.

The silence that followed was deafening, a void where the anticipation of the evening had once thrummed with possibility. Here I was, stood up by technology and man alike, my evening's plans dissolving like sugar in my steadily emptying glass. The realization dawned, bitter and unwelcome, that perhaps the only company I'd be keeping tonight was my own, serenaded by the ghosts of texts unsent and the soft crooning of my playlist.

At this juncture, any sane individual might have gracefully bowed out, perhaps with a dignified tear or a spoon deep in a pint of 'Forget Him' fudge ripple. But not me, Annie. The thought of surrendering to the silence and nursing the wound of rejection was about as appealing as singing karaoke sober —unthinkable. The disappointment was one thing; the sheer volume of hope I'd piled onto this evening made the void left by his absence feel like a chasm.

Cue the spectral wisdom of Gramps, floating through my thoughts with the gentle chiding of a man who'd seen it all, "Never set your eyes on ANY man completely, they will always let you down, they are after all only men, instead keep your eyes on Jesus." "Yeah, Gramps, I know, you're right,you're right I know" I sighed into the emptiness, acknowledging the advice I'd been too stubborn to heed.

Misty, the bearer of inconvenient truths, had once branded me 'Marie', a nod to that character from "When Harry Met Sally" who, despite better knowledge and advice to the contrary, always veered towards romantic disaster. And here I was, proving her point, ignoring both Misty's ground-level guidance and Grandpa's posthumous proverbs, walking headlong into emotional quicksand.

CHAPTER 13
MISTAKES WILL
BE MADE

Having navigated through two relationships that were more about control than companionship, my social circle had shrunk to resemble something more akin to a social dot. Misty, my beacon in the fog of life's more questionable decisions, was unfortunately 500 miles too far to play cavalry this evening. Then there was Annie, my namesake and dear friend, dubbed A1 to my A2 by the family I'd gained through our bond. Her sudden departure from this world a year ago left a void that still echoed with the sharp pangs of loss, as vivid and painful as the moment I received that life-altering call.

It's funny, in a tragic sort of way, how a single week of hopeful flirtation followed by a ghosting can dredge up a sea of losses that I'd carefully navigated around for the past five years. The list was heartbreakingly extensive: my husband, my brother-in-law who'd been a fixture since I was fourteen, A1, my rock of a grandmother, and Kingsley, the dog who had been my first baby, my four-legged shadow of 16 years, whose loyalty knew no bounds. Each loss was a story, a chapter of my life that ended too abruptly, leaving me to soldier on, often feeling more alone than not.

And now, here I was, reeling from the absence of a man who'd barely had a week to etch his initials on the surface of my life. Yet, his silence managed to stir the sediment of grief I'd worked so hard to keep settled, bringing it swirling up until it threatened to spill over. Perhaps, if I had taken a moment to truly reflect on the turmoil within, or even dared to lay it all before God, I might have found a way to begin healing these festering wounds. But tonight wasn't the night for introspection or divine consultations. Tonight, I had a bonfire that demanded to be lit, a house too clean for its own good, and an emptiness that begged to be filled, even if just superficially.

In a moment of inspired desperation, I thought of Jarrod, an old friend of my late husband's who had made it his unspoken mission to drop by and check on me and the girls from time to time. Perhaps he'd be up for a night of drinks, music, and pyrotechnic therapy. After all, if I couldn't have the company I'd yearned for all week, I could at least salvage the evening with someone who knew the value of a good bonfire and, hopefully, the art of conversation that strayed from the realm of the painfully superficial.

So, with a mixture of defiance and determination, I fired off a message to Jarrod: "Bonfire tonight. Music, drinks, and the therapeutic burning of things. You in?" Because if there's one thing I've learned, it's that when life hands you a ghost, you make ghost s'mores—or something like that.

Jarrod, ever the antithesis to Josh's digital ghosting act, shot back a message faster than I could refresh my inbox: "I'll be there in 10 min." His promptness was like a gust of fresh air in the stale atmosphere of anticipation and disappointment that had been my evening thus far. With a drink firmly in one hand and my trusty Bluetooth speaker in the other, I ventured outside to confront my next adversary: the bonfire.

Now, igniting a fire, for me, is less of a chore and more of an event—a primeval dance between woman and the elements. And tonight's performance was set to be particularly enthralling, given the wood's recent baptism by rainfall. But I've never been one to shy away from a challenge, especially not when armed with a secret weapon: diesel fuel. Some might call it cheating; I prefer to think of it as leveling the playing field.

As I poured the diesel with the care of a sommelier decanting a vintage wine, I couldn't help but feel a twinge of excitement. The anticipation of the first spark, the gradual catch and spread of the flame—it was all a prelude to the evening's main event, a ritual that promised warmth, light, and, with any luck, a decent distraction from the evening's earlier debacle.

With a flick of the lighter, the fire roared to life, a testament to my pyrotechnic prowess and perhaps a slightly concerning indication of my enjoyment of controlled danger. The flames danced, casting flickering shadows that seemed to beckon Jarrod to hurry up and join the party. Tonight, the bonfire wasn't just a source of heat or a beacon for camaraderie; it was a symbol of defiance, a fiery middle finger to the ghosters of the world and a reminder that, sometimes, all you need to salvage a night is a bit of fire, a good friend, and enough diesel fuel to make a dragon jealous.

Jarrod's arrival was heralded by the crunch of gravel under the tires of his trusty old red truck, a vehicle that had seen more life than most reality TV stars. There I was, stationed at the bonfire's helm, wielding a long stick like some kind of suburban witch performing a ritual.

The night air was filed with the serenade of tree frogs, their croaking a backdrop to our impromptu gathering. "Hey there, Jarrod, would you like a Tito's and soda?" I called out, trying to sound hospitable and not at all like I was desperately grateful for the company.

"Sure," he replied, his voice muffled slightly by the large joint he'd just brought to life. Jarrod, it seemed, was a man who embraced the concept of pre-gaming with a fervor I could only admire from a distance. The sweet, pungent aroma of marijuana wafted towards me as he offered, "Wanna hit?"

Now, pot and I have a complicated history. There were days, now shrouded in the haze of youthful exuberance (and, well, actual haze), when I'd partake without a second thought. But these days, my relationship with it was more akin to nodding acquaintances than close friends. Experience had taught me that marijuana had a way of turning me into a bundle of nerves or a desert-thirsty pilgrim on a quest for more alcohol —a quest I was already well on my way to completing, sans additional encouragement.

So, with a polite shake of my head, I declined Jarrod's offer, choosing instead to nurse my drink and bask in the glow of the fire we were gathered around. The flames crackled and leaped, as if celebrating our resistance to solitude and societal expectations of mature adult behavior. Jarrod's presence, joint in hand and a Tito's and soda soon to join it, was a reminder that sometimes, companionship comes in the most unexpected and pleasantly unconventional forms.

Sitting around the bonfire, with Jarrod contributing his own personal smoke cloud to the ambiance, we decided to take a trip down memory lane. It was less of a leisurely stroll and more of a rollercoaster ride through the absurd and the hilarious. Now, let me clarify something: My feelings for Jarrod have always been strictly in the friend zone. Think of him as a comfortable, well-worn shoe—not exactly what you'd choose for a night out, but perfect for when you just need to feel grounded.

Among the treasure trove of memories we unearthed that night was the tale of Bella, my intrepid middle child, and her encounter with One-Eyed Willie. Not to be confused with any seafaring scallywag, this Willie was the pond's reigning amphibian overlord, a bullfrog so majestic he might as well have had his own lily pad throne. One fateful night, under A1's headlamp-lit supervision, my girls embarked on a frog-hunting expedition. I returned home to a scene straight out of a Spielberg movie—four beams of light dancing across the water, converging on Bella as she triumphantly hoisted Willie into the air like a trophy. This frog was so enormous, I half expected him to start croaking the national anthem.

It's funny, in a world that seems determined to outdo itself with each passing day's absurdity, how some memories, like catching a two-foot-long frog on a warm summer night, remain golden. As we laughed and swapped stories, the night sky above us ablaze with stars, I couldn't help but feel grateful for old friends, middle daughters with a penchant for amphibian wrangling, and the reassuring permanence of the friend zone.

With our glasses betraying the thirsty truth of an evening well spent, Jarrod, ever the resourceful guest (or perhaps just too accustomed to the peculiarities of my kitchen), took it upon himself to play bartender. As he vanished into the house, the void he left was quickly filled by the kind of silence that, when combined with a bloodstream generously infused with alcohol, becomes a breeding ground for emotions I'd been diligently ignoring.

Josh had become somewhat of a taboo topic, a chapter of my recent history that I preferred to keep closed, especially around Jarrod. The thought of even mentioning him felt like admitting to a crime I wasn't entirely sure I hadn't committed. So there I sat, alone with the fire and the frogs, watching the private screening of my life's latest tragicomedy unfold behind my eyes. This particular feature film, however, was far from entertaining. When Jarrod returned, drink in hand, he found me not so much in the moment as lost in the cinema of my mind, where the current showing was a stark reminder of my apparent expertise in the art of being left behind. My face, usually an open book, must have been broadcasting the grim plot of my internal monologue in high definition.

"Um, does your face right now have anything to do with all the Natty Daddy's in your fridge?" he asked, his tone walking that fine line between concern and the kind of teasing familiarity that comes from years of friendship. Jarrod knew me well enough to understand that Natty Daddy—the kind of beer chosen by people who consider taste an optional beer quality—was not my usual drink of choice. It was his way of lightening the mood, of asking what was wrong without making me feel cornered.

In that moment, his question felt less like an inquiry about my questionable beverage selection and more like a gentle nudge back to reality, a reminder that, despite the somber movie playing in my head, I wasn't as alone as I felt. With a single, lighthearted question, Jarrod managed to pull me back from the edge of my own introspection, reminding me that sometimes, the best way to deal with life's less-than-stellar script is to find the humor in it, even if that humor comes in the form of inexplicably finding yourself with a fridge stocked full of Natty Daddy.

In an alternate universe where good decisions are the norm and self-control isn't just a myth peddled by self-help gurus, calling it a night after extinguishing the bonfire and partaking in a modest amount of adult beverages would've been the sensible finale to our evening. However, Jarrod and I, citizens of a reality far removed from such rational conduct, opted instead to keep the party going. The night was ours, and we were determined to wring every last drop of enjoyment from it, consequences be damned.

As the music continued to spill into the darkness, creating

a soundtrack for our increasingly blurry escapade, I found myself lounging with the kind of abandon that only comes from having indulged in one too many drinks. My feet, seeking a throne of their own, had claimed an empty chair between Jarrod and me as their domain. Then, in a move as unexpected as finding a vegetarian option at a barbecue festival, Jarrod reached across the void, seizing one of my feet and commencing an impromptu massage.

"WTF is happening?" The thought barely had time to race through my foggy brain before the shock of the situation was eclipsed by the sheer oddity of it all. Yet, beneath the layers of inebriation and bewilderment, I found the sensation of his hands working away at my feet not entirely unpleasant. As he looked at me, something in his gaze shifted, stirring a cocktail of emotions within me—unease mingled with curiosity, all swimming in a sea of surprisingly competent foot massage.

And then, as if the night hadn't already taken enough unexpected turns, boundaries were blurred, lines were crossed, and we kissed. It was a moment as confusing as it was fleeting, a culmination of too much alcohol, too much nostalgia, and perhaps too little thought for the repercussions.

Realizing the precarious ledge upon which we now teetered, I declared my need to retreat to the sanctity of my bed, my mind a whirlwind of confusion, exhaustion, and a lingering sense of disquiet from the day's rollercoaster of emotions. Jarrod, ever the gentleman in the oddest of times, made his departure, his truck's departure rumble serving as a punctuation mark to the evening's bewildering sentence.

Stumbling inside, I was left to navigate the labyrinth of my own thoughts, the evening's events a bizarre tapestry woven from the threads of companionship, spontaneity, and an unexpected foot massage.

CHAPTER 14 THE ICK

Saturday dawned with the kind of hangover that felt less like a consequence and more like a cosmic punishment for the emotional gymnastics of the preceding week. Annie's mind was a merry-go-round of confusion, spinning from one disorienting thought to the next, all while nursing the physical aftermath of a vodka spree. She embarked on a mental excavation of the previous evening, starting with the perplexing case of the disappearing man.

Josh, who had been all but tethered to her phone with interest and intrigue, had vanished into thin air as suddenly as if he'd been a figment of her imagination. Had she said something, done something, to prompt his ghosting? Or, as a nagging voice in her head suggested, had he found a shinier toy to play with? The thought struck a chord, a painful twang that resonated with a truth she'd been dodging all week: the fear of being no more significant than a quarter machine trinket, momentarily amusing but ultimately disposable.

If she dared to peel back the layers of her feelings about Josh's abrupt exit, she might confront the unsettling realization that the real issue wasn't his apparent disregard for her; it was her own belief in her unworthiness. In her heart, a part of her felt undeserving of anything more substantial, anything more lasting—hell, she'd started to believe she hadn't even been good enough for Josh.

But, as was her custom when emotional depths beckoned, Annie slammed that door shut with all the finality of a vault.

Delving into those waters was a risk she wasn't ready to take. Instead, she redirected her focus to another equally unnerving chapter of her Friday night saga: Jarrod.

The involuntary journey of Annie's stomach contents, prompted by the recollection of a kiss with Jarrod, resembled an ill-fated roller coaster ride, one that she, with the determination of a cat avoiding a bath, managed to reverse. The aftermath? A buffet of guilt seasoned with a pinch of horror. Had she, in a moment of vodka-induced vulnerability, sent Jarrod the wrong smoke signals?

The mission now was akin to navigating a tightrope while juggling flaming swords: How to gently inform Jarrod that their brief foray into romance was less a path to be pursued and more a detour never to be taken again, all without causing an emotional uproar? Yet, as Annie dissected the evening's events, a rebellion stirred within her. Cast adrift on the tumultuous seas of rejection, had Jarrod not, in fact, commandeered her moment of weakness? This was not entirely her circus, nor her monkeys.

Still, a solution was required, one preferably devoid of soap opera-worthy drama. Secretly, Annie harbored hope that Jarrod would opt for the convenient route of collective amnesia, allowing this kiss to fade into the mist of 'oops, let's pretend that never happened,' alongside other well-intentioned but ultimately regrettable life choices, like bangs or thinking one could 'just stop at one' chip.

The sudden vibration of Annie's phone catapulted her into a dual realm of speculation. First, the fluttering hope that Josh, the Houdini of modern romance, had decided to grace her inbox with his presence. This possibility sent her heart into a frenetic tap dance, even as another part of her recoiled in self-reproach, berating her for the lingering attachment to a man who had mastered the art of disappearance.

Then there was the second possibility: Jarrod, signaling round two of what could only be described as the World's Most Awkward Foot Massage Championship, might be looking for a rematch. The mere thought was enough to stir a cocktail of emotions, blending a shot of regret with a twist of "What on earth was I thinking?"

Hovering in this limbo, Annie was swamped by 'the ick'—that all-encompassing feeling of dread that creeps up like a B-movie monster, half ridiculous, half terrifying. The phone, once her lifeline to social interaction and potential romance, now felt like a grenade with the pin pulled, each vibration a countdown to emotional chaos.

With a sense of trepidation that would've been comical if it weren't so painfully real, she reached for the device as if it were a snake ready to strike.

As Annie's gaze fell upon the illuminated screen, the name "Jarrod" flashed up like a neon sign in the dim light of dawn, heralding a message that sent her internal world into a tailspin. "Hey there, I was wondering if maybe I could take you out to breakfast this morning?" The words, seemingly innocuous to the untrained eye, ignited a chorus of internal alarms, causing an almost physical reaction as if someone had suggested ketchup on a well-cooked steak—a profound, guttural, internal scream of "nooooooooooooooooooooooooo."

There it was, the feared box flung wide open, its contents sprawling messily before her. This wasn't just any box; it was Pandora's, teeming with potential awkwardness, misunderstandings, and the need for explanations she had no interest in crafting.

"Not today," thought Annie, her brain staging a mutiny at the thought of navigating the treacherous waters of a post-misstep breakfast with Jarrod. So, with the nimble fingers of a seasoned diplomat crafting a treaty, she quickly composed her escape clause. "Sorry, can't today, kids will be home and I have some things I need to get done." The message, a masterpiece of evasion, was sent off, carrying with it her hopes of a graceful exit from the situation.

Annie exhaled a sigh of relief, a weight lifted off her shoulders with the press of a send button. In her mind, this tactful dodge might just be the life raft she needed. Perhaps Jarrod would read between the lines, see the polite rebuff for what it was, and she could maintain their friendship without venturing into the murky waters of "what if" and "what was that." In a world that often demanded confrontation, Annie opted for the path of least resistance: aloofness and unavailability.

With the morning's potential for awkward encounters skillfully dodged like a pro dodgeball player, Annie reverted to her tried-and-true trinity of survival tactics: reading material that made her feel slightly smarter than she probably was, cold showers that were less about invigoration and more about shock therapy, and exercise routines that suggested she was preparing for a marathon she'd never run.

Motherhood had been her Everest, a peak she had climbed with the determination of a Sherpa. The birth of her first daughter had hit her with the force of a revelation, imbuing her life with a sense of purpose so profound it was like discovering a new color. But as her daughters grew, asserting their independence with the subtlety of teenagers declaring war on curfews, Annie found herself on the cusp of redundancy. The realization that her full-time gig of 'World's Most Needed Person' was being downsized left her oscillating between pride in her daughters' strides toward autonomy and the dread of her own impending obsolescence.

"Is this the end?" Annie pondered, her workout now feeling

like she was physically trying to outrun her existential crisis. The notion that her tenure as CEO of Mom, Inc. was drawing to a close, without a clear succession plan, plunged her into a state of limbo. Sure, the thought of freedom was as tantalizing as a forbidden midnight snack, but the reality felt more like opening the fridge to find nothing but expired milk and wilted lettuce. She longed for the next chapter, yet feared it might be titled "Annie and the Great Expanse of Nothingness."

There she was, a seasoned matron of motherhood, simultaneously yearning for liberation and dreading the vacuum it promised. The closing of one life chapter loomed like the final episode of a beloved TV show, leaving her to wonder, "What now?" The future, once a horizon brimming with promise, now felt like stepping into a room where someone had forgotten to pay the electricity bill—exciting in theory, but in practice, just dark and slightly terrifying.

As she wrapped up her routine, Annie couldn't shake the feeling that while she was ready to embrace the next act of her life, the script was still being written. And as any seasoned sitcom viewer knows, when one door closes, you're either left standing in the hallway or, in Annie's case, doing squats in it, hoping the next door opens somewhere less metaphorically daunting.

CHAPTER 15 SOME KIND OF LUCK

For the past fortnight, Annie has been ducking and weaving through her social life with the grace of a seasoned boxer, evading Jarrod's attempts to reconnect like they're poorly aimed jabs. Meanwhile, Josh has achieved the status of a ghost, haunting her with his silence, an impressive feat considering his corporeal form was hardly present even when he was supposedly around. The dating apps, those digital catalogs of hope and despair, have been exiled from her phone, though a few brave souls managed to parachute into her messages and social media before she slammed the door shut.

Among these intrepid adventurers is Jack. He's not going to be setting any hearts on fire with his looks anytime soon, but he's got something—probably found in the intersection of a solid career and not being a total disaster. At the wise old age of 55, Jack's life seems like a well-oiled machine, if his texts are anything to go by. He brings Annie the rare gift of laughter, a treasure in the arid desert of online banter. Yet, Jack is the embodiment of "Where in the World is Carmen Sandiego?" Always on the move, his presence in Annie's life is more theoretical than practical, save for the daily texts and calls that somehow find their way through his globe-trotting schedule.

They've penciled in a rendezvous upon his return, marking it with the cautious optimism usually reserved for groundhog sightings and weather forecasts. But today, as the hour approaches for her offspring to scatter to the winds, Annie finds herself ankle-deep in a necessary pastime of shoveling goat excrement. AirPods jammed into her ears, she channels her inner diva, belting out tunes with the reckless abandon of someone performing at Madison Square Garden, her audience —a group of utterly unimpressed goats—munching away, oblivious to her concert.

In this sublime moment, surrounded by the smells and sounds of the farm, Annie is a picture of pure, undiluted joy. The complexities of her love life, with its ghosts and globetrotters, fade into the background, upstaged by the simple act of scooping poop and serenading livestock. Here, in the goat pen, Annie finds an odd sense of peace, a reminder that happiness can be found in the most unexpected of activities. The goats, for their part, offer no critique of her performance, their silence a testament to either their appreciation or their complete indifference. Either way, Annie is too caught up in her impromptu performance to care, embracing the absurdity and beauty of the moment in equal measure.

Just as Annie had nestled comfortably into the embrace of farmyard bliss, shoveling goat contributions with the glee of a child in a sandbox, the cosmos, in its infinite jest, lobbed a glittering curveball her way. The buzz of her phone cut through the air, a beacon of unforeseen possibilities. "Angel T" materialized on her screen, the "T" not so much a surname as a breadcrumb trail leading back to Tinder, the digital jungle where they had first crossed paths.

Ah, Angel. The man whose profile photo had the kind of pearly white grin that could sell ice to Eskimos or convince skeptics of the merits of flossing. Tall, dark, and sculpted from the dreams of those who penned romance novels, his message jolted Annie from her muck-raking reverie. "Hi Annie, I was wondering if you would let me take you out tonight for dinner and drinks?" Straight to the point, his invitation was as refreshing as a cold drink on a scorching day, a stark contrast to the nebulous "let's hang out" that usually hinted at less culinary-focused encounters.

In this unexpected moment, Annie's world, previously measured in goat pen square footage, expanded to include the tantalizing prospect of real human interaction. With her adrenaline pumping louder than her playlist, she faced a choice: continue her solo symphony of farm chores or dive headfirst into the potential whirlwind of an evening with a man who, for all intents and purposes, was a living, breathing novela protagonist.

Without so much as a second thought—a testament to her undying allegiance to the gods of spontaneity and thrill-seeking—Annie's fingers danced across her phone's keypad. "Sure that sounds great!" she fired back, her heart racing with the kind of reckless abandon usually reserved for action movie heroes or people who eat sushi from gas stations.

This was Annie in her element, a seeker of adventure and new horizons, even if those horizons occasionally included awkward first dates or men who existed primarily in the realm of digital flirtation. As she confirmed her plans with Angel, a man she knew little about beyond his dental hygiene and geographic origin, she couldn't help but marvel at her own impulsivity. With a mix of giddy anticipation and the faintest whisper of "what am I doing?" echoing in her mind, Annie prepared to step into the evening's unknown adventures. The path of adventure had called, and Annie, ever the enthusiast for life's unexpected twists, had answered with a resounding yes.

CHAPTER 16
PUTTING LIPSTICK
ON A PIG

As Angel, with the commanding air of a military strategist planning a covert operation, had nonchalantly set our rendezvous at a sushi spot in downtown Tulsa for the oh-so-specific time of 6:30 PM, I was awash in admiration. Here was a man who orchestrated dinner plans with the precision of a Swiss watch, a refreshing change from the usual wishy-washy, "I dunno, what do you wanna do?" brigade.

Here I stood, the driveway just emptied of children, inspecting my current fashion statement: a blend of mud—or so I fervently hoped—and nature's own palette smeared across my person. The time was 4:30 PM, which left me exactly one hour and a half to metamorphose from a woman who looked like she'd wrestled a pig in a bog to someone fit for public viewing at a "nice" restaurant. This was not just any date; this was a date that screamed for elegance, sophistication, and most crucially, clean clothes.

A quick inventory revealed more horrors: my legs harbored a fuzz thick enough to be declared a new habitat for endangered species, my fingernails housed enough soil to start a small garden, and my toenails lamented a pedicure that had seen better days, possibly in a previous geological epoch. Panic wasn't just knocking; it had barged in, sat down, and made itself at home.

But the real kicker, the cherry on top of this disaster sundae, hit me as my stomach gave a treacherous gurgle. Lunch. Two gargantuan bowls of beans consumed with the gusto of a woman unaware of her impending doom. As the age-old jingle unhelpfully played in my head—"beans, beans, the magical fruit..."—I could practically hear the ticking time bomb within me. In a night destined for potential romance, had I unwittingly laid the groundwork for my own digestive downfall?

Hyperventilating now, with visions of being remembered as "that woman who cleared the restaurant," I knew there was only one course of action. CALL MISTY. The woman was less a friend and more a crisis management team in human form, having guided me through fashion emergencies, hair disasters, and now, it seemed, beans-induced panic.

Fumbling for my phone, I dialed her number, each ring a lifeline thrown to a woman drowning in her own tragicomic predicament. "Misty," I whispered to the dial tone, "you're my only hope." Against the backdrop of an impending beanpocalypse and the daunting challenge of scrubbing up for a high-stakes date, Misty's wisdom was the beacon I sought in the storm of pre-date jitters.

Misty picks up, and instantly, her voice is like a tranquilizer dart shot from the phone, hitting me square in the chaos of my pre-date meltdown. We jump onto FaceTime, and she guides me through the wreckage of my wardrobe like a search-and-rescue team navigating a disaster zone. Together, we unearth a black dress that says, "I'm trying, but not too hard," and a pair of nice black flip-flops that scream, "My feet are a pedicure-free zone, and I've made peace with that." She orders me to strip my toenails of their chipped, ancient polish—evidence of a spa day long past—and, above all, to take a chill pill.

For the next hour and fifteen minutes, I'm a whirlwind of activity, moving through my preparations with the grace of a chicken sans head. Misty, through the screen, is the eye of my hurricane, her calming presence and timely advice steering me clear of total implosion. She's less a friend now and more a drill sergeant for the emotionally unstable, barking orders that somehow bring me to a state of semi-readiness.

As the clock ticks down, the frazzled nerves, the remnants of my bean-induced panic, and the lingering doubt about my wardrobe choices coalesce into a singular focus: the urgent need for that drink. The mad dash to transform from farmyard chic to dinner date decent has left me teetering on the edge of sanity. I glance in the mirror, taking in the sight of myself— dressed, polished (sort of), and holding together by a thread of hope.

"Okay, Misty," I say, a hint of desperation in my voice that I hope sounds more like optimism, "I'm as ready as I'll ever be." The reflection staring back at me is a woman on a mission, albeit one who's not entirely sure what that mission entails beyond surviving dinner without a beans-related catastrophe. I take a deep breath, square my shoulders, and with a final glance at my trusty flip-flops, I step out the door, ready to face whatever the evening has in store. After all, in the grand adventure of life, a little chaos is just par for the course.

CHAPTER 17 FIRE

There I was, navigating the urban jungle of downtown Tulsa in search of that elusive beast: a parking spot. As fate would have it, the skies chose that exact moment to open up, as if to add a little atmospheric drama to my evening. Rain, the bane of well-planned hair and makeup, began its descent. Spotting a space at precisely 6:29 PM—a minute to spare, a minor miracle —I executed a maneuver worthy of a stunt driver and claimed it as my own. "Well, I guess it's a sprint in flip-flops through the drizzle for me," I thought, rationalizing that this impromptu dash would serve as a convenient excuse for any appearance shortfalls upon arrival.

As I prepared to brave the elements, my phone erupted into life —it was Angel, also circling the parking labyrinth. We agreed to rendezvous inside, a plan that seemed simple enough. I bolted from the car, my flip-flops slapping against the wet pavement with a rhythm that echoed my racing heart, and made a beeline for the shelter of the restaurant.

Damp but determined, I took refuge at a table, my breath catching up as I scanned the room for Angel. Moments later, he materialized at the entrance, his entrance marked by the kind of radiant smile that could easily be weaponized for charm offensives. Spotting me, he approached, and with a voice dripping in a thick Latin accent, he declared, "Oh my God, you are so beautiful! Are you hungry?"

"Not yet, really," I replied, my mind a battleground where the forces of hunger clashed with the memory of those traitorous beans. Introducing sushi into this delicate ecosystem felt akin to throwing a match into a tinderbox.

Undeterred, Angel's hand found the small of my back, his touch guiding me with the assurance of a captain steering his ship through stormy seas. "Here, there's seating at the bar; let's go sit there," he suggested, leading me to a pair of vacant chairs that promised a front-row seat to the evening's unfolding drama.

As we settled in, the bar's intimate lighting and the buzz of conversation around us felt worlds away from my earlier fears and the sprint through the rain. Angel, with his disarming smile and accent that made everything sound like an invitation to dance, seemed unfazed by my less-than-stellar entrance.

As the night unfurled like the plot of a novel you can't put down, Angel—ever the attentive date—made sure my vodka soda was never more than half empty. The tension that had initially clung to me like the rain on my dress began to dissipate. With a casual yet decisive move, Angel pulled my chair closer to his, positioning my legs squarely between his, as he embarked on the narrative journey of his life.

He painted a picture of himself that was as complex as it was intriguing: an accountant by day, a martial arts aficionado by night. Not just any enthusiast, but a 3rd degree black belt in karate with aspirations of securing a similar accolade in jiu-jitsu. His tales of youth included a stint as a lieutenant in the Venezuelan army, a detail that added layers of depth to his already rich backstory. And, as if his life needed any more spice, he mentioned his origins from a small island off the coast of Spain, adding an air of mystery and romance to his already captivating persona.

Angel's passion was not just reserved for his hobbies and his heritage; it spilled over into his interactions with me. Within the first hour, his conversation was peppered with compliments, each one wrapped in the warmth of his thick, exotic accent. He spoke of his admiration for me, declaring me beautiful and amazing, and confessing his burgeoning feelings with the intensity of a telenovela protagonist.

Before I knew what was happening, I found myself ensnared, spellbound by the combination of his megawatt smile, those soulful deep brown eyes, and the fervor of his words. It was as if he'd woven a magic spell, his accent the incantation, drawing me deeper into his world with every syllable.

There I was, seated at the bar next to a man who seemed to have stepped out of an adventure novel, feeling an unexpected connection. The Annie who had sprinted through the rain in flip-flops, worried about the aftermath of a bean-heavy lunch, seemed a world away. In her place was a woman momentarily captivated by a story that felt both improbable and irresistibly charming.

With each refill of my drink, the evening slid further into a realm of enchantment, the kind you read about but seldom experience. Angel, with his stories of martial arts and military service, his ties to distant lands, and his unabashed passion, had momentarily transported me from the humdrum of my daily life to the pages of a story I was eager to continue reading.

CHAPTER 18 SEXY SEXY RAIN

Angel, deploying the kind of charm that should be regulated by international treaties, cracked a joke that had me smiling wider than I thought physically possible. Before I could even process the wit that had unfurled before me, he leaned in with the precision of a marksman and planted a kiss that was so swift, so sure, that I barely had time to realize my mouth was still curved in a smile. It was unexpected, yes, but unpleasant it was not.

He pulled back, his smile widening as if he'd just pulled off the world's greatest magic trick. "There's a rooftop bar around the corner with a covered patio. Shall we go check it out?" he proposed, his eyes twinkling with the promise of continued adventure despite the rain's insistence on setting a moodier scene.

Ever the enthusiast for spontaneity, I agreed. "Where did you park?" he asked, as if logistics were the only thing tethering us to reality at this point. "Just across the street. You wanna take my car?" I offered, ready to dive headfirst into whatever the night had in store.

"Sure," he said, a man of decisive action. He settled the tab with the efficiency of a seasoned diner-dasher (sans the dashing part, thankfully), then led me by the hand through the deluge that had chosen this moment to unleash its full fury. "Don't worry, they have valet," he assured me, as if valet parking were a shield against the chaos of the universe.

Once we arrived and dashed inside the hotel, Angel's excitement was palpable, stopping every few steps to kiss me with a fervor that seemed to say, "Why waste a perfectly good journey with mere walking?" The elevator ride up was a scene straight out of a rom-com, with a kiss that lasted until reality, in the form of a noisy, crowded rooftop bar, intruded upon our little world.

Angel, unfazed by the bustle, steered us toward a cozy loveseat tucked away from the throng. Before I knew it, he was back with drinks, his hands seemingly drawn to me by some magnetic force, leaving me both startled and strangely flattered. The whirlwind of dinner and drinks had morphed into something else entirely, a rapid ascent into intimacy that I hadn't anticipated but wasn't entirely opposed to.

Then came the declarations, echoes of a not-so-distant past with a different suitor who had promised the world only to evaporate into thin air. "I want you to be my girl. I need you to be mine. You don't see anyone else, only me." His words, though dripping with the intoxicating blend of desire and commitment, sent a jolt of reality through me. I hesitated, memories of recent ghostings whispering caution into my ear. "Wow, I like you, and this is amazing, but can we just slow down a little? We just met a few hours ago," I managed, trying to steer us back to a pace that didn't feel like we were breaking the sound barrier.

His response, a mixture of incredulity and a dash of manipulation, "So you want me to see other girls?" caught me off guard. "Well, no, but—" I started, only to be cut off with a swift, "We will see only each other then," followed by another kiss that was meant to seal the deal.

In that moment, the memory of Jack and our planned date loomed in my mind, a reminder of the complexity of my current dating landscape. The sudden exclusivity with Angel felt both exhilarating and suffocating, a whirlpool of emotions that left me dizzy. "Let's just have this night and see where it goes," I suggested, a compromise to myself as much as to him, in a world where the next adventure—or heartbreak—was just a swipe away.

In the dimly lit ambiance of the bar, where the night had gently unfolded, the intensity of our connection had escalated beyond the confines of polite public display. Angel, ever the strategist with a solution for every predicament, suggested a more private venue—the car. The rain, which had started as a mere drizzle, now unleashed its full fury, transforming the world outside into a blurred, watery canvas. As Angel took the wheel of my car, offering to navigate through the storm, his confidence was as palpable as the rain was relentless.

He drove us to a secluded parking lot, where the rain's relentless onslaught ensured privacy, each drop a curtain shielding us from the prying eyes of the world. Angel, with his thick, fiery Latin accent, whispered fervent declarations into the steamy air—words of desire, of an attraction so intense it seemed to defy reason. His voice, laced with passion and an accent that curled around each syllable like smoke, enveloped me, drawing me deeper into the vortex of our mutual longing.

As the rain drummed a wild rhythm on the car roof, Angel spoke of his insatiable yearning, how the scent of me drove him wild, how the taste of my lips was something he could never get enough of. Each proclamation, more intense and passionate than the last, was a testament to the whirlwind that had engulfed us—a maelstrom of desire, of need, of a connection that seemed as inevitable as the storm raging around us.

In the cocoon of my backseat, with windows fogged to opacity, the world outside ceased to exist. There was only the sound of the rain, the warmth of our bodies, and Angel's accent, thick and enveloping, promising me the world in a voice that made every nerve ending sing. It was a moment suspended outside of time, a passionate interlude that defied the ordinary and flirted with the extraordinary.

Eventually, the fervor of our encounter ebbed as the storm outside began to wane, leaving us to navigate the aftermath of our impromptu intimacy. I drove Angel back to his sleek Mercedes, the night now quiet except for the soft patter of raindrops. He sealed our parting with a kiss that held promises of future storms, his accent wrapping around his farewell like a warm embrace, urging me to meet again soon.

As I drove home, the streets slick with rain and my heart aflutter with the remnants of our passion, I found myself ensnared by the memory of his voice, of the way his accent seemed to dance around each word, imbuing it with a heat that lingered long after the sound had faded. The night with Angel, marked by a passion as intense as the storm that had witnessed it, left me wondering about the nature of desire, the promises whispered in the heat of the moment, and whether the forecast would indeed bring more storms our way.

CHAPTER 19
PRINCESS

Annie, emerging from the cocoon of her sheets, found her morning already alight with a message from Angel, "Good morning, My Princess." It was a title she'd never claimed, yet the idea of being someone's princess was unexpectedly enchanting. She quickly replied with a "good morning," only for her phone to burst into life with a call from Angel himself. His voice, brimming with energy and warmth, greeted her, "Good morning my princess, how are you? I miss you!" The immediacy of his affection was startling—it hadn't been more than a few hours since their parting kiss under the veil of night.

"I'm good, last night was so much fun!" Annie responded, her mind racing to categorize Angel's fervent affection. Was this a parade of red flags, or merely the cultural flair of a passionate Latin lover? Opting to bask in the glow of her newfound fairytale, she shelved her doubts under 'cultural differences.'

"I can't stop thinking about you, I need to see you, when can I see you again, how about tonight?" Angel's eagerness was palpable. Annie paused, contemplating the rapidity of their budding romance. Two nights in a row? She pondered her own worthiness, a smirk playing on her lips at the thought. Last night had been a whirlwind of enjoyment, and the prospect of another evening with Angel was enticing. Besides, the girls were old enough to manage a few hours on their own. "Yes, I think I can get free for a few hours tonight, but I can't stay out as late as last night," she ventured.

"Perfect," Angel responded, his voice a blend of excitement and anticipation, "I can come meet you somewhere close to your house, how about 6?" The ease with which plans were made, the simplicity of arranging a sequel to their romantic interlude, left Annie both thrilled and slightly unnerved. "That works!" she agreed, and thus, date number two was etched into the fabric of the day.

As she set down her phone, Annie couldn't help but marvel at the swift current pulling her into Angel's orbit. Was she truly ready to be swept away again so soon? The thrill of the unknown, of Angel's unabashed ardor, offered a tantalizing escape from the ordinary. Yet, somewhere beneath the surface, a flicker of caution whispered warnings she chose to ignore. For now, the promise of another night with Angel eclipsed all else, casting her into a whirlwind of anticipation and, perhaps, a touch of recklessness.

Amid her contemplations of an evening enlaced with Angel's fervent declarations, Annie's phone sprang to life, jolting her back to a different reality. It was Jack, greeting her with the kind of nickname that never failed to amuse: "Hey dilla killa." This little moniker had its roots in an adventure with A1, during which Annie, had taken aim at an armadillo. The result was not only a direct hit but also the discovery of an armadillo's surprising vertical leap—turns out they could launch into an almost cartoonish airborne panic when faced with existential threats.

The chuckle that Jack's message evoked was swiftly quenched by the sudden recollection of their impending date. Panic fluttered in her chest—a sensation not unlike the startled armadillo's leap. She had utterly spaced on their plans, what with being swept up in the tempest of Angel. Guilt gnawed at her, a curious feeling given her tactical sidestep of any commitment chat with Angel. And Jack? His laid-back vibe had never once hinted at exclusivity; he was probably as entangled in the web of online dating as she was.

Torn between simplifying her suddenly complicated love life and honoring her plans, Annie was on the brink of crafting a polite bow-out to Jack when his next message hit her inbox. He shared the heartrending news of his dog's passing, a companion of 13 years. The upcoming date with Annie, he confessed, was a silver lining in his grief.

Well, that settled it. There was no backing out now. Backpedaling on plans with a man mourning his furry friend felt like a betrayal too cruel even for online dating standards. So, she decided on a tactful silence about her whirlwind with Angel. What Jack (and Angel, for that matter) didn't know wouldn't hurt them, she reasoned.

Now, Annie found herself performing a delicate balancing act between Angel's passionate pursuit and Jack's comforting camaraderie. Here she was, a sharpshooter turned inadvertent heartthrob, navigating the murky waters of dating where one wrong move could send everything jumping into the air, much like that armadillo on its ill-fated day.

CHAPTER 20 THE SHOW MUST GO ON

Annie's sequel date with Angel felt like a rerun of the first, filled with the same firework display of passion and Angel's not-so-subtle nudges towards locking it down officially. Annie, however, had become a pro at dodging these romantic grenades, weaving through the evening like a secret agent avoiding laser beams. Angel's pout at her unavailability the next evening was Oscar-worthy, but Annie's lips were sealed about her clandestine rendezvous with Jack.

Cue the universe throwing a wrench—or rather, a slight fever —into her plans via Eliana. This minor hiccup seemed like a cosmic signal: maybe the universe was telling her to put the brakes on her date with Jack. But when she floated the idea past Jack, his disappointment was almost palpable over the phone. "Aw, but I have gifts for you!" he lamented, throwing Annie into a whirlpool of guilt and intrigue. Gifts? For her? The concept was as novel as it was flattering.

Jack's next move was a masterstroke: offering to play knight in shining armor by bringing over dinner for the family. And just like that, Annie found herself agreeing to a backyard picnic under the guise of chivalry. "Um, okay sure, that is too kind. I suppose you and I could have a little picnic on the back deck," she replied, her voice a mixture of gratitude and bewilderment.

Now, Annie faced the task of explaining to her daughters why Jack, the mysterious bearer of gifts and dinner, would be dining with their mother on the back deck. The girls, ever the keen observers of their mother's suddenly vibrant social calendar, agreed to the arrangement with a mix of amusement and curiosity, promising to keep their distance.

As the evening set in, Annie prepared for her picnic under the stars, her life resembling less a fairy tale and more a sitcom episode where the protagonist wonders how on earth she ended up here.

CHAPTER 21
SHOOTER MCGAVIN

With my brood safely corralled indoors and the anticipation buzzing through me like a live wire, I hear the distinct growl of Jack's custom Ford Bronco as it makes its grand entrance into my driveway. The moment is upon me. I step outside, my heart doing that peculiar dance between excitement and the kind of dread you feel when you've invited a near-stranger into your personal world.

Jack unfolds himself from the driver's seat with a smoothness that contradicts the ruggedness of his vehicle, and as he rounds the Bronco, he greets me with a nervous grin that somehow manages to be both endearing and slightly awkward. "Hi, can I get a hug?" he asks, as if we're long-lost friends rather than two people who know each other through a series of texts and a shared appreciation for armadillo-based humor.

"Sure," I say, committing to a hug that's brief enough to be polite but not so long as to suggest any deeper connection. As we break apart, Jack begins to unload the car like a magician pulling an endless chain of handkerchiefs from his sleeve. Boxes of food appear one after another, followed by a cooler that looks like it's seen its fair share of adventures, and then, the pièce de résistance: a gift bag so meticulously adorned it could have been the work of a team of elves. It's so over-the-top, I half expect a choir of angels to burst into song as he hands it to me.

Offering to help with the load, I lead Jack to the back deck, mentally preparing myself for whatever this evening has in store. I ferry the food intended for my daughters indoors, delivering it with a "Don't disturb us unless it's an emergency" look that I hope they understand. Then, I return to Jack, who's now making himself comfortable on the deck.

I shuffle over on the small outdoor love seat to make room for Jack, feeling like we're about to embark on some sort of bizarre blind date orchestrated by the universe itself. With the precision of a DJ setting the mood for a party, I connect my phone to the Bluetooth speaker I had strategically placed earlier. Jack, ever the eager beaver, can hardly contain his excitement. "You wanna go ahead and open your gift?" he asks, eyes twinkling with anticipation.

"Sure," I say, my grin mirroring his enthusiasm. I grab the gift bag, which looks like it could have been wrapped by a team of competitive gift-wrappers on steroids. The first thing I pull out, after navigating through an ocean of silver and white tissue paper, is a bottle of Corralejo tequila. I'm impressed; Jack remembered my offhand comment about my appreciation for good tequila. This wasn't just any tequila, though. This was the kind that made you forget about your troubles—or at least made them funnier.

Next, a bag of limes and some margarita salt tumble out of the bag, eliciting a genuine giggle from me. But then comes the pièce de résistance—a large box containing what can only be described as the ultimate party weapon: a gun that shoots alcohol directly into your mouth. My laughter bursts forth, a mix of surprise and delight at such a wonderfully absurd gift.

And as if he hadn't already secured his place in the Hall of Fame for Thoughtful and Slightly Quirky Gifts, I pull out the final item: a personalized flask engraved with "Dilla Killa." Jack really has outdone himself, blending humor, personal touches, and a dash of the unexpected into one unforgettable gift.

Not to mention, he's come prepared with an ice chest stocked with Dos Equis, catering to yet another one of my favorites. Sitting there, surrounded by gifts that so perfectly captured the essence of our budding friendship (or whatever this was turning into), I felt a mix of gratitude, amusement, and a hint of bewilderment. Here was a man who had listened, really listened, to the ramblings of a woman he barely knew, and had turned them into the most perfectly tailored gift.

There we were, Jack and I, nestled on my back deck like two connoisseurs of the absurd, our taste buds tingling from the eclectic spread he'd brought and our spirits buoyed by the chilled embrace of our beers. That's when the brilliant (or so I thought) idea to christen the tequila gun emerged. Jack, the eternal skeptic with a cautious eye, wasn't exactly thrilled at the prospect of becoming a human target for an alcoholic weapon. My inner stunt double, however, was all too eager to volunteer for what promised to be a highlight reel moment.

Unboxing the tequila gun felt like opening Pandora's Box, but with less impending doom and more potential for shenanigans. We loaded it with Corralejo. Jack took aim with the seriousness of a sommelier about to decant a rare vintage, his target: my wide-open maw.

What ensued was not the graceful arc of liquor one might expect from such a sophisticated device but rather a torrential downpour, a veritable firehose of tequila that sucker-punched my uvula with the ferocity of a Mike Tyson right hook. In a panicked flurry, Jack attempted a course correction, only to douse my eyeballs in a baptism of fire.

There I was, spluttering and blinded, tequila searing my

retinas while my mascara surely ran rivers down my face. Amid the chaos, a part of my brain idly wondered if I was about to get inebriated via ocular absorption, a thought both terrifying and utterly ridiculous. Had Jack masterminded this bizarre eyeball cocktail? No time to ponder—my body was too busy oscillating between fits of laughter and bouts of coughing.

Jack, meanwhile, stood frozen in horror, looking as if he'd accidentally opened a portal to the tequila dimension. "I'm going to go in and wipe my face," I declared, still chuckling like a lunatic. Jack, now a statue of remorse, could only nod dumbly, his earlier enthusiasm washed away by the tequila tsunami.

Standing before my bathroom mirror, I discovered that tequila, in addition to being a drink best enjoyed in moderation, doubles as an aggressive makeup remover. The once painstakingly applied mascara had been unceremoniously stripped away by either the liquor itself or the sheer force with which it was delivered. My eyes, now devoid of any cosmetic enhancement, bore the slightly bloodshot evidence of my recent altercation with the alcohol cannon. After a quick rinse to remove any lingering traces of my impromptu tequila eye bath, I ventured back outside to rejoin Jack, feeling oddly refreshed and slightly amused by my own disheveled state.

No sooner had I settled back into the rhythm of our evening, the laughter and music abruptly interrupted by the insistent buzzing of my phone. Angel. The first call I diverted to voicemail without a second thought, a minor hiccup in an otherwise enjoyable night. But then, one call became two, then three, until the tally reached an unsettling eight calls in rapid succession. Each refusal to answer felt like poking a bear, or in this case, a very determined suitor with an apparent aversion to boundaries.

I caught Jack's eye and offered a sheepish shrug, an apology without words for the interruption. He didn't pry, for which I was grateful, and we seamlessly returned to our evening of shared stories and sporadic laughter. That was, until the inexorable march of time caught up with us, and Jack glanced at his watch, the realization dawning that it was already 11 pm. He'd come from two hours away, a fact that still baffled me—was I really worth that kind of effort? Perhaps I was someone's princess after all, but the jury was still out on whose royalty I'd claim.

As Jack stood to leave, that familiar prelude to a kiss hung in the air between us. Sure enough, he leaned in, and the kiss that followed was gentle, a slow burn that promised more but stopped just short of igniting fully. His hands found mine, and for a moment, the world narrowed down to the warmth of his touch and the soft pressure of his lips. But as quickly as the heat had built, Jack stepped back, a look of resolve etched on his face. "Oh lord, I need to go, or I won't want to stop," he confessed, almost breathless.

With a flurry of thanks and well-wishes, Jack returned to his Bronco, the rumble of its engine fading into the night. Left in the wake of his departure, I couldn't help but feel a twinge of... something. Was it regret? Anticipation? Or perhaps just the lingering buzz of tequila and unexpected companionship? Whatever it was, it fluttered quietly in my chest as I pondered the strange, serendipitous turns my life seemed to take —always unpredictable, occasionally messy, but never, ever boring.

I retreat inside, still feeling the peculiar mix of exhilaration and confusion that seems to be my constant companion these days. Knowing Misty will be both horrified and amused by the evening's escapades, I grab my phone to give her a rundown.

As I type out the tale of tequila cannons, unexpected gifts, and late-night kisses, I can almost hear Misty's laughter through the screen.

Her response doesn't disappoint. After a brief pause that I imagine was filled with her cackling, my phone lights up with her verdict. "From now on, he's Shooter McGavin to me," she declares, a reference that sends me into a fit of giggles. The absurdity of my life, distilled into a nickname based on a tequila gun mishap and a character from Happy Gilmore, feels oddly fitting.

CHAPTER 22 WHY IS CRAZY SO COMFORTABLE

Awakening to a fresh dawn, Annie's phone greeted her with digital tokens of affection—one from Shooter, charming and sweet, another from Angel, dripping with the same saccharine intensity that had become his signature. Yet, it was Angel's messages that sent her heart racing, not with excitement but with a familiar, unsettling dread. The barrage of missed calls from the night before loomed over her like a storm cloud, each one a reminder of the tightrope she found herself walking once again.

Confronted with the prospect of explaining her silence, Annie's mind raced. The truth was too complex, too fraught with potential for conflict. She had danced with anger before —its fiery steps burned into her memory, from the volatile outbursts of her father, whose temper could turn on a dime, to the darker, more dangerous fury of Mark, her husband, whose charisma masked a rage that left destruction in its wake. Even after Mark, she had stumbled into the arms of another whose temper mirrored the storms she'd vowed to escape, a relationship that left her more than just emotionally scarred.

Angel's intensity, his relentless pursuit and possessiveness, stirred the ashes of those old fires, awakening a fear Annie thought she'd buried deep. His affection, while intoxicating, carried an undercurrent of something she recognized all too well—control, a desire to consume and possess, masked as devotion. And so, despite every alarm bell ringing in her head, Annie reverted to her well-rehearsed dance of appeasement, crafting a lie as flimsy as tissue paper. "Goodmorning, sorry I couldn't take your calls. I was busy with mom stuff," she texted back, each word tasting like ash in her mouth.

Lying, especially poorly, went against every fiber of her being. It twisted her stomach into knots, a physical manifestation of the moral dissonance she felt. Yet, the alternative—confronting Angel, possibly inciting his wrath—terrified her more. The shadows of her past, of men whose anger could turn her world upside down, loomed large, guiding her hand even as her conscience screamed in protest.

Should she have cut ties then and there, erasing Angel from her life as easily as swiping a name from her contacts? In a world governed by reason, perhaps. But Annie's world was one of emotions run wild, of fear and longing entangled in a dance that left no room for reason. And so, she clung to Angel, a decision that promised companionship but tasted of desperation, a familiar pattern replayed on a loop, ensnaring her once again in its intricate, dangerous ballet.

As the sun rose on yet another day in the life of Annie, it brought with it an invitation from Angel for what would mark their third date in just four days. This time, however, the venue was to be his place—a request that sent a shiver down Annie's spine, not of anticipation but of apprehension. With logistical precision, she managed the calendar of her children's activities, ensuring their evenings were accounted for, before reluctantly agreeing to Angel's proposition.

The anticipation that once sparked a fire within her was conspicuously absent, replaced by a chilling dread that seeped into her bones. Angel's demand for exclusivity, a chain she had neither chosen nor desired, felt like a noose tightening around her neck, a specter of control that dredged up dark waters of her past. Memories of Mark's tempestuous anger and Steven's brutal violence surged forward, not just as recollections but as vivid, living nightmares, engulfing her in waves of fear so tangible, they left her gasping for air.

In a futile attempt to escape the encroaching shadows, Annie sought solace in her daily rituals, the music from her AirPods turned up in a desperate bid to drown out the cacophony of her thoughts. Yet, the notes that once offered comfort now mocked her, a cruel soundtrack to her impending descent into the abyss.

The approach of evening, and with it the moment to venture into Angel's world, found Annie wrestling with her inner demons. The palpable dread that enveloped her was not just about the evening ahead but also a reflection of her own entrapment in a cycle she seemed doomed to repeat. Despite the clear signs urging her to flee, an irrational part of her clung to Angel, driven by a deep-seated need for love, for validation, for a change in her stagnant existence.

This need to be loved, to be desired, paradoxically chained her to a path littered with red flags, a path that promised nothing but a return to the lessons she had twice failed to learn. It was as if she was drawn, moth-like, to the flame of her own destruction, compelled to seek out the very situations that had shattered her before.

Standing at the precipice, the music in her ears unable to drown out the dread that gripped her heart, Annie faced a harsh epiphany. Her pursuit of something, anything, to fill the void within had led her back to the edge of a familiar cliff, one she had teetered on before. And yet, despite the screaming alarms in her mind, despite the visceral fear that coursed through her veins, she stepped into the night, drawn inexorably towards a fate she had yet to escape, a prisoner of her own yearning for a love that remained just beyond reach.

CHAPTER 23
EVERYTHING IS FINE

Annie's journey to Angel's apartment unfolded with a predictability that was both comforting and unnerving. His doorstep welcomed her with the customary shower of adulation and a kiss that, while warm, sparked a flicker rather than a flame within her. The evening's sequence was scripted in familiarity: dinner, a setting where compliments were served more liberally than the wine, followed by a retreat to his sanctum for drinks and solitude.

As the night draped its velvet curtain around them, Annie found the shadows of her fears retreating to the corners of the room, yet a profound connection failed to bridge the distance between them. She moved through the evening like an actress on stage, delivering her lines with practiced ease but devoid of genuine emotion. The familiar sensation of treading on eggshells beneath her feet, a dance she knew all too well, underscored each moment. Her focus, laser-trained on maintaining Angel's contentment, left no room for the pursuit of her own joy.

Rationalizing the void between them as a mere cultural discrepancy, Annie cast Angel in the role of the passionate Latin lover, while she, perhaps, played the part of the so-called ice queen. It was a convenient narrative, one that allowed her to overlook the deeper dissonance that thrummed beneath the surface. Annie's strategy in the face of conflict was a silent retreat into her inner fortress, a pattern forged in the fires of childhood memories filled with parental disputes and the instinctual drive to flee from confrontation.

Yet, in Angel's presence, there was no overt conflict to flee from. He was a flurry of passion and promises, his intensity surrounding everything from whispered endearments to the grand plans he spun out of the night air. But Annie, ever the observer, found herself lost in translation, unable to decipher whether his fervor was the flame she sought or simply another kind of smoke.

In this dance of desire and detachment, Annie grappled with the reality that, despite Angel's fervent declarations, she remained an outsider to her own story. The passion that should have ignited her soul felt more like a performance, a role she had been cast in without an audition. As the night unfolded, she remained adrift, caught between the need to play her part perfectly and the silent, gnawing awareness that the script she followed was not her own.

In the grand opera of Annie's romantic endeavors, where alarm bells chimed like off-key sopranos, our heroine maintained her role as the eternal optimist. She was like a gambler doubling down with a smile, blissfully ignoring the dealer's knowing smirk. In Angel, Annie saw not just a man but a mosaic of potential, piecing together his commendable work ethic and his hobbies with the enthusiasm of a child with a new puzzle. His mature demeanor and the way he crowned her his princess eclipsed any doubts—a feat comparable to ignoring a parade because you found a penny.

The quirks of their relationship, such as Angel's mysterious need to tuck Annie away in the exercise room during unexpected late-night visits from his children, might have raised eyebrows in a less trusting soul. Yet, to Annie, these moments were just quirky footnotes in their love story, not the glaring plot holes they might have seemed to a more cynical observer. Where one might see red flags, Annie saw a peculiar shade of rose, viewing each oddity with a glass-half-full cheerfulness that was both her shield and her blindfold.

As their dates evolved from princess-worthy outings to more humble hangouts at his place, Annie adjusted her expectations with the grace of a contortionist, bending over backward to see the silver lining.

Focusing solely on Angel's better traits, Annie treated each warning sign not as a stop but as a mere yield, slowing down only long enough to rationalize it away before speeding ahead. It was as if she was wearing life-preservers as earrings —acknowledging the possibility of drowning but convinced she'd float based on sheer willpower alone.

In her heart, Angel's designation of her as his princess wasn't just a pet name but a title she was determined to live up to, even if it meant overlooking the increasingly casual nature of their encounters. To Annie, every moment with Angel was a brick in the foundation of what could be, if only she focused hard enough on the blueprint of potential she'd drafted in her mind, ignoring the actual architectural integrity of what was being built.

In this way, Annie sailed through their relationship with the wind of optimism in her sails, navigating through a sea of denial with the skill of an experienced captain, steadfastly ignoring the iceberg of reality looming in the mist.

CHAPTER 24
THE FIZZLE

In the peculiar universe of Annie's life, where the constants were her children, her unwavering dedication to fitness, and those lifesaving cold showers, Angel had become a sort of erratic comet, brightening her sky with the promise of excitement but never quite delivering the spectacle expected. Their rendezvous, while anticipated with a blend of hope and habit, often dissolved into evenings that whispered of what could have been, leaving Annie feeling more adrift than anchored.

The cadence of their courtship had settled into a rhythm as predictable as her morning routine, punctuated by dates that felt increasingly like echoes of their first few meetings. There was a pattern to the disappointment, a familiar ache in the realization that the fireworks she'd hoped for were more akin to sparklers—bright, but fleeting and far from the grand display she'd imagined.

Then came the Friday when Angel, citing a jiu-jitsu injury, called off their plans. His foot was hurt, he'd said, and while Annie offered her usual blend of concern and willingness to help, his assurance that he needed nothing felt like a gentle but firm closing of a door. In the silence that followed, no further plans blossomed. The abrupt end to their whirlwind was as anticlimactic as their dates, fading out not with a bang but with a whimper.

Strangely, Annie found herself not mourning the end but feeling a sense of liberation, as if she'd been holding her breath underwater and was finally allowed to surface. There was no rush to text, no urge to call and mend what had unraveled. Instead, she embraced the conclusion of their chapter with a sense of relief, a silent acknowledgment that this ending was perhaps the most fitting epilogue to their story.

The absence of tears or turmoil wasn't coldness but clarity— the recognition that what had ended was less a romance and more a detour, a scenic route that had promised vistas but delivered mostly fog. In letting go without a struggle, Annie accepted the end not as a loss but as an escape, a release from the cycle of anticipation and disappointment that had become their relationship's hallmark.

CHAPTER 25 NEVER REALLY ALONE

I'm lounging in my fortress of solitude—my room, that is —surrounded by the comforting buzz of adolescent energy somewhere in the vicinity of my backyard. The rest of the house might as well be a different country for all I care. I'm knee-deep in the kind of show that's like comfort food without the calories, the kind you've watched enough times to lip-sync the dialogue, yet here I am, chuckling like it's brand new. My phone, that treacherous gateway to the outside world, sits idly by, until it doesn't. It buzzes with the audacity of a cold caller at dinnertime. "David has added you on Snapchat." David? Do I know a David? I rifle through the mental Rolodex of Davids and come up empty. But what's life without a little mystery? And let's be honest, the vodka tonic might be whispering sweet nothings about adventure into my ear.

With the reckless abandon of a pirate diving into uncharted waters, I add David back. The alcohol coursing through my veins has transformed me from a mild-mannered, show-binging hermit into an intrepid explorer of the digital age. I whip out a quick snap video, a casual "Hi David, what's up?" with all the nonchalance of a spy exchanging secret codes. There I am, in the dim glow of my phone's light, offering a digital olive branch to a stranger named David, because why not? The night is young, I'm feeling bold, and David... well, David is an unknown quantity in the equation of my Friday night.

I tap the screen with the enthusiasm of a squirrel discovering a new bird feeder. David's video loads, and suddenly, there's this guy grinning back at me like he's won the lottery but hasn't decided if he's more excited about the win or the fact that he got to meet the oversized novelty check.

"Holy shit! WHO are you??? You are stunning? I thought I was adding an Annie from the bar I was just at, but OMG you are so much better!!!" His smile is so wide, I'm momentarily concerned for the structural integrity of his face. His eyes twinkle with the kind of mischief usually reserved for cartoon characters plotting an elaborate but ultimately harmless prank.

And just like that, something flutters in my chest. It's either the early signs of a heart attack or, more likely, a case of the feels. I, Annie from Oklahoma, have just been hit by a digital cupid's arrow, fired from the bow of a guy named David, through the unlikely quiver of Snapchat.

Feeling bold, buzzed, and slightly bewildered by this turn of events, I shoot back a video. "Hi, I'm Annie from Oklahoma. Wasn't sure who you were so I thought I'd see." I grin, hoping it's more 'mysterious and intriguing' and less 'I've had one too many vodka tonics.'

I set my phone down, now feeling like I've accidentally auditioned for a reality dating show I didn't sign up for. The buzz from my drink is suddenly overshadowed by the buzz of anticipation. Who knew Snapchat could be a portal to such unexpected connections? It's like finding a dollar in your pocket but instead of a dollar, it's a guy with a killer smile and possibly the same level of boredom as me on a Friday night.

As I wait for his response, I can't help but wonder: is this the start of something new, or just another anecdote for my future memoir, "Snapchat Giveth, Snapchat Taketh Away: The Annie Chronicles"? Only time, and maybe a few more vodka tonics, will tell.

The digital volley continues, and I'm suddenly picturing David, this enigmatic Snapchat sorcerer from the swamps of Florida, wandering a boardwalk aglow with nightlife, his beer hand waving like a flag of casual revelry. He's surrounded by the kind of vibrant scene that usually demands one's full attention, yet here he is, fixated on his phone, engaging in a transcontinental flirtation with me, an Oklahoman hiding from a mini-adolescent apocalypse.

"Oh my kids have friends over and they are all out running amok, so I'm just hiding back in my room enjoying my vodka sodas," I snap back, trying to sound as cool and collected as one can be when they've essentially admitted to using alcohol and self-imposed isolation as coping mechanisms for parenting.

David's response comes quickly, filled with the kind of compliments that make my cheeks burn—a sensation I attribute equally to the flattery and the vodka. He talks about my smile, my eyes, my laugh, as though he's known them for years rather than minutes. It's like receiving accolades from a celebrity judge on a reality show where the grand prize is a boost in self-esteem, and suddenly, my mundane Friday night feels dipped in glitter.

The unexpected turn of events leaves me somewhere between bemusement and exhilaration. Here I am, nestled in the chaos of my home, now part of this spontaneous connection with a stranger hundreds of miles away, under the neon lights of Orlando. It's absurd, unexpected, and, frankly, a delightful deviation from the norm.

As I volley snaps back and forth with David, I can't help but marvel at the serendipity of technology, the internet's ability to forge connections in the most unlikely of circumstances. Who needs fairy tales when you've got Wi-Fi? This could be the beginning of a beautiful friendship, or just a very entertaining chapter in the story of my life, titled "The Night Florida Came to Oklahoma, Via Snapchat." Either way, I'm here for it, vodka soda in hand, ready to see where the conversation takes me.

The digital tango with David continues well past what any respectable adult would call a reasonable bedtime, stretching into those hazy hours where the night starts to flirt with morning. By the time David retreats to the confines of his hotel room, our conversation hasn't lost a bit of its momentum—it's as if we've found an endless seam of common ground to mine.

Discovering that David, with his sun-kissed 6'2" frame, not only shares my passion for music in all its different forms but also lives within whispering distance of the ocean, only fuels my intrigue. And when he mentions his former life as a nursery owner, bonding over botany of all things, I can't help but feel a jolt of excitement. Here's a man who knows his way around both a surfboard and a soil pH testing kit.

His snapshots, lit by the soft glow of hotel lighting, reveal a man whose handsome features are animated by a genuine warmth and humor. It's the kind of combination that could easily make a woman forget the more pragmatic concerns of long-distance flirtations. And so, as our exchange winds down and I finally surrender to sleep, I find myself ensnared by a smittenness I hadn't anticipated.

As I drift off, wrapped in the comfort of my own bed but mentally strolling some distant Floridian beach alongside David, I can't help but marvel at the night's turn of events. In the span of just a few hours, my world has been subtly but unmistakably expanded, thanks to a serendipitous snap and a willingness to engage in the art of late-night banter.

The optimism that so often guides me, sometimes blindly, through life has once again taken the wheel, steering me into dreams filled with sandy shores, shared playlists, and the burgeoning hope that maybe, just maybe, this unexpected connection could grow into something more tangible. For now, though, I'm content to let my imagination and optimism carry me off to sleep, with the promise of more snaps, more laughs, and perhaps more shared dreams with David waiting on the horizon.

CHAPTER 26
GATEWAY STRANGER

Annie's week unfolds with its usual rhythm of self-improvement and domestic routines, punctuated by moments of unexpected delight every time her phone signals a new message from David. These digital interruptions quickly morph from curious novelties into the highlight of her days, injecting an element of excitement into the otherwise predictable flow of her life.

This burgeoning digital companionship with David begins to take on the qualities of an addiction. Each notification from her phone sends a rush of anticipation through her, breaking through the monotony of daily life with a promise of connection. David's virtual presence becomes a beacon in Annie's routine existence, a spark of something thrilling and new.

Their exchanges, ranging from the mundane to the deeply personal, fill Annie's days and spill into the nights, culminating in lengthy FaceTime calls that seem to make the distance between them vanish. David, with his quick wit and easy charm, captivates Annie. She finds herself deeply drawn to him, enjoying the escape he offers from her solitude, even if it's just through the screen of her phone.

As predictably as a cat chasing a laser pointer, Annie had once again launched herself wholeheartedly into the digital arms of a man, David, whose existence in her life was as tangible as a hologram. This latest chapter in her series of romantic misadventures was underscored by the familiar chorus of divine caution, a blend of Grandpa's wisdom and possibly God's nudge, advising her to redirect her gaze heavenward for guidance. But Annie, ever the optimist and thrill-seeker in the realm of heart matters, chose instead to silence these whispers under the sweet symphony of notification pings.

David, the dashing protagonist of her digital dalliance, danced through her days and nights via the glowing screen, filling her with a cocktail of excitement and anticipation. Every snap, every call, was like a spark in the darkness, illuminating a path to a fantasy so vivid and compelling, it rendered the warnings of her inner council mute. Why listen to the sage advice of celestial beings and departed relatives when the promise of virtual romance beckons with the allure of a siren's call?

But as the laws of internet engagements dictate, the vibrant blaze of their virtual connection began to dim, flickering out into the cold reality of digital silence. The snaps ceased, the calls dwindled, and texts fell into the abyss of unreturned messages, leaving behind not the heartache of lost love, but the hollow mourning for a future that never moved beyond the confines of her imagination.

Annie wasn't so much grieving the absence of David, whom she never met outside the parameters of pixels and data, but rather the loss of the elaborate future she had crafted around their digital encounters. It was a peculiar kind of void, one filled not with the sorrow of separation but with the quiet lament for the dreams and fantasies that had provided her with such vibrant escapism. Once again, Annie found herself standing at the edge of reality, peering into the fading light of a romance that fizzled out as silently as it had ignited, leaving her to wonder what adventure awaited her next in the unpredictable saga of her heart's journey.

CHAPTER 27 PAST PRESENT FUTURE

In the relentless march of her daily routines, with the echoes of recent virtual heartaches receding into the background, Annie found herself grappling with an all-too-familiar adversary: her own anxiety. It was a shadowy companion that lurked beneath the surface of her seemingly unfazed exterior, a constant undercurrent in the river of her life. But Annie, ever the paradox, had discovered long ago that the best way to confront her fears was to dive right into them.

Her approach was akin to a tightrope walker deciding that the best way to conquer a fear of heights was to simply walk higher, without a net, believing in the safety of their skill alone. It was this audacious spirit that led her, one fateful, alcohol-fueled evening, to enroll in what could only be described as the most daunting challenge of her life: a televised boxing match. The realization of what she had committed to in a moment of inebriated bravado hit her with the force of a freight train the morning after. The very thought of stepping into a ring, gloves laced, facing an opponent with the intent of physical confrontation, was antithetical to every instinct of self-preservation she possessed.

Yet, when the moment of truth arrived, Annie, fueled by a mixture of dread and adrenaline, stepped into that ring. Under the glaring lights and the gaze of hundreds of spectators, she found something within herself: a resilience she hadn't known she possessed, a strength that went beyond the physical. The experience was exhilarating, a baptism by fire that left her with not just a champion's jacket as a trophy but a profound sense of empowerment. It was a reminder that she could indeed face the seemingly insurmountable, that the act of confronting her fears head-on could transform them from towering monsters into manageable challenges.

This incident became a touchstone for Annie, a vivid illustration of her capacity to not just endure but to thrive in the face of fear. It reinforced her belief in the efficacy of facing anxiety with action, of the transformative power of daring greatly. And as she continued to navigate the complexities of her life, this memory served as a beacon, illuminating the path forward whenever the shadows of doubt and anxiety threatened to engulf her. This moment stood out as a bold stroke of color, a testament to the unpredictable beauty of a life lived courageously.

Within the mosaic of Annie's life, there were segments not colored by her own choices, where she was not the one stepping into the ring by choice, but rather, fate had cast her into battles unbidden. The most seismic of these was the sudden passing of her husband, Mark. In a singular, devastating blow, Annie found herself a solo navigator of the ship that was her family life, tasked with steering her three young daughters through the turbulent waters of grief and adjustment.

Mark had been the financial anchor of their family unit, leaving Annie in uncharted waters when it came to the practicalities of day-to-day life without him. Yet, in his foresight, Mark had laid financial preparations that stood as a testament to his care and love, ensuring that, in his absence,

Annie and their daughters would remain secure. It was in these harrowing times that Annie felt the presence of God most acutely, a silent, steadfast companion offering solace through dreams and whispers, assurances that, despite the trials, they were not adrift alone.

This chapter of her life, fraught with potential for heightened anxiety and fear of the unknown, paradoxically served to fortify Annie's faith in the divine safety net that seemed to unfurl beneath her whenever the ground threatened to give way. It could have been an opportune moment for Annie to fix her gaze firmly on God, to lean into that faith as a guiding light. Yet, human as she was, Annie found herself caught in the inertia of the immediate, living life one task, one day at a time, without pausing to contemplate the morrow or to untangle the web of emotions from her past still ensnared within her.

In the whirlwind of responsibilities — from bill payments to homeschooling, from physical fitness routines to the endless cycle of household chores — Annie maintained the semblance of control, a ship's captain in calm waters. Yet beneath the surface, there lurked undercurrents of unresolved grief, unaddressed fears, and the nagging sense of directionlessness. It was as though, in her bid to keep the ship steady, Annie had neglected to chart a course for the future, to heal the old wounds that subtly steered her journey. In her steadfast commitment to the here and now, she inadvertently overlooked the healing and growth that lay in introspection and in a deeper communion with the divine guidance that had never once failed her.

CHAPTER 28 PRETTY SURE THAT'S NOT WHAT JESUS MEANT

Armed with the thrill of a digital debutante on the brink of her grand entrance, I prepared to accept a cavalcade of new friend requests on Snapchat. "Welcome, potential confidantes and conversational cohorts!" I silently heralded to the array of unknown avatars, each a pixelated promise of future interactions. The charm of this virtual salon? The power vested in me to disappear any bore or brigand with the tap of a 'Block' button—a digital guillotine for the socially insufferable.

Chuckling to myself, I mused, "Here stands Annie, the illustrious Fisher of Men, casting her net into the teeming cyber-seas." Each acceptance was like turning the knob on a door to an unknown dimension. The fleeting nature of these connections was the evening's pièce de résistance; unlike a tangible gathering, where the departure of guests is a matter of their own volition, here, I wielded the power of instantaneous exile.

As I clicked 'Accept' on each invitation, a ripple of excitement and a dash of anticipation coursed through me, much like the thrill of untying ribbons on a collection of mystery presents. Who would emerge from the shadows of anonymity? Might I encounter a kindred spirit, a riveting raconteur, or the rare jewel of the internet—a soul as mesmerized by the enigmas of theoretical physics as I am?

Yet, amidst this intellectual quest, the prospect of stumbling upon a dashing digital Adonis—a man whose mere digital footprint could send my heart into fluttering frenzies—lingered enticingly in my mind. With my drink in hand and a playlist that could either serve as the backdrop for profound dialogues or light-hearted jesting, I dove headfirst into the night's potential escapades.

In the vast, unpredictable ocean of the internet, who knows what or who might be reeled in? And if the catch proves less than satisfactory, there's solace in the digital age's mantra: there's always a new dawn to cast the net once more, in search of camaraderie, intellectual stimulation, or perhaps even a heart-throbbing encounter. As I waded into the digital swamp that is my newfound social life, it became clear that the wildlife here was... varied. The first message I opened was less "hello" and more "hell no," a visual assault that had me scrambling for the block button faster than a cat on a hot tin roof. I mean, come on, gents, first impressions matter, and that's not the foot (or other body part) you want to put forward.

Then came a "hello" that didn't immediately make me want to wash my eyes with bleach, so I sent back a hello of my own, albeit through video. It's the 21st century; let's see the goods, and by goods, I mean your face, not your... other assets. Lo and behold, Johnny from Ohio pops up, looking like he's never sent an unsolicited crotch pic in his life. A true unicorn in this bizarre digital forest.

While Johnny and I exchanged what could pass for normal human interaction, my inbox continued to ding with the fervor of a slot machine, each message a gamble. More often than not, the payoff was a jackpot of the anatomical variety.

It's a peculiar phenomenon, this conviction some men have that the fastest way to a woman's heart is through showcasing their southern hemisphere.

Ladies and gentlemen of the jury, I submit to you: when has the history of courtship ever been advanced by the unsolicited reveal of the family jewels? Show me a chapter in Jane Austen where Mr. Darcy wins Elizabeth's affection with a well-timed genital portrait, and I'll show you a very different Pride and Prejudice.

What's truly baffling is the sheer optimism of these digital flashers. Do they really think, in the vast encyclopedia of online interactions, that theirs will be the crotch shot that launches a thousand ships? Or is it a more primal urge, a digital "look what I can do," shouted into the void of the internet, hoping someone, anyone, will look? Perhaps they're under the mistaken impression that we're all here playing a bizarre game of Pokémon Go, eager to catch 'em all.

But here's the kicker, folks: the real catch isn't found in pixelated privates but in the potential for genuine connection, in laughter shared over silly snaps, in the mutual discovery of interests and idiosyncrasies. So, to the men of the internet, let's flip the script: try dazzling us with your wit, your smile, or your thoughts on whether pineapple belongs on pizza (the correct answer is yes). Trust me, it's a far more effective—and less legally dubious—strategy than the alternative.

Embarking on a digital odyssey that vodka-soaked evening, I braced myself for the virtual equivalent of a thrift store —expecting a few hidden gems among heaps of, well, less-than-desirable offerings. The incoming messages were a smorgasbord of the good, the bad, and the downright puzzling, kind of like finding a designer jacket next to a collection of used socks.

Amidst this electronic bazaar, a tantalizing proposition caught my eye: "hey want to see a magic trick?" Intrigued and slightly buzzed, I thought, "Why not?" After all, my evening's highlight thus far had been debating the artistic merits of various potato chip crumbs stuck to my couch.

The spectacle that unfolded was less David Copperfield and more... I'm not even sure there's a comparison for it. The initial act featured a member of the male anatomy so modest, it could have easily gone undercover as a piece of uncooked orzo. But then, as if by some dark sorcery (or perhaps a side effect of my drink), it metamorphosed into a behemoth that seemed to defy the very laws of nature.

This digital sideshow, while disturbing, was also inexplicably riveting. It was like watching a B-movie that's so bad, it loops right back around to being a cult classic. There I was, caught between horror and amusement, witnessing what could only be described as the wildest party trick gone wrong—or right, depending on your level of intoxication.

This unexpected turn of events led to a moment of introspection. What does it mean about me, or us as a society, that amidst a sea of potential human connection, I'm here, entranced by the most bizarre show on Earth? Is this the digital age's version of rubbernecking at a traffic accident, or is it a deeper dive into the human psyche's insatiable appetite for the odd and the outrageous?

As the night progressed and my vodka levels dangerously depleted, I came to appreciate the odd beauty in this virtual vaudeville. It was a reminder that behind every carefully selected profile picture lies a universe of weird, wonderful, and sometimes disturbing desires and expressions.

Thus, as I reflected on the "magic trick" that had captured my attention, I found myself simultaneously appalled and entertained. It seemed that this journey through the digital wilderness wasn't just about the shock value or the laughs; it was about the strange, sometimes terrifying, but always fascinating exploration of what it means to be human In the digital coliseum of modern courtship, where the thumbs-up is the new thumbs-down, perhaps it's not enough to merely be seen. One must astonish, dazzle, and—if all else fails—bewilder. So, as you stand on the precipice of potential infamy, consider this: Will your unsolicited contribution to the annals of internet oddities be just another forgettable flash in the pan, or will it be the stuff of legend, whispered about in hushed tones and recounted with a mix of disbelief and reluctant admiration?

In the end, while I can't condone the practice of digital flashing, if you're going to hurl yourself into the abyss of online notoriety, why not do so with a flourish? After all, in the grand tapestry of human folly, it's the threads of absurdity and whimsy that often catch the eye, for better or worse.

CHAPTER 29
MODERN DAY
ANTHROPOLOGIST

In the grand odyssey of Annie's digital explorations, her evenings have become less about winding down and more about spinning the globe on its digital axis. Her Snapchat, a once humble app relegated to the exchange of occasional pleasantries and pet pictures, has transformed into a veritable United Nations of male suitors. Each "add friend" click is akin to stamping her passport to another realm of the male psyche, a sort of digital version of "Eat, Pray, Love" without leaving her living room.

Amidst the backdrop of her mundane daily rituals, Annie's phone buzzes with the promise of another adventure. There's the skier from Utah, who sends breathtaking snaps from his mountainous abode, his living room a window to snow-capped serenity. A banker from Tennessee regales her with tales of finance and whiskey, his southern drawl seeping through every video. The musician from New York, surrounded by the chaos of creativity, shares snippets of symphonies yet to be, while men from Vienna to Australia, Argentina to Germany, and the tropical allure of Hawaii to the homegrown charm of most of the 50 states, parade across her screen.

As Annie delves deeper into these digital dialogues, she

becomes a connoisseur of characters, her Snapchat a canvas for the eclectic and the eccentric. The banker, the skier, the musician—they all become pieces in a puzzle that Annie is too intrigued to solve, their stories a buffet from which she indulges her boundless curiosity. This virtual voyage spans continents and cultures, a testament to the unifying (and sometimes dividing) power of technology.

Yet, with each new acquaintance, Annie's role evolves from passive observer to active participant in this global gathering. Her evenings, once a solace of solitude, are now vibrant vignettes of lives lived loudly and quietly across the globe. From the palace in the mountains to the hustle of the Big Apple, each man is a window to a world Annie never knew she wanted to explore, their uniqueness a reminder of the endless variety the human experience offers.

And so, with the world at her fingertips, Annie finds herself an armchair anthropologist of the digital age, her phone a portal to a thousand different lives. Each night, as she navigates this mosaic of masculinity, she marvels at the diversity, the depth, and sometimes the sheer oddity of her digital companions. In this vast network of fleeting connections, Annie discovers not just the multifaceted nature of men from every corner of the earth but also the universal quest for connection that binds them all. It's a quest that, for now, keeps Annie clicking "accept," ever eager for the next tale to unfold in the grand adventure of her digital dominion.

In the swirling vortex of Annie's inbox, a tempest of flattery and proposals, she finds herself riding the digital waves with both excitement and a hint of trepidation. The incessant pings of her phone, once a source of mild amusement, have transformed into the siren calls of potential adventures, or misadventures, as fate would have it. Three times a day, like clockwork, the words "marry me" flash across her screen, each proposal more earnest than the last, from suitors spanning the globe, their avatars and usernames a parade of the hopeful and the hopeless.

And yet, for all the exotic promises and flights of fancy offered by these digital Don Juans, Annie remains firmly grounded in her little corner of the world. The thought of jet-setting to meet a stranger from the internet is quickly dismissed with a pragmatic shake of the head and a chuckle. After all, there's adventurous, and then there's reckless, and Annie prefers to walk the line somewhere safely in between.

But it's not just the virtual world that keeps Annie's days interesting. Poor Jarrod, with the tenacity of a bulldog and the subtlety of a freight train, refuses to fade into the background. His random appearances and calls, meant to woo and win her over, have become a part of the chaotic tapestry of her life. Despite Annie's declarations of friendship and nothing more, Jarrod seems to be on a different frequency, his signals crossed, his intentions muddled by wishful thinking.

Annie, ever the gentle soul, finds herself in a quandary. Too kind-hearted to sever ties with blunt cruelty, yet too weary to entertain Jarrod's unyielding advances, she navigates their interactions with the grace of a diplomat. Each "we're just friends" reminder, delivered with patience and a smile, seems to bounce off Jarrod like rain off a duck's back, leaving Annie to wonder if the message will ever truly sink in.

As the days blur into nights, and the nights into mornings, Annie's digital escapades continue unabated, her inbox a never-ending storybook of what-ifs and maybes. Each new message, each marriage proposal, adds another layer to the rich tapestry of her virtual existence. And through it all, the specter of Jarrod's unrequited affections looms, a bittersweet reminder of the complexities of human connections.

CHAPTER 30
WHERE DID YOU
COME FROM?

Settled into my nightly nook, my room—a hybrid of a recluse's cave and a digital launchpad—I brace for another dive into the social media sea. Clicking "accept" on a new batch of friend requests feels akin to opening a mystery box. Who knows? Maybe I'll unearth a gem among the digital flotsam. Or perhaps I'll stumble upon another showcase of the male species' inexplicable fascination with photographing their nether regions. The world of online connections is nothing if not a mixed bag.

"Hi," I venture, sending out a digital probe. Back comes a video, pulling back the curtain on a new character in my ever-expanding digital theater. Enter Aaron: robed like a monk, ensconced in a chaos of screens and papers, his dark curls bouncing with each excited gesture, a visual symphony of disarray.

"Um, hi," he stutters, looking genuinely shell-shocked at the prospect of talking to a real human woman. "You are, um, stunning." The words fumble out like he's handling delicate china, too precious, too surprising. His desk, a testament to the creative mind's perpetual storm, sets the backdrop for this intriguing new dialogue.

Our digital volley gains momentum. Aaron confesses to a looming academic doom, procrastination having steered his ship perilously close to the rocks. "You might wanna focus on that," I suggest, half-amused at his predicament, wholly charmed by his earnest panic.

But no, Aaron seeks refuge in distraction, sending snap after snap, each more frenzied than the last, a detailed account of his self-inflicted academic siege. From his Seattle fortress, this former Marine turned techno-sentinel is now battling an alien mathematics, symbols resembling crop circles more than equations.

His frantic updates are a whirlwind, capturing me in the narrative of his procrastination odyssey. "Where did you even come from?!" he marvels, as if I've materialized from the digital ether to save him from algebraic damnation.

As the clock ticks down to his final moments of freedom before academic judgment, Aaron, ever the dramatist, sends a snapshot from his doorstep—still in his trusty robe, now a flag of procrastination—puffing on a cigarette like it's his last, his silhouette framed against the Seattle drizzle.

His chaotic charm, a mix of vulnerability, humor, and raw humanity, pulls me in. And so, as Aaron dashes back to his battle station, leaving me to the quiet of the night, I'm reminded of the unexpected magic that lurks within the digital world—a place where connections are forged in the crucible of shared laughter, and where even a procrastinator in a bathrobe can become a knight in shining armor, if only for a night.

CHAPTER 31
CREEEEEEEPED OUT

Under the warm glow of my kitchen lights, I, swaddled in the comforting fluff of my oversized pink robe, was serenading the shadows with Otis Redding's soulful melodies, my spirit buoyant with the promise of a tranquil evening. The vodka soda in my hand was a testament to the small joys that punctuated my solitude, a perfect companion to the melodies that filled the air. But as I rounded the corner, my sanctuary was breached. A figure, uninvited and startlingly out of place, stood at the sink, his gaze fixed on the unseen mysteries of the floor.

My heart, in an act of rebellion against the calm of the night, catapulted into my throat, threatening the serene facade I had so carefully constructed. The glass, now a precarious symbol of my shock, teetered on the edge of disaster. It was Jarrod. His presence, unexpected and unexplained, sliced through the evening's serenity like a blade through silk.

Despite the palpable alarm painted across my features, he remained oddly unfazed, his demeanor steeped in an unsettling blend of melancholy and disregard for the sanctity of my space. My voice, when it finally broke the heavy air between us, was laced with incredulity and a faint trace of dread. "Hi.. what are you doing?" His reply, something about bringing glasses for the girls for an upcoming eclipse, did nothing to assuage the rising tide of discomfort.

His intrusion, though not malevolent, was profoundly disturbing. A once-familiar face now cast in the shadow of unpredictability. I yearned for the solace of solitude, for the return to my nightly rituals and the freedom to sing along to Otis without the oppressive weight of his unexpected presence.

Attempting to navigate the situation with grace, I hinted at my desire for solitude, hoping he would grasp the unspoken plea for his departure. But he lingered, a specter of awkwardness and unvoiced turmoil, until finally, he trudged towards the door with the heavy steps of defeat. His parting words, a self-deprecating murmur, hung in the air, a stark reminder of the evening's unwelcome turn.

As he sat in his truck, a silent figure in the glow of my driveway, the night's promise of peace was irrevocably altered. The realization that my trust had been misplaced, that the sanctuary of my home had been compromised, settled over me with the weight of a thousand worries.

I retreat to the sanctuary of my room, the lingering unease from Jarrod's unannounced visit seeping into the fibers of my plush pink robe. As I navigate the labyrinth of skincare, I find solace in the rhythmic tapping of my fingers on the screen, firing off messages into the digital void where my eclectic collection of snap acquaintances reside. It's odd, comforting even, to divulge the evening's eerie turn to these faces without places, these friends without physical form.

Aaron, with his chaotic charm, responds with a half-joking offer to fly over and "handle" Jarrod. The notion sparks a flicker of amusement amidst the residual tension, a wild, fleeting fantasy that Aaron, in all his disheveled, spastic glory, could swoop in and save the day. Despite the impracticality, his readiness to leap to my defense, even in jest, endears him further to me, adding layers to our burgeoning digital rapport.

The consensus is unanimous among my virtual circle: the security code must be changed posthaste. Their distant concern acts as a balm, easing the initial shock into a manageable disquiet. The conversations meander on, each message a stepping stone away from the night's unsettling beginning, with vodka lending its steady hand to guide me back to equilibrium.

Eventually, the digital murmurings and the soothing burn of alcohol coalesce into a semblance of peace. The laughter shared over absurd hypotheticals and the collective indignation at the breach of my sanctuary by an all-too-real ghost from the past lulls me into a state of calm. The virtual world, with its boundless conversations and infinite escapes, wraps around me, a reminder that even in solitude, I'm never truly alone.

But as the night winds down, and the glow of my phone casts long shadows across the room, I'm reminded of the tangible steps I must take to reclaim my peace. The code will be changed, a simple sequence of numbers acting as a ward against unwelcome intrusions. For tonight, though, I'm content to let the laughter of distant friends carry me off to sleep, the digital echoes of their support a testament to the unexpected connections that sustain us in our most vulnerable moments.

CHAPTER 32 WHERE IS THE LINE

Annie updated her home's security code with a sense of purpose, a minor adjustment that symbolized a larger commitment to safety and privacy for herself and her daughters. They understood the change as a necessary measure, a collective step towards maintaining their sanctuary against unwelcome intrusions.

As days melded into nights, Annie's virtual explorations became a constant in her life, an expedition into the hearts and minds of strangers that spanned the globe. Among these digital interactions, a young man from Washington D.C. emerged as a beacon of intellectual and emotional alignment. Their discussions wove through the complexities of philosophy, the depth of literature, engaging in the rich tapestry of thought that Dostoevsky and C.S. Lewis offered. This connection, set against the backdrop of the Washington Monument framed by his apartment's expansive windows, was a source of genuine intrigue and affinity for Annie.

Yet, this world of connection also revealed its darker underbelly, where Annie encountered souls lost to their shadows. Some sought humiliation, others a reprieve from their torment in the anonymity afforded by the screen. These interactions, while deeply unsettling, prompted Annie to question the roads that had led them to such despair. What series of events, what singular moment, could drive a person to embrace such darkness?

Despite the draw of these mysteries, Annie knew there were depths she dared not delve too deeply into. The conversations with her young intellectual friend provided a stark contrast to these darker exchanges, offering a glimpse of human connection that was both enriching and enlightening. This dichotomy of experiences—both the refreshing intellect of shared thoughts and the harrowing revelations of the internet's darker corners—served as a continuous reminder of the vast spectrum of human experience. For Annie, each interaction was a step on her own path, a journey marked by the search for meaning, understanding, and perhaps, a way forward through the digital landscape that had become her world.

Amid the kaleidoscope of faces and stories that filled Annie's new world, Aaron stood out like a beacon in the dark, a kindred spirit in the sea of fleeting connections. Their conversations meandered from the mundane to the profound, with Aaron's travel tales offering Annie glimpses into foreign landscapes. His spontaneous tours, shared through the lens of his camera, brought the beauty of distant mountains and serene streams right to her screen, each snapshot a testament to their growing bond.

Aaron's quirky confessions like his affection for rest stops, those transient havens for travelers, further endeared him to Annie. He cherished these spots for their panoramic views and the unmatched people-watching opportunities they offered. Annie likened Snapchat to the ultimate rest stop of the internet—a place where people from all walks of life paused briefly on their journeys, offering glimpses into their worlds.

Their friendship blossomed against this backdrop of shared laughs and mutual understanding, a beacon of light in Annie's otherwise predictable days. Then, the bombshell: Aaron revealed he was married, his home life a shell of its former self, cohabitation without the closeness. This revelation sent ripples through the foundation of their friendship, leaving Annie to grapple with the moral implications of their connection.

Despite the flare gun of warning signs, Annie chose to navigate the murky waters of this revelation with the same pragmatic optimism that defined her. She rationalized the situation, focusing on the companionship and the escape Aaron provided from the loneliness that often enveloped her. Their bond, built on shared secrets and digital intimacy, remained untouched by the complexities of Aaron's real-world commitments.

In her quieter moments, Annie pondered the parallels between her willingness to overlook Aaron's marital status and the shadowy paths of those she encountered in the digital depths. Yet, she couldn't bring herself to sever the ties with Aaron, their connection a lifeline in the vast sea of her solitude.

Aaron's presence in her life became a constant, a source of joy tinged with the complexity of unspoken truths. The rest stop analogy echoed in their connection—both finding in each other a brief respite from their journeys, a moment of rest and reflection before moving on.

CHAPTER 33 DAY OF THE DEAD

I nestle deeper into the sudsy warmth of my bathtub sanctuary, the familiar tingle of vodka soda at my lips, when the intrusive ping of my phone shatters the tranquility. "Who could this be?" I muse, my fingers prune-like as they swipe the screen. Ah, it's Josh... yes, *that* Josh. The Houdini who vanished without so much as a "see ya." His message, devoid of any semblance of remorse or even a cursory "been abducted by aliens, my bad," simply reads, "Hey, I thought we could get together again. What are you doing tonight?"

I'm momentarily transported back to the whirlwind of our first date—the spark, the laughter, and yes, that intoxicating rush of being whisked off my feet, quite literally. But as quickly as the nostalgia arrives, it's bulldozed by the cold, hard memory of his subsequent vanishing act. With a newfound resolve simmering beneath the bubbles, I tap out, "sorry I can't I'm busy tonight." Take that, Casper. A small victory for womankind, or at least for Annie-kind.

Flush with the thrill of asserting my worth, I prepare for a peaceful retreat into the realm of sleep when another digital intruder makes its presence known. But this time, it's Shooter, aka Ghost of Dates Past, part deux. "Hey, Dilla Killa, I was wondering if maybe I could finally take you out on a real date?" The text conjures a smile, tinged with the guilt of my own neglect. Shooter, with his unexpected gifts and earnest charm, was a casualty of my whirlwind romance with Angel, and perhaps, of my own indecision.

"Hey Shooter," I type back, a mix of excitement and trepidation coursing through me. "I'd love that." And just like that, I'm back in the game, but this time with a little more wisdom, or so I tell myself.

As I lie in bed, pondering the peculiar timing of these resurrected romances, I can't help but marvel at the universe's sense of humor. Was rejecting Josh's belated overture a test I passed, paving the way for Shooter's return? Or is saying yes to Shooter setting me up for another lesson in the unpredictable curriculum of love and loss?

Life, with its bizarre twists and serendipitous turns, continues to baffle me. Yet, here I am, perpetually strapped in for the ride, my heart perennially on my sleeve and my spirit ever willing to leap into the unknown. So, let's leap with Shooter and see where this next adventure leads. After all, in the grand odyssey of love and connection, I am, above all, an intrepid explorer, ever in search of my next great escapade.

CHAPTER 34 A NIGHT OUT

I'm pacing like a caged animal, each tick of the clock punctuating my increasing anxiety. The house is abuzz with the usual pre-date electricity, but it's tinged with a dash of paranoia, courtesy of my last ghosting experience. As the clock's hands sneer at me, indicating it's already 6:30 and no sign of Shooter, I begin to entertain all sorts of dismal scenarios. Is this another no-show? A cruel joke at my expense? My fingers itch to text him, to demand an ETA or even a hint of his whereabouts, but I resist the urge. I don't need to unveil my inner neurotic just yet—not before the appetizers, at least.

I send a quick, somewhat manic video to Aaron, seeking solace in his unflappable demeanor. "Looks like I might be dining with my shadow tonight," I half-joke in the clip. Aaron's response is swift, his face crinkled in mock outrage on my behalf. "If he doesn't show, I'm booking the next flight over to give him a piece of my mind… or a friendly shove," he jests. His words are the comfort food of our friendship, filling the hollow uncertainty with warmth.

Just as I consider swapping my shoes for slippers, my phone buzzes—a message from Shooter. "Caught behind a train, but I'll be there in a shake!" he texts. Relief washes over me, followed by a wave of embarrassment for my earlier panic. I relay the update to Aaron, who's been virtually holding my hand through the ordeal. His parting message, "Have fun and text me when you get back, okay?" is sprinkled with brotherly concern. I quip back, "You're now officially on Misty's team of bodyguards," and share my live location. "Consider yourself deputized as my backup guardian angel," I add, which earns a hearty laugh and a solemn vow of vigilance from him.

As I dab on a final touch of lip gloss and glance out the window, Shooter's headlights cut through the dusk. The evening is back on track, and with it, my heart skips back to its regular rhythm, hopeful and cautiously optimistic about what the night might bring.

As I totter out to meet Shooter, who's beaming beside his Bronco, I'm instantly faced with an engineering marvel: a seatbelt that could easily double as a harness for scaling Mt. Everest. "This is…intense," I comment as he demonstrates the intricate click and pull required to secure me into the passenger seat.

We make our way to a local Mexican spot, settling in at the bar where margaritas flow and tacos appear as if by magic. Shooter is on his A-game, recounting tales that could rival any Netflix comedy special, and I'm impressed—this man has somehow catalogued every rambling story I've ever tossed into our conversations. Post-margarita, we venture into a dive bar that's as charming as it is dimly lit, with karaoke crooners who take their craft far more seriously than the Olympic judges.

The bar is nearly empty, save for a cowboy who might have been a backup singer for Johnny Cash in another life, and a lady whose age is as ambiguous as her song choices. Shooter and I claim a pool table, and he's quick to score the games on a chalkboard with the flair of a seasoned bookie—his victories stacking up as swiftly as my dignity diminishes. But hey, I snag one win, even if it's by his sheer misfortune.

In between his triumphant rounds, Shooter steals a moment to pull me close for a kiss that's more electrifying than any karaoke rendition we've heard tonight. It's the kind of kiss that could make a girl forget she's in a bar with more echoes than patrons.

Eventually, the night winds down, and Shooter drives me home, where we share a few more moments of passion in the sanctuary of his Bronco. As he departs, I'm left pondering the potential of 'us.' Could there be more? Maybe. But as Shooter disappears into the night, I find myself content with the evening's adventure, whatever it may portend.

Back in my room, I send off a final video to Aaron—my long-distance cheerleader—recounting the night's escapades. "Well, I survived, and I might even go for round two," I quip as I sign off and curl into bed. As sleep pulls me under, I'm grateful for whatever comes next—be it more dates with Shooter or solo nights with karaoke cowboys. Either way, life's looking up from here.

CHAPTER 35 THE DAM BREAKS

It's yet another night in my fortress of solitude, armed with vodka and navigating the digital sea of messages from a constellation of virtual souls. Yet tonight, there's a shift in the air—a subtle crack in the sturdy façade of my relentless optimism. Depression, like a stealthy intruder, begins to weave its dark threads through the tapestry of my thoughts.

Anyone familiar with the dual nature of alcohol knows its treacherous power; how it can elevate the spirits to euphoric heights or plunge them into shadowy depths without warning. I've always been the merry drunk, the life of the party, never veering towards the belligerent or the morose. But now, a change is upon me, a somber turn in my usually buoyant journey.

During a video chat with Aaron, who's long preached the ills of alcohol—calling it a poison in his matter-of-fact, yet strangely endearing way—I feel a noticeable shift. His casual admonishments had always seemed like background noise, part of his quirky charm. Yet tonight, as he detects something amiss in my expression, his concern cuts through the haze of my inebriation. He asks what's wrong, and that simple question is like a pin to a balloon, bursting the barrier I had meticulously maintained around my emotions.

For once, I don't reach for my mask of joviality. Instead, I take the plunge into uncharted waters, sharing the turmoil churning within me. Overwhelmed, I can't bring myself to send a video, fearing he wouldn't make sense of my tear-soaked babble. So, I text him instead, pouring out my fears and frustrations, revealing the shadows lurking beneath my usually sunny disposition. It feels alarmingly out of character, this confession. I'm exposing parts of myself that usually never see the light of day, guided by a trust in Aaron's steadfast presence on the other side of the screen. It's a leap into vulnerability, but somehow, it feels like the only path forward.

As our late-night digital dialogues evolve, they begin to peel away layers of joviality, revealing the raw undercurrents of our lives. Aaron, typically a beacon of offbeat humor, shares the oscillations of his mood with a vulnerability that mirrors the weight of his words. This sharing transforms our interactions, deepening them beyond the casual snaps and witty banter about the world's peculiarities.

Here we are, two internet wanderers, now anchoring each other amidst our personal tumults. The conversation that started as a way to stave off the monotony of my evenings now serves a more significant purpose. It's not about romance; it's about a mutual recognition of our battles and a shared commitment to navigating them.

Aaron's openness about his struggles and the earnest, almost therapeutic, exchange that follows my own confessions make me realize something profound. Perhaps he's not meant to be the knight in digital armor I whimsically hoped for, but rather a crucial ally in my fight against the emotional whirlpools that sometimes threaten to pull me under.

In this unexpected twist of fate, my relentless optimism finds a new companion—not in the romantic sense but in a deeply human one. Aaron, with his chaotic desk and heartfelt verses, turns out to be not just a friend but a lifeline, thrown across the miles, just as I'm learning to admit that even the sunniest of dispositions can use a little shade now and then.

CHAPTER 36 OPEN YOUR EYES

As Annie's daily video chats with Aaron become a cornerstone of her routine, their conversations spark a much-needed transformation within her. Guided by Aaron's sagely advice, albeit delivered with a characteristic mix of humor and seriousness, Annie faces a sobering reality: her relationship with alcohol needs to change. This isn't just about cutting back —a full pause is necessary. For Annie, who used the liquid crutch to navigate through her evenings of solitude, the idea of quitting seemed as daunting as swimming across the Atlantic.

Yet, the real torment wasn't the thought of giving up her nightly vodka sodas; it was the perpetual stasis, the maddening cycle of sameness that had ensnared her life post-breakup. Each day blurred into the next, a Groundhog Day of minimal variations, tethered tightly to her past traumas and present fears. The promise of change, then, came not as a threat but as a lifeline.

Making the decision to quit drinking, even just for a while, was like choosing to stop circling the same drain and start swimming towards a new horizon. It wasn't just an act of refusal but an affirmation of life's possibilities. With each sober day, the fog of aimlessness began to lift, replaced by a clarity that had been dulled by alcohol. This wasn't the whimsical hope of her usual flights of fancy but something sturdier, forged in the commitment to personal evolution.

Hope, then, took on a new color in Annie's life, shaded with the hues of personal growth and self-care. It was a hope not just to escape the old but to embrace the new, each small step marking a significant stride towards a future she could genuinely believe in.

Annie had been plodding through life with the precision of a well-programmed automaton, her vision constricted by the blinders of routine. Oblivious to the broader vistas around her, she navigated the familiar terrain of daily chores and obligations, never pausing to question the path laid before her. But as she sobered up, the blinders fell away, and a vivid, unfiltered world sprang into focus. It was overwhelming, this sudden influx of sensation and perception, as if she had been submerged in grayscale and now faced the daunting spectrum of reality.

The sedation of alcohol had dulled her to the vibrancy and potential horrors of the world alike, but now, with her newfound sobriety, Annie felt both invigorated and vulnerable. Every sharp edge and soft curve of her existence was felt acutely, every emotion magnified. It was akin to walking into daylight after years spent in a dim room.

But with this clarity came a strength Annie hadn't known she possessed. The fog of inebriation had obscured not just her view but her own capabilities. Now, she stood firm, ready to face whatever demons had lurked in the shadows of her mind. She confronted painful memories that bubbled up, faced fears about a future unscripted, and began to chart a course through unexplored territories of her own psyche.

Annie's journey was marked by a resolve to no longer evade the uncomfortable or unknown. Her eyes, once closed in denial, were now wide open, scanning the inner landscape for signs of old wounds and hidden dreams. Each step forward was a deliberate act of defiance against the inertia that had once defined her days. Though the path was lined with challenges, each encounter fortified her, sculpting from the raw materials of her experiences a new identity, one not defined by the past or limited by fear.

It was not just about recovery or rediscovery but about reclamation—of agency, of passion, of potential. Annie was no longer just surviving; she was learning to thrive, each day a fresh canvas on which to draw a new vision for her life.

CHAPTER 37 DAWN

This morning burst into my consciousness with a peculiar brand of zeal that's been missing for more years than I care to count—like a long-forgotten song suddenly blaring through the speakers. Here I am, fizzing with an effervescence that could rival a freshly popped bottle of champagne, wondering if perhaps I've accidentally stumbled into a manic episode. Could I be bipolar? Is this what mania feels like? If so, hats off to mania—it's downright exhilarating!

My mind races, skipping from thought to jubilant thought like a stone skimming over the surface of a sunlit lake. I'm practically vibrating with ideas, each one more thrilling than the last. With the newfound clarity of a monk but the energy of a caffeinated squirrel, I suddenly feel invincible, unstoppable. As I hop onto my climber, it isn't just my body that's ascending; my spirits are skyrocketing alongside. Could it be that the simple act of cutting out vodka has uncorked a wellspring of untapped potential?

The idea that ambushes me mid-climb isn't just good; it's nuclear-grade inspiration. I should write a book! Not just any book—a novel! As I pedal furiously, powered by a frenetic playlist of gospel and glory, the idea doesn't just grow— it explodes, showering me with the glittering possibilities of what might be. Who knew sobriety could be such a wild ride? I'm ready to strap in and see where this rocket fuel of newfound zest will take me.

This morning's brain menu featured an extravagant buffet ranging from quantum entanglement to C.S. Lewis' musings, and now, as I'm doing squats and leg lifts, it feels like my neurons are hosting a wild party. The thoughts are like bubbles in a soda, popping faster than I can keep track. I'm scribbling notes between sets, afraid these fleeting moments of brilliance might vanish into thin air.

It's exhilarating but also slightly concerning—this surge of ideas has me half-convinced I'm tiptoeing into madness. I mean, is this what going crazy feels like? Or is it just God giving me a cosmic thumbs-up for finally getting my act together? As I jot down another potential chapter title, I can't help but wonder if I'm not just catching a divine nudge in the right direction. Maybe this is what I've been praying for, or maybe it's just the adrenaline from exercising without a hangover. Either way, it's a rush of inspiration that's so intense, I half expect my sneakers to start smoking from the mental workout.

As I toggle between manic note-taking and a series of lunges and push-ups, I'm also firing off a barrage of video snippets to Aaron—my own private broadcast of what might generously be called a cerebral meltdown. He's living a few time zones away, blissfully unaware of the avalanche of enthusiasm that's about to hit him when he checks his phone. I imagine his sleepy confusion morphing into amused bewilderment as he listens to me chatter like a caffeinated squirrel about every lofty thought that's bounced through my head this morning.

Then, amidst my flurry of activity, my phone pings with a message from Shooter. He texts occasionally since our last outing, his messages spaced out like those awkward silences you're never sure how to fill. "Hey Dilla Killa, I'm heading down to Dallas today. What are you up to?" Oh, if only he knew what he was stepping into.

With the reckless abandon of someone who's just discovered the theory of relativity but can't find anyone to tell except their goldfish, I unleash a torrent of texts upon him. My morning revelations about the novel I plan to write, ruminations on our bizarrely interconnected yet emotionally disjointed world, a touch of undulation theory, and how Schrödinger's equations might just explain more about human interactions than particle behavior.

If he actually takes the time to digest that, he'll either think I've lost my marbles or that I'm on to something profound. But hey, today's another groundbreaking discovery: I shouldn't have to dial down my own frequency to match someone else's. If this scares him off, it's his loss, not mine. At least he'll have something to ponder on his drive to Dallas.

In typical Shooter fashion, his response doesn't disappoint. Within moments, a GIF animates my screen—a cartoon brain detonating into fireworks—and his accompanying text reads, "Wow, you are full of surprises. Didn't know you had it in you." I'm pretty sure I've rendered him speechless, which is no small achievement. This is a man who once penned a ballad in my honor—yes, the now infamous 'Dilla Killa'—and strums his guitar as naturally as breathing, always weaving his thoughts into lyrics or conversation. Yet here I am, having possibly stupefied him with my quantum physics-cum-philosophical ramblings.

I can't tell if he's horrified, impressed, or a bit of both, but no matter what, I'm not about to slow down. This intellectual buzz is too exhilarating to dampen. So, I'll keep riding this wave, reveling in the sheer joy of sharing my unfiltered self. If my frenzied discourse on the mysteries of the universe and the human condition can shake even the unshakeable Shooter, then surely I'm onto something grand.

I swipe through to Aaron's messages, almost reluctant to see his reaction; it could either fan the flames of my manic inspiration or douse it with the cold reality of his pragmatic brain. But there he is in his latest video, cocooned in what I affectionately call his 'viking robe', looking like a character plucked from a Norse saga if it were set in a Silicon Valley startup. His room, a jumbled lair of tech and trinkets, forms the perfect backdrop to his tired yet undeniably contented smile.

"Annie," he starts, his voice thick with sleep yet bright with enthusiasm, "this is the version of you I absolutely adore. You're all lit up, a beacon of ideas and excitement. Whatever this book turns out to be, I know it's going to be as brilliant and chaotic and wonderful as you are. You're a force, the total package. You've got everything it takes to make your dreams reality. I'm here, cheering you on. Proud doesn't even cut it."

As his message sinks in, I can't help but smile, feeling a rush of warmth that's so much better than any vodka buzz. If I'm steering my ship towards the whirlpool of the bizarre and the new, at least I have one steadfast supporter who's ready to dive into the vortex with me. With Aaron's encouragement echoing in my ears, the prospect doesn't just feel possible—it feels inevitable.

"So," I whisper to myself, buoyed by his belief in me, "let's write that book." And for the first time in what feels like forever, the path ahead doesn't just seem less daunting; it sparkles with the promise of something genuinely extraordinary.

CHAPTER 38 DON'T GET STUCK

Annie is resolute, yet her path is not lined with assurances. The journey of writing a book is strewn with obstacles that might deter the faint-hearted. Every blank page is a test, a stark reminder of the potential for monumental failure. However, Annie's spirit, imbued with an innate optimism passed down from her beloved grandmother, doesn't waver. She would often recall how Grams found joy in everything, from mundane chores to life's small adventures, always maintaining a cheerful disposition.

This learned positivity is what Annie clings to whenever doubt creeps in—which it does, frequently, and with force. Each time the shadows of uncertainty try to cloud her purpose, she conjures the memory of Grams' unwavering ability to see the silver lining. It's this skill, more than any other, that propels her forward.

"Even if this book never sees the light of day, even if it remains unread by others," Annie muses to herself, "it will still be something amazing for me, a personal triumph over the inertia that once defined my days." She holds onto the belief that the very act of writing, of pouring out her thoughts and confronting her inner turmoil, is transformative. It's not just about the potential literary success; it's about the journey, the personal evolution that comes with daring to step into the unknown. Armed with Grams' legacy of optimism, Annie presses on, finding in each word typed a reason to continue, a testament to the power of keeping on the sunny side, no matter the outcome.

Annie's routine still involves her airpods firmly in place, creating a barrier between her and the world, drowning out the noise and often her own thoughts. Yet, she's beginning to adjust her approach. Now, as she goes about her daily activities, she occasionally pauses her music to allow real thoughts to seep in, turning these moments into opportunities to talk to God.

Her approach is cautious, akin to someone tiptoeing into cold ocean waves. Each conversation with God is like a step deeper into the water, a slow wading into a more meaningful relationship with Him. These aren't marked by profound theological inquiries or extended prayers, but by brief, honest dialogues—asking for patience while managing daily tasks, or expressing gratitude for small moments of calm.

Through these short but sincere exchanges, Annie experiences a revelation. She realizes that articulating her thoughts aloud isn't just for God's benefit—He already knows everything—but it helps her clarify her own desires and questions. It makes it a lot easier to listen for God's replies when she knows the questions her heart and soul are asking.

Speaking to God becomes a way for her to understand what her heart and spirit are truly seeking. This realization deepens her spiritual connection, not overwhelmingly so, but like the gradual warming of her toes as she edges further into the sea, promising greater depth and understanding the more she engages.

Annie, while inching deeper into her conversations with

God, stumbles upon a trepidation that rattles her newfound spiritual routine. She's heard sayings before—like asking for patience might lead God to put her in situations that test her limits, or requesting strength could mean facing trials that demand she prove it. The prospect of inviting such challenges is daunting; she isn't sure she's ready to have her prayers answered in ways that might stretch her too thin.

Then, amidst these swirling fears, C.S. Lewis's words from The Problem of Pain echo through her mind, shedding light on the nature of true love. Lewis argued that love isn't merely about seeking happiness for the beloved but about encouraging them to grow into the best version of themselves. Real love, therefore, involves not only comfort but also challenges—it's not about easing paths but about preparing the beloved for the road ahead.

This reflection leads Annie to a deeper understanding of God's love. Like a parent who must sometimes allow their child to face difficulties to build character, God's challenges are acts of profound love meant to foster growth, however unfathomable they may seem at the moment. With this in mind, Annie musters the courage to embrace whatever may come. She starts to pray more boldly, asking not just for immediate comforts but for wisdom, patience, strength, and —most courageously—for God's will to be done in her life, trusting that whatever challenges arise, they come from a place of divine love, and that God will be closer than ever, ready to provide comfort and guidance.

CHAPTER 39 SHIT

Sitting in the parking lot, waiting for Eliana's dance class to end, my phone erupts with a startling ring. It's Bella, whispering frantically, "Mom, there's someone in the house!"

My heart drops. "What? Where are you?" I manage, trying to keep panic at bay.

"I'm hiding in your bathroom. I can hear a man's voice. I think he's in the kitchen," she replies, her voice a barely audible tremble.

Flashes of a misunderstanding months ago, where a similar panic was just Eliana unexpectedly at home, flicker through my mind. "Bella, are you sure it's not just the TV?" I ask, though her certainty sends chills down my spine.

"It's not the TV, Mom. Someone is here!" she insists, her whisper sharp with fear.

"Stay put. I'm calling Angie next door to check from their side. I'll call you right back," I say, dialing Angie with shaky fingers.

Thankfully, Angie answers quickly. "Angie, it's Annie. Bella thinks there's someone in our house. Can Travis check it out?"

"We're on it, Annie. Travis will head over now. Stay on the line," Angie's calm voice is reassuring.

I switch back to Bella to keep her calm, "Stay hidden, honey. Help is on the way. I'm just a few minutes out."

CHAPTER 40 IM THE WORST

In an instant, all of Annie's past traumas and missteps crashed over her like a merciless wave. She had dedicated herself to protecting her daughters from the world's darker corners, creating a sanctuary of education and affection at home. Yet, the harsh realities of life had a way of infiltrating even the tightest defenses. Mark, who had been a loving father, was also a storm in Annie's life, his outbursts witnessed just enough by the girls to leave unseen scars. Sophia, being the eldest, had seen enough to sense the undercurrents that troubled the waters.

Then, Mark's sudden departure from this world had shaken their foundation violently. One day, their robust protector was there; the next, just echoes in the halls of their home. This brutal lesson in life's fragility had clung to the girls, haunting them with the fear of losing Annie too. They had clung to her, their lifeline, with a desperation that was heart-wrenching, fearing every goodbye might be the last.

Annie knew this fear lingered in the quiet moments, in the unguarded whispers at night, and now, with Bella's frantic call, it reared its head once more. They had endured, yes, but at what hidden cost?

Under the crushing pressure of realization, Annie felt herself sinking, tethered to the heavy anchor of her daughters' stolen innocence. It wasn't just the shadow of Mark that darkened their past—it was also Steven, her own misguided attempt to fill the void left by loss. In her loneliness, she had latched onto Steven, whose charm was a thin veneer over a volatile core of immaturity and blame. He had brought nothing but instability, his presence a whirlpool that threatened to pull them all under.

The weight of having introduced such chaos into their lives now suffocated Annie. She was drowning in the aftermath of her choices. Steven's departure from their lives had been violent. The house had echoed with screams and turmoil that day. Annie remembered the blood, how it had seemed to paint the walls of their once-safe haven, a vivid scarlet that marked the violence endured.

Bella, only a child yet forced into a corner of unimaginable fear, had stood trembling with a cell phone in one hand and a pepper grinder in the other as her mother staggered from the bedroom, a mask of blood obscuring her face. When Steven, drunk and stumbling in false penitence, had followed, Bella had acted with a child's instinct to protect, striking him with the grinder. The sound, a sickening crack, was a chime of reality that echoed still in Annie's ears.

As Annie waited in her car, trembling with the phone pressed to her ear, she couldn't escape the flood of guilt for the scars her children bore. Each decision she had made, each step taken in desperation, had woven into a net that now entangled her family in threads of trauma. The weight of this reality was a current against which she continually swam, fighting for a breath of clarity, a chance to make things right.

In the rush of the moment, the road blurred under the sweep of headlights as Annie drove, her mind churning like the wheels that ate the miles back to her home. Beside her, Eliana sat, unknowingly shielded from the terror that gripped her mother's heart. On the phone, Bella's whispers were a thin thread of fear that Annie clung to, a live wire that kept her connected to the immediate danger lurking in their family sanctuary.

What had she done? The thought pounded in her head with each throb of her pulse. The image of Jarrod, uninvited and unsettling, loomed in her mind, an omen of vulnerability. Her digital escapades, a seemingly harmless diversion, now took on a sinister cast. Had her flirtation with anonymity drawn a shadow to her doorstep? The very idea sent a shiver sharp as a knife down her spine.

God, she prayed silently, let this be nothing. Let my fears be just the echo of past horrors and not the prelude to new ones. She implored for protection, for forgiveness for her recklessness that might have endangered her most cherished —the innocent souls of her daughters who had already seen too much shadow in their young lives.

As Annie speeds home, the weight of her world feels slightly lighter knowing Bella has been found safe by Travis. Upon her arrival, the reassurance solidifies when she sees her daughter unharmed, with Travis having thoroughly checked the house and surrounding area. Still, the unease lingers as she double-checks Bella's certainty about hearing a man's voice. Bella insists, though shaken, that she heard someone, and that it wasn't just the television.

After expressing their thanks, Angie and Travis head home, leaving Annie to settle her daughters and restore some semblance of normalcy. It's during a routine chore of taking out the trash that Annie's brief calm is shattered. There, by the firepit, she notices two cigarette butts. This is not a place where passersby could have casually dropped them; her home, nestled away in the countryside, sees no such accidental visitors. The butts look freshly discarded, one barely smoked at all, gleaming eerily in the pale moonlight.

A cold shiver runs through Annie as she picks them up, a tangible sign of an unwelcome presence. Opting to shield her daughters from further distress, she disposes of the cigarette butts quietly, choosing not to share this unsettling discovery. The night's events have carved a deeper notch of vigilance into her already burdened heart.

CHAPTER 41 PAUL

Sitting alone in my room at night, I sift through my messages, searching for something—though I'm starting to question what exactly it is I'm hoping to find. Now that I'm sober, well mostly, the emptiness of these Snapchat interactions echoes louder. The constant flattery from perfect internet strangers doesn't buoy me like it used to. Without the rosy haze of alcohol to make every shadowy figure seem intriguing, I'm beginning to see how mundane this all is.

There are a few people I talk to daily, and Aaron is a staple in my virtual life, but I had become hooked on the thrill of possibility that each new "friend" might offer. I'm slowly realizing, though, that most men aren't here for friendship; they're after something else. Maybe someone did too good of a job building up my confidence, convincing me I'm so fascinating that everyone wants to be my friend. And maybe I am that fascinating—but let's be honest, most of the people trolling the internet are just trying to satisfy their base desires. I've read that's often a trauma response. If that's true, then it seems there's a whole world of traumatized souls out there. Including me.

So, I continue to poke through my messages, navigating past the barrage of wildly sexual requests and the all-too-familiar "Hey" or "Hi." My interest in uncovering something genuinely intriguing is waning by the second.

Here I am, delving into my extensive collection of Canadian

acquaintances—I'm not entirely sure how I've amassed such a crowd from the north, but there they are. One in particular catches my eye tonight. I've exchanged brief messages with him before, but only in fleeting moments. He's tall, at least according to his photos where he towers over everyone else. And he's in Vegas. Ah, Vegas! I have fond memories of that place, not from gambling—I'm too much of a miser to get a thrill from that—but from the sheer spectacle of it all.

My one trip there was with Misty. It surprised me with its excess and its vibrancy, a city that catered to every sensory indulgence. We didn't bother with the slots or cards. Instead, we feasted on lavish meals, shot giant guns in the barren desert, raced dune buggies, and even took a leap off the Stratosphere. There was that one dinner with professional drift racers; I had no clue who they were until the meal was halfway through. Talk about being clueless but entertained.

And now here's Paul, standing in front of that new mammoth theater they've built in Vegas, a marvel that's all screens, both inside and out. It definitely piques my interest.

I reply to Paul, "Wow, you got to see U2 at The Sphere? Was it as mind-blowing as it looks?" Almost instantly, he fires back, "Absolutely amazing—I've never seen anything like it." Next thing I know, my phone is buzzing like a disgruntled bee, vibrating with about thirty photos from his Vegas escapade. Each picture looks more spectacular than the last, like a visual symphony, transporting everyone to otherworldly places from the comfort of a seat inside this futuristic colosseum. It's official; The Sphere just made it onto my bucket list.

Paul, a seemingly normal IT guy, promises a refreshing change of pace: no unsolicited anatomical exhibitions or creepy requests for ratings. I laugh as I tell him, "Yeah, you wouldn't believe the audacity of some dudes. It's like a bad carnival game—'Step right up and rate my...'" He chuckles, and we spiral into a conversation about the oddities of digital interaction, a pleasant change from the usual online weirdness.

As I tuck myself into bed, my last thoughts flit to my conversation with Paul. He's definitely getting a slot in my eccentric digital rolodex. I chuckle to myself, thinking, "Maybe I'm the real oddball on the internet, keeping a collection of people like some kind of digital stamp album." But as I drift off, it occurs to me that there are worse collections to have—at least mine tells good stories.

CHAPTER 42 PUT
IT IN 4WD

Annie's finger hovered over the delete button on her Snapchat app, feeling a stuck sensation that had been gnawing at her lately. Sure, quitting drinking had initially sparked a wave of positivity and growth, but now the novelty had worn off, leaving her feeling stalled again. The excitement had dulled into a routine, and the constant distraction of Snapchat, though once a delightful escape, now felt like a chain holding her back from truly moving forward.

She needed a change, a new step, to keep the momentum of self-improvement going. The thought of eliminating Snapchat from her daily distractions seemed like the right move—a way to cut through the noise and focus on deeper, more meaningful projects and relationships. With a mix of trepidation and determination, she pressed delete.

As she explained her decision to Paul, he responded with encouragement, deciding to join her in this digital detox. But simply deleting the app didn't seem like a significant enough step to shake the sense of stagnation that clung to her like a stubborn shadow. She needed something more—a gesture that would mark a true commitment to change. That's when she opted for a 72-hour water fast as well, doubling down on her resolve to reset both her digital and physical intake.

Paul, ever the enthusiastic companion in Annie's forays into self-improvement, didn't just support her decision—he joined her in both endeavors. Their pact to undertake this dual challenge was set with an air of mutual encouragement that seemed to bridge any distance between them. It was a leap towards something new, a conscious effort to regain control and induce a much-needed shift in their routines.

As they embarked on the 72-hour journey of fasting, only consuming water, the initial hours felt empowering. The clarity that began to emerge from eschewing physical nourishment mirrored their digital detox, as both seemed to clear away the accumulated clutter of unnecessary interactions and unhealthy habits. They shared their experiences and challenges in real-time, their camaraderie deepening as each hour passed.

Annie found the fast to be a revelatory experience. It wasn't just the absence of food that was transformative, but the very act of reclaiming control over her body and mind. She was making a statement to herself more than anyone else—that she had the strength to forego immediate gratifications for longer-term benefits. This wasn't just about detoxifying her body; it was about resetting her life's compass.

CHAPTER 43 RIGHT IN TO A BRICK WALL

As Thanksgiving faded and the festive lights of Christmas began to twinkle around her, Annie felt a heavy sense of dread settling over her like a dark cloud before a storm. It wasn't just the looming debt—a relentless beast that grew hungrier during the holiday season, demanding gifts, decorations, and expensive outings she could scarcely afford. No, it was deeper than that, a more profound dread that rooted itself in the darkest soils of her past.

December and January were no ordinary months for Annie; they were specters of past traumas, haunted by anniversaries of loss so deep and raw they seemed to burn into her very soul. The festive joy that filled other homes with laughter and warmth seemed to mock her solitude and sorrow, turning every Christmas carol into a cruel joke and every bright light into a glaring reminder of her darkness.

Even the New Year, which should have symbolized hope and renewal, loomed like a grim reaper, promising not new beginnings but a continuation of her silent torment. Each cheerful jingle and sparkly light was a stark contrast to the horror and foreboding that clutched at her heart, reminding her not of what she had but of what she had endured and lost.

Haunted by these shadows, Annie approached the holiday season not with joy but with a sense of impending doom. Each festive symbol, each gathering, intensified the dread, her body tensing as if bracing for the next shock, the next trauma. It was as if her very nerves remembered the pain and were tensing, preparing defensively for the next inevitable horror.

Thus, as the calendar pages turned, Annie steeled herself against the coming festivities, not with anticipation, but with a warrior's resolve, armored against the emotional trials that awaited, ready to endure yet another season marked not by celebration but by survival against the inner demons that the holidays never failed to awaken.

Annie had been diligent in her therapy sessions, collecting a toolbox of strategies for those moments when the past's shadows grew too large, threatening to swallow her whole. Like a boxer bracing for a punch, she learned to spot the swing —those crippling waves of emotion that could buckle her knees and steal the breath from her lungs as effectively as a blow from Mike Tyson.

Her therapist had taught her to pause and visualize a safe space whenever these feelings ambushed her. For Annie, that refuge was her grandparents' home, a place wrapped in layers of warmth and security, where she had felt loved and protected as a child. Usually, this technique shepherded her through the storms of her mind, but the holiday season was a different beast altogether. It wasn't just a fleeting shadow or a momentary cloud that she could dispel with thoughts of her grandparents' cozy kitchen or the smell of her grandmother's cooking. No, this was a relentless, oppressive mountain of grief and fear, immovable and daunting in its permanence.

Annie believed in a God who could move mountains, yet as the holidays drew nearer, she found herself turning away from that potential miracle. Instead of confronting the mountain with her faith, she sidestepped it, masking her dread with a performance of festive cheer for her daughters, who undoubtedly bore their own burdens from the shared traumas of past Decembers.

She would sometimes gently probe, asking the girls how they were holding up, acknowledging the heavy air that December brought into their home. Yet, when it came to her own struggles, Annie clung to her mask of resilience. She buried her own despair beneath layers of Christmas lights and holiday activities, wrapping their home in every cheerful distraction she could muster.

Inside, however, Annie was not decking halls but laying sandbags against a flood of memories, each strand of lights a barrier against the darkness, each batch of holiday candy a sweet defiance against the bitterness of the past. Yet no amount of sugar could truly sweeten the reality of the season for her, and no number of lights could fully illuminate the dark corners of her heart. Still, she persisted, a silent sentinel guarding her daughters from the depths of her own despair, all the while wondering if perhaps this year, she might finally find the strength to climb the mountain rather than simply live in its shadow.

CHAPTER 44
CHRISTMAS PARADES

As I'm barreling down the backroads, my car's heater working overtime against the December chill, I can feel every parent's worst nightmare clenching at my guts like a vice. Bella's voice, laced with fear, replays in my head, sending a shiver that's not from the cold straight through me.

"Mom, I hear a man outside the house, I'm scared!"

Great. Just great. Because we really needed another episode of 'Creeper by the Countryside' to round out our holiday season. And here I thought the Christmas parade was the finale, not this impromptu horror show.

Poor Bella. She'd chosen the warmth of her bed over the chilly celebration, probably dreaming of a quiet evening with her YouTube videos and a bag of Cheetos, not a live reenactment of a suspense thriller. The last incident had left her jittery, jumping at shadows and mistaking the wind for whispers. Now, this.

With the car's engine growling beneath me, I push the pedal a bit harder. We turn off the highway. Two minutes. Just two minutes away.

Eliana and her friend are in the back, buzzing with post-parade adrenaline, blissfully unaware of the drama unfolding. I keep the worry corked up tight inside, where it bubbles and hisses, threatening to make a liar out of my calm exterior.

The phone call hangs in the air, heavy and ominous, as we make the final turn toward home. My mind races through the possibilities—Is it a real threat or just shadows and sounds? Is it the same situation as last time? But deep down, the primal part of me that's all mama bear and raw nerve doesn't care about probabilities. It only cares about getting to Bella, about sweeping her up and proving that it's nothing, just the wind, just the house settling.

"Stay on the line, Bella, I'm almost there," I assure her, my voice a steady lie that I'm not sure I believe.

As we pull into the driveway, my headlights slash through the darkness, casting long, eerie shadows that dart away like specters caught mid-scheme. I'm out of the car before it's fully stopped, my heart thudding a frantic Morse code of dread and hope, ready to face whatever waits in the darkness. Tonight, I'm all simmering rage, half-hoping to catch some miscreant lurking in the yard just so I can unleash this pent-up fury. But as I sweep the yard with my phone's flashlight, it's just shadows and silence—no villain to confront, just the crisp night air.

I barricade myself in the bedroom, leaving the kids with their sleepover staples—microwave pizza rolls and animated movies that are supposed to ensure a magical night. They're set. They're safe. They're happy. Me? I'm a cocktail of adrenaline and exasperation, shaken and stirred.

In the solitude of my room, the earlier rush of motherly fury gives way to a crash—the kind that leaves you not just questioning the universe but also ready to file a complaint with its management. I'm furious, truly. Furious that my home, my fortress, feels breached even without proof of an intruder. Furious with God, who I'm sure has more pressing matters than my backyard drama but who I wish would cut me some slack. And let's be honest, I'm mostly furious with myself, because if there's a screw-up to be had, I'm your woman.

As I sit on the edge of my bed, the night's excitement morphs into a leaden weariness. Maybe I am just tired. Tired of being on edge, tired of second-guessing every creak of my too-old house, and tired of feeling like I need to be the superhero in a cape when I can't even keep my own anxieties in check. There's no villain lurking in the shadows tonight, just the all-too-familiar specter of my own thoughts.

As the house falls silent after the evening's chaos, I find myself sitting alone, the weight of my responsibilities pressing down on me with unbearable force. I'm not alone in the strictest sense—I have my girls, my beautiful, lively daughters who fill my days with laughter and love. Yet, when it comes to life's decisions, fears, and burdens, I stand alone. There's no partner to share the load, no confidante to lean on when the night grows dark and full of terrors.

I ponder this solitude, crafted by a God who must have known the path my life would take. Here I am, sculpted for a role that often feels too grand and solitary for one soul to bear. Even when I was married, even when Steven was around, companionship felt like a myth. They were like extra children, large and unwieldy, adding layers of complexity rather than partnership.

Tonight's scare has thrown my emotions into sharp relief, highlighting the stark loneliness that accompanies the holiday season. The joy and warmth of festive lights seem to cast longer shadows in my home, shadows filled with anxiety, loneliness, and an unshakeable dread.

As I sit here, embraced by the night's stillness and the chilling touch of solitude, I'm struck by a harsh realization: even if the perfect companion were to appear, I am not in a state to give or receive the love that a relationship requires. This realization adds another layer of hopelessness to my burden. I recognize, on some level, that I am part of the problem, yet I have no idea how to begin to fix myself. This not only deepens my sense of isolation but also leaves me yearning for a beacon—a light or a soul to guide me to a haven where I might find respite from this relentless sea. Tonight, however, it's just me, grappling with the shards of broken expectations and a dwindling whisper of hope for a less solitary path ahead.

CHAPTER 45 SISTERS

Annie's childhood home in Sapulpa was a hub of youthful energy, nestled in a neighborhood that served as the perfect playground for her and her sister Jeana. Their modest Craftsman house, always well-kept by their industrious parents, was the starting point for daily adventures. With both parents often busy working and studying, Annie and Jeana grew up as latchkey kids, a common scenario in the 80s and 90s.

From a young age, they were granted a level of independence that fueled their explorations. Their days were filled with the simple joys of childhood: biking to the local store for candy, racing to the park to claim the best swings, and organizing impromptu games with neighborhood friends. The freedom to roam the streets and alleyways, to feel the wind in their hair as they pedaled furiously down the block, was exhilarating.

This carefree existence was punctuated by the clinking of bike chains and the distant calls of "Dinner's ready!" echoing down the street as the sun began to dip below the horizon. Annie and Jeana, often muddy-kneed and sun-streaked, would return home with stories of the day's escapades, their laughter a constant soundtrack to their adventures.

These were golden, untethered days, where the biggest concerns were skinned knees and who would be the seeker in the next game of hide and seek. Annie's early years were filled with freedom, camaraderie, and the kind of innocent mischief that only childhood can offer

Annie's knack for people-pleasing wasn't just a superficial trait; it was a survival mechanism, deeply rooted in her aversion to conflict and her yearning for harmony. Growing up in Sapulpa, her home was often charged with the undercurrents of parental disputes. The sharp crescendo of raised voices between her mother and father could instantly douse the warmth of their small home, replacing it with a cold tension that seeped into every corner.

This environment, where domestic storms were frequent and unpredictable, instilled in Annie a profound fear of discord. Each argument felt like a crack in the foundation of her family's stability, and she believed, perhaps naively, that she could fill these fissures with her own conduct. By aligning her behavior with the expectations of those around her—smoothing her edges, silencing her doubts, perfecting her role as the compliant daughter—she hoped to keep the peace.

Her efforts extended beyond her family life. In school, she was the child whose hand shot up not merely to answer but to affirm her teachers' expectations. In church, her prayers were whispered pledges of good behavior, each word a brick in the barricade she built against potential chaos.

The very thought of causing disappointment or, worse, igniting further conflict, was unbearable. It was as if she held herself responsible for maintaining an equilibrium, believing that her perfect performance could somehow mend the cracks in her world. This pressure to be the glue, the fixer, the peacekeeper, was a silent burden she carried, often at the expense of her own voice and desires.

Jeana, the fiery counterpart to Annie's placid demeanor, blazed through life with a spirit that often perplexed their parents.

Where Annie sought approval, Jeana challenged authority from a tender age. Her rebellious streak was ignited early; a memorable episode unfolded when their mother was summoned to the principal's office because Jeana, barely in first grade, had sauntered into class, propped her feet on the desk, and declared that the teacher had no right to boss her around.

This audacity set the tone for Jeana's school years. Each September brought a new teacher's hopeful smile, expecting another student like Annie—meticulous and eager to please. Instead, they met Jeana, whose vibrant personality couldn't be more different. Although not a troublemaker in the traditional sense, Jeana wore her independence like armor. She questioned everything, which teachers often mistook for disobedience rather than an intelligent, inquisitive mind engaging with the world on her own terms.

Her struggles in school weren't due to a lack of intelligence or ability, but rather a profound sense of how mundane and constraining the educational system felt to her. Jeana possessed a robust sense of justice and a compassionate heart, attributes that made her a fiercely loyal friend and a defender of underdogs. However, these traits often put her at odds with a system that, in her view, rarely addressed the things that truly mattered. Where Annie found safety in conformity, Jeana found her identity in resistance, a dynamic that painted their sibling story in starkly contrasting hues.

As Annie and Jeana journeyed deeper into adolescence, the rift between them widened, transforming into a chasm filled with mutual resentment and frustration. Annie, entrenched in her academic and extracurricular pursuits, found herself increasingly exasperated by Jeana's defiance and the chaos it invited into their family life.

Their parents, already stretched thin by their commitments,

were now utterly consumed by efforts to steer Jeana back on a more conventional path, their worry and disappointment palpable in every strained conversation and tense family dinner.

Jeana, for her part, harbored a growing resentment towards Annie, whom she saw as the quintessential people-pleaser, effortlessly embodying their parents' ideals of success and propriety. This perceived perfection only deepened Jeana's feelings of inadequacy and rebellion. She didn't aspire to reach the bar Annie had set; in fact, she rejected it entirely, yet the constant comparisons drawn by teachers and even their parents left her feeling alienated and misunderstood within her own family.

The sisters, once bound by childhood camaraderie, now found themselves embroiled in a silent battle of wills —Annie increasingly angry at Jeana for the turmoil she caused, and Jeana feeling marginalized and defiant, convinced that her identity was being overshadowed by her sister's accomplishments. This growing animosity only added another layer of tension to an already strained household, marking their teenage years with conflict and emotional distance.

CHAPTER 46 LIFE GETS HARD

At fifteen, Annie grappled with a gnawing sense of abandonment. Her efforts to excel—whether in academics or extracurriculars—had always been partly motivated by a desire to garner her parents' attention and approval. But now, with her parents' focus laser-locked on Jeana, Annie felt like a background character in the drama consuming her family. Jeana, just thirteen, had already dropped out of school and was in the throes of a tumultuous relationship with a seventeen-year-old. She seemed to drift further from the family each day, appearing at home only sporadically, her visits usually motivated by need rather than affection.

Annie's home life, once a realm of safety and encouragement, had transformed into a landscape of neglect. The constant crises surrounding Jeana left Annie feeling invisible. Her achievements, once celebrated, now barely garnered a nod. This erosion of familial support left Annie profoundly isolated, battling feelings of worthlessness and rejection. This shift not only deepened the divide between the sisters but also altered Annie's relationship with her parents. They, consumed by the fear of losing Jeana , inadvertently widened the emotional gap with Annie. Each passing day, as Jeana's shadow grew larger and more troubled, Annie's sense of isolation intensified, forging a chasm that seemed too vast to bridge with mere grades or school awards. The family unit, once close-knit, was fraying, and Annie felt powerless to stop it.

The escalating chaos surrounding Jeana reached a breaking point for Annie's mother, who, exhausted and defeated by the constant worry, capitulated to the turmoil. The house, once a haven of order and discipline, became a den for Jeana and her unruly friends. Central to this shift was Jeremiah, Jeana's older and decidedly troubled boyfriend, who effectively commandeered the role of ringleader within their home.

Jeremiah's presence marked a stark transformation in the household dynamics. Annie's mother, having exhausted every recommended strategy from countless parenting books and tough love methods, felt powerless. Her decision to relent was born from a desperate hope that keeping Jeana close was better than the agony of endless nights wondering if her daughter was safe.

This surrender, however, came at a significant cost to the family's structure and Annie's sense of security. The home was no longer a place of safety and nurturing but a stage for the reckless escapades of Jeana and her cohort. The constant flow of strangers and the air thick with rebellion suffocated any remaining semblance of normalcy.

Annie watched as her family's values were trampled under the feet of uncaring interlopers. Her mother's defeat, while perhaps stemming from a place of maternal desperation, allowed dysfunction to root deeply within their home. Annie felt the sting of abandonment more acutely than ever, as her environment spiraled into chaos, leaving her to navigate the wreckage of what was once her sanctuary.

In the tumultuous environment of her home, Annie's efforts to maintain a focus on academics felt like clinging to a life raft in stormy seas. The house that once provided a sanctuary was now perpetually drowned in noise from her sister Jeana's reckless entourage. Their drug-fueled revelry and endless nights of drinking transformed her safe haven into a den of chaos.

Annie's parents, when they were around, drifted through the house like shadows, seemingly oblivious or powerless against the upheaval. This detachment not only deepened Annie's sense of isolation but also bred a profound resentment. It felt as though they had chosen Jeana's side, surrendering to her chaotic lifestyle at the expense of Annie's well-being.

With each day, Annie harbored a growing rage—a silent, simmering fury not just at the stolen peace but at her parents' apparent abandonment. Why, she often wondered, did they sacrifice her sense of security to appease Jeana? It felt as if she had been discarded, thrown out like garbage, left to cope alone in the mess her sister created.

This toxic brew of emotions—anger, despair, and a feeling of utter powerlessness—converged to cast a shadow over her once hopeful spirit, coloring her world with a relentless gray of resignation and deep-seated sorrow.

In the cramped quarters of their shared bedroom, each sister had claimed a twin-sized bed as their own tiny island of privacy. Yet for Annie, this small space of refuge was frequently invaded. Returning from school, she would often find Jeana's boyfriend, Jeremiah, sprawled across her bed, his presence an unwelcome intrusion. The remnants of his occupancy—sunflower seed shells, chicken wing bones, and empty beer cans—strewed across her sheets, desecrating what little personal space she had.

This daily violation of her sanctuary deepened Annie's sense of powerlessness. Even though Jeremiah would move when asked, the disrespect lingered, tainting her bedding and the air around her with a palpable sense of contamination. This constant breach not only eroded her comfort but also ignited a smoldering anger within her.

As the chaos of her sister's life increasingly dominated their home, Annie's attempts to maintain some semblance of normalcy and achievement felt futile. The stark contrast between her striving for approval and her family's indifference to her needs sharpened her feelings of worthlessness. The pain of feeling like an afterthought in her own home was a heavy burden, making each day a test of her resolve and endurance.

CHAPTER 47 IF YOU CAN'T BEAT EM

As the days wore on, the weight of Annie's ignored pleas and trampled privacy pushed her to a breaking point. The constant invasion of her space and disregard for her feelings eroded her once steadfast determination to excel and please. Why maintain the facade of the perfect daughter when it seemed to gain her nothing but more neglect? With her resolve crumbling, Annie began to experiment with the same vices that had taken over her home—alcohol and drugs—though she kept her new habits well concealed beneath her good girl veneer.

The turning point came when Annie's paternal grandmother passed away, leaving her house empty. Sensing perhaps a sliver of remorse—or maybe just wanting to ease their own burdens —Annie's parents allowed her to move into the vacant house at the start of her senior year. Overnight, Annie's social status underwent a drastic transformation. Previously unnoticed, she suddenly found herself at the center of attention; her new, adult-free home became the hotspot for her classmates. The girl who had felt invisible and unvalued was now the linchpin of high school social life, a bittersweet twist that left her more bewildered than fulfilled.

For the first time, Annie was popular, but the irony was not lost on her: the newfound popularity was not for who she was, but for the freedoms her home afforded. As she navigated this unexpected social limelight, Annie wrestled with the complex feelings of enjoying the attention while questioning its sincerity. This sudden shift in her social standing brought with it both excitement and a deeper sense of isolation, highlighting the stark contrast between her public persona and her private struggles.

In this newfound social whirlwind, Annie found herself the sudden center of attention, not just from her classmates in general, but from the boys as well. Previously, she had always felt awkward, towering over her peers with her height, which chipped away at her self-esteem. Yet now, boys swarmed around her, drawn in by the allure of her adult-free space. Deep down, Annie understood that their interest was more in her house than in her as a person. This realization only drove her self-esteem lower, making her newfound popularity feel hollow and somewhat perilous.

As the school year progressed, Annie's academic focus began to waver. The house became a haven not just for parties but also for truancy. "Friends" would often impersonate her parents over the phone, concocting excuses to pull her from class. More than once, Annie found herself summoned to the office, clueless about why she was being excused, only to discover someone had arranged her early departure. Each unauthorized leave, each hallway whisper about her next rendezvous, chipped away at the facade of control she tried to maintain. Caught in the rush of her sudden social status, Annie felt her life spiraling out of control, each day straying further from the student and daughter she had once strived so hard to be.

In the shifting sands of Annie's rapidly changing life, she clung to one vestige of her former self—a promise she had made to herself about her virginity, a boundary she was determined to maintain until marriage. It was her line in the sand, one of the few aspects of her life over which she felt she still had control.

But then came a night that would fracture even that resolve. A long-time school friend visited her, someone she had trusted. As the evening unfolded, he mixed her a drink. The night's memories would only come to her in fragmented flashes; her consciousness ebbed and flowed like a menacing tide. She could vaguely recall the echo of her own voice, weakly protesting, "No, no, no..." but her body felt disconnected, unresponsive, robbed of the will or strength to resist.

That night, the last bastion of her autonomy was breached. The violation was not just physical but profoundly personal, stripping away the final semblance of control she had clung to amidst the chaos swirling through her life. It marked a profound violation of trust and a deep, indelible scar on her spirit.

In the aftermath, the horror of what happened was compounded by the boy's brazenness. He bragged to Annie about taking her virginity as if it were a consensual trophy, a shared victory rather than the violation it truly was. This blatant distortion of reality plunged Annie deeper into a well of humiliation and shame.

The descent into recklessness was as rapid as it was ruinous. Annie, feeling utterly powerless and stripped of worth, surrendered herself to a maelstrom of partying, alcohol, and drugs. It was a desperate bid to numb the pain, to blur the harsh lines of her reality into something tolerable, if not entirely forgettable.

Eventually, her parents noticed the downward spiral and intervened, dragging Annie back to the family fold. But things at home had changed: they had moved to a sprawling house perched on a hill, equipped with a pool and a hot tub, and most importantly, offering Annie a large room of her own. The space was a sanctuary, a much-needed barrier between her and the constant chaos that Jeana and her unruly entourage continued to create.

Despite the new settings and her own space, Annie's life continued its downward trajectory. She clung to her job and community college classes with a white-knuckled grip, managing to maintain these last vestiges of normalcy amidst her tumultuous personal life. The partying didn't stop; if anything, it intensified, as if the greater the heights from which she had to fall, the harder she tried to fly. Annie was walking a tightrope, balancing between the demands of daily responsibilities and the escape offered by her nocturnal escapades.

CHAPTER 48
GODS MERCY

Amidst the turmoil of Annie's spiraling lifestyle, a profound transformation was unfolding in her sister Jeana's life. At the brink of adulthood, Jeana found herself pregnant— a revelation that could have spiraled into more chaos, but instead served as a pivotal moment of clarity. Raised in a church-going family, Jeana knew the sanctity and value of life, and this foundational belief guided her decision in ways she hadn't anticipated.

When Jeana broke the news to her parents, the response was enveloped in nothing but support and love. There was no room for shame or guilt; only a deep, abiding gratitude permeated their household. Her parents saw the pregnancy not as a crisis but as a divine intervention—a merciful wake-up call from God that Jeana desperately needed. This support system became her bedrock, reinforcing her decision to turn her life around.

Jeana quit smoking, drinking, and using drugs, choosing instead to dedicate herself to the well-being of the child growing inside her. She reconnected with her faith and her family, finding strength in the very relationships she had once strained with her rebellious streak. The birth of her son, Mason Lee, marked not just a new beginning for him but a rebirth for Jeana as well. Her transformation was a testimony to the power of support, love, and second chances, underscored by her family's unwavering belief in redemption and the grace of God. Her parents' support was unyielding, their joy immense at the prospect of welcoming a grandchild, seeing it as a blessing that brought renewed hope and purpose into their lives.

In the midst of Jeana's life blossoming anew with the arrival of her son, an unexpected transformation was also occurring in the life of Jeremiah, Jeana's troubled boyfriend. While Jeana was embracing her new role as a mother, Jeremiah found himself in the stark confines of a prison cell—a place that forced him into sobriety and introspection, starkly different from the chaotic life he had led on the outside.

Jeremiah's past was marked by deep trauma. Raised by a mother who was deeply troubled and intermittently absent, he and his brother had faced a tumultuous childhood. His life took a darker turn when, at just ten years old, his brother, the only constant in his young life, tragically took his own life in the woods near their home. This event left an indelible scar on Jeremiah, burdening him with an unwarranted and heavy guilt that he carried into his adult life.

Raised in an environment filled with disdain for Christianity and rampant with drugs and alcohol, Jeremiah's path seemed irrevocably set towards destruction. However, the solitude and forced withdrawal of prison life led to a profound personal revelation. For the first time, he truly heard the message of Jesus Christ, and it resonated deeply within him, prompting a radical transformation. He committed his life to Christ, finding solace and redemption in his newfound faith.

Simultaneously, Jeana and Annie's parents, moved by the transformations they witnessed and the struggles they understood all too well, became regular visitors to the jail. Their visits weren't limited to supporting Jeremiah; they extended their compassion to other inmates as well. This experience profoundly impacted them, eventually leading them to become deeply involved in jail ministries. They felt a compelling call to reach out to others in similar situations, sharing the hope and redemption they had witnessed in their own family. This new commitment added a layer of healing and purpose to their lives, intertwining their faith with a practical expression of love and redemption.

In the winding corridors of Annie's family life, which had long been shadowed by discord and pain, a remarkable transformation began to unfold, echoing through the hearts of each family member. The birth of Mason, Jeana's son, marked a pivotal moment of renewal and hope. This tiny, innocent life seemed to act as a catalyst for healing, drawing everyone into a collective embrace of change and redemption.

Mason, with his infectious giggle and wide, curious eyes, was more than just a beloved addition to the family; he symbolized a fresh start, a tangible testament to God's grace. Each coo and smile from the little boy seemed to mend the frayed edges of the family's troubled past. For Annie, who had weathered the storm of her own tumultuous adolescence alongside her sister's struggles, Mason's presence was a daily reminder of the possibility of redemption and the power of love.

Jeremiah, too, played an unexpected role in this unfolding narrative of restoration. His journey from a life marred by bitterness and misguidance to one of faith and purpose was nothing short of miraculous. Through his transformation, he not only redeemed himself but also brought a sense of closure and healing to a family long plagued by his chaotic influence.

The entire family, once fragmented by turmoil and conflict, found themselves united in their affection for Mason and in their support for Jeana's newfound strength and responsibility. Annie, watching these changes, felt a profound shift within herself. The bitterness and resentment that had once clouded her view began to dissipate.

God's grace, manifested in the joy of a new life and the redemption of a lost soul, was a powerful force, turning years of pain into a story of hope. It was a reminder that no situation was beyond His reach, that every act of genuine repentance and every step towards love could pave the way for miraculous healing.

Jeana and Jeremiah, both fiery spirits with a penchant for passionate exchanges, found themselves perfectly matched in temperament and resilience. Their communication style—often intense, sometimes comical—seemed to work for them in a strangely effective way. No matter the challenge or how heated their arguments became, their deep-rooted love for each other, their children, and their faith always pulled them back together.

Their relationship, though tumultuous at times, was a testament to their commitment to continuously show up for each other and their family. Even after significant setbacks, like Jeremiah's struggle with addiction following his surgery, their bond remained unshaken. They tackled each hurdle with a shared determination to emerge stronger, not just for their sake but for their children.

CHAPTER 49 MARRY YOUR BEST FRIEND

In her roaring twenties, Annie's life was a roller coaster of impulsive road trips to see her favorite bands, unpredictable camping adventures, and non-stop social gatherings. During this electrifying period, she struck a deep friendship with Mark—a lanky, uproarious soul who could effortlessly turn any dull moment into a riot of laughter. Their affinity for spur-of-the-moment escapades made them inseparable.

As their friendship deepened, Mark revealed his clever wit and sharp humor, captivating Annie further. One unexpected evening, the dynamics shifted dramatically: Mark made a bold move that transitioned them from platonic pals to romantic partners. From then on, they were a dynamic duo, fused by both friendship and love.

Despite his occasional bouts of jealousy and immaturity, Mark's intelligence and humor shone through, endearing him even more to Annie. His love was genuine—flawed, perhaps, but deeply rooted. Annie cherished him, not just for the laughter he brought into her life, but for his unwavering commitment to their shared happiness.

Everything shifted for Annie at the age of 25 when she discovered she was pregnant. This news wasn't just a surprise

—it was a seismic shift in her self-perception and purpose. For years, Annie had felt like an afterthought in the lives of those around her, but the realization that she would soon become a mother brought an intense mix of excitement and profound anxiety. Could she handle such a monumental responsibility? The doubt loomed large, yet intertwined with it was an overwhelming love and a fierce protective instinct towards the tiny life growing inside her.

This mix of emotions was compounded by a deep-seated fear: What if God had made a mistake in entrusting her with this new life? However, this fear was gradually overshadowed by a powerful sense of validation. The very fact that she had been blessed with this child seemed to signal a divine vote of confidence. It suggested that, perhaps, God believed in her capability more than she believed in herself. This thought brought her a comfort she hadn't expected, reinforcing her resolve to rise to the challenges of motherhood.

Mark, who until this pivotal moment had navigated life with the breezy carelessness of an overgrown child, albeit a charming and clever one, found himself abruptly anchored by the gravity of impending fatherhood. The news of Annie's pregnancy ignited a transformative spark within him. Known for his wit and humorous antics, Mark's usual lightheartedness was now paired with a newfound purpose. With palpable excitement bubbling through his usual jest, he threw himself into the task of securing their future. He scoured the job market with a vigor that was both surprising and heartening, determined to provide for the family that was about to expand. His efforts, driven by a blend of joy and responsibility, marked the beginning of a new chapter for both him and Annie as they prepared to navigate the uncharted waters of parenthood together.

In a whirlwind of spontaneity that mirrored their entire relationship, Mark and Annie decided to elope, tying the knot in a humble yet heartfelt ceremony only a couple of months before their first daughter, Sophia, was due to arrive. The decision was impulsive, yet deeply significant, reflecting their shared desire to solidify their commitment in the face of their impending new responsibilities. As they stood together, exchanging vows in a modest setting, there was an unspoken understanding that this was not just the culmination of their wild adventures together but the beginning of their most profound adventure yet. With little fanfare but plenty of genuine emotion, they stepped into marriage, ready to welcome their daughter into a newly formed union.

CHAPTER 50 A LIFE WITH PURPOSE

After Sophia's birth, the years seemed to whirl by in a blur of joy and diapers, bringing Isabella into the world and, not long thereafter, Eliana—each child adding more noise, more chaos, and infinitely more happiness to their lives. Annie embraced motherhood with a ferocity that surprised even herself; she found a profound sense of purpose in nurturing these small beings, her life suddenly anchored in a way it had never been before. She poured her entire soul into raising her daughters, infusing their days with as much magic and love as she could muster.

Mark, for his part, was smitten with his girls, each new arrival wrapping him a little tighter around their tiny fingers. Committed to their well-being, he worked, balancing a demanding job with night classes, driven by the determination to provide a stable and prosperous future for his rapidly expanding family.

Mark, though often a loving husband and adoring father, had a darker side that brewed beneath the surface, a volatility that Annie felt with increasing frequency. His affection for her was undeniable, yet it was tainted by an underlying aggression that surfaced during his bouts with alcohol. These episodes transformed him, making the walls of their home feel more like prison bars to Annie as she became the target of his drunken tirades.

With the break of dawn, Mark would often wake with regret thick in his voice, issuing apologies steeped in sincerity but lacking permanence. Annie, well-versed in the art of appeasement from her youth, maneuvered through her days on a tightrope of caution, her movements calculated to evade the landmines of his mood swings. Despite her careful choreography, the threat of another outburst hovered constantly, a dark cloud over their domestic landscape.

Her efforts, no matter how delicately executed, seemed only to postpone the inevitable. Each cycle of reconciliation and disruption chipped away at her, leaving her to navigate the dual burdens of hope and helplessness. In her deepest moments of despair, she felt trapped, reliving the helpless anxiety of her childhood, now compounded by the fierce desire to shield her daughters from the shadow that loomed unpredictably over their lives. The love that bound her to Mark was complex, woven with threads of deep connection and frayed by fear and uncertainty.

As Annie embraced her role as a mother with fervor, finding in it a fulfillment that saturated the deepest recesses of her being, she also confronted the irony of her domestic life. She had envisioned a partnership in this grand venture of parenthood, a shared journey with Mark, her companion who once made her world a happier, funnier place. Yet, more often than not, the weight of family life seemed to rest solely on her shoulders.

Mark, who could light up a room with his humor and whose love had once seemed a steadfast pillar, now flickered erratically like a lamp in a storm. His moods were a pendulum swinging from warmth to chilling aloofness, leaving Annie to tread carefully around him, nurturing her children's joy while tempering their exposure to his darker days.

She poured herself into motherhood with dedication, yet found herself navigating the unpredictable currents of Mark's discontent. Her days were a ballet of managing smiles and soothing frowns, of keeping the children aloft in a bubble of wonder, all while attending to Mark's ever-shifting needs. In this complex dance, Annie often felt less like a partner and more like a caretaker managing an overgrown child, whose bouts of sullenness could eclipse the joy she worked so hard to cultivate.

Despite the joy her daughters brought her, there was an undercurrent of loneliness in her role as a mother, a sense of solo navigation through the choppy waters of family life, where she was the sole captain responsible for keeping the ship afloat.

After the worst of Mark's outbursts had subsided, leaving emotional wreckage in their wake, Annie would gather her daughters and escape to the temporary haven of her parents' home. These escapes were her way of drawing breath, brief interludes from the relentless turbulence at home, yet they were always short-lived. Bound by a mix of fear and loyalty, she inevitably found herself returning to Mark.

Mark, ever controlling, had chillingly vowed that he would rather end her life than let her leave him permanently—a threat that Annie took to heart. It was a stark and horrifying declaration from a man whose darker sides were all too familiar to her. Her love for him, entangled with intense fear, created a complex relationship where affection was overshadowed by dread.

In moments of deep despair, when the burden of her life grew too heavy to bear, Annie's recourse was prayer. She cried out to God, her words laden with the desperation of someone caught between hope for change and the fear it might never come. She prayed for Mark's transformation, for him to find redemption and return to being the man she once loved. Simultaneously, she pleaded for liberation from his oppressive presence, should change prove impossible. Each prayer was a fragile whisper into the chaos, a mix of hope and skepticism, as she grappled with the reality of her love and the terror it entailed. Her faith was her sanctuary, yet it flickered in the shadow of the relentless storms she endured.

CHAPTER 51 THE HOLIDAYS

It's the heart of December, and Christmas is breathing down Annie's neck with its frosty breath. Somehow, she has mustered the scraps of her finances to buy presents for Sophia, Isabella, and Eliana. It won't be a mountain of gifts, as the financial quagmire left by Steven still clutches at her ankles, but it will be enough. Tomorrow, they plan to brave the cold to buy ingredients for homemade candies, a tradition that brings a semblance of sweetness to their strained festivities.

As the holidays tighten their icy grip, so too does anxiety constrict around Annie's heart. The joy of the season is tarnished by a haunting past that revisits her each year, a ghost more chilling than any winter wind. The atmosphere at home grows heavy, a silent acknowledgment of shared pain as they all engage in the motions of merriment.

In the midst of this emotional tempest, Paul's presence, once a beacon, becomes another wave crashing against her weary shores. His attempts to anchor her with calls and messages only seem to drive her further into the storm. As he presses for closeness, she recoils, adrift in her sea of turmoil. When he finally confronts her, pleading to understand her retreat, Annie's response is a resigned whisper of impossibility. She tells him she's sorry, but she cannot be the harbor he seeks, not now, perhaps not ever.

Feeling increasingly isolated, Paul's voice becomes another echo she can't face, and their connection frays until it snaps. Distraught and disconnected, Annie finds herself reopening her Snapchat account. The digital platform, dormant yet not erased, welcomes her back with open arms, preserving her connections like specters in a machine. In a moment of weakness or perhaps necessity, she plunges back into the virtual crowd, seeking anything to fill the void left by withdrawn affections and the spectral pains of December.

CHAPTER 52 NOT A DREAM

It's a chilly Thursday night, and I'm deep in the kind of dreamless sleep that only comes when you're truly exhausted. Suddenly, Gracie's deep, menacing growl cuts through the silence. Her bed is nestled in the corner by the window, and this sound from her is not the usual attention-seeking whimper but a guttural warning that sets every nerve in my body alight.

My heart catapults into my throat as I lie frozen, half-consumed by the fog of sleep, half-alert to the creeping danger. Then, the faint beep of the front door's electronic lock pierces the stillness, followed by a sinister clicking noise, like the tumblers of fate aligning against me. Is someone attempting to invade my sanctuary? Panic claws at my chest, fierce and quick. I mentally tally the whereabouts of my gun, then my trusty golf club. But as abruptly as they began, the sounds cease. Gracie, too, settles back down as if the night has reassured her of its innocuous intentions. She curls up and resumes snoring.

And then, a wave of inexplicable peace washes over me, drowning my fears in a gentle, insistent tide. Moments ago, adrenaline had primed me for battle in the confines of my bedroom, but now a heavy tranquility anchors my limbs to the bed. The readiness to spring into action dissipates, replaced by an overwhelming urge to sleep. My eyelids grow heavy, impossible to keep open.

As I teeter on the edge of consciousness, a warm hand gently touches the top of my head, a tender kiss lands softly on my forehead. It's a gesture so filled with safety and love that it banishes any remaining shred of fear. I don't even question the presence; the comfort it brings feels ancient and immeasurable. Surrendering to the sensation, I drift back into a deep, protective slumber, enveloped in a sense of security that feels both otherworldly and intimately familiar.

It's a bright, crisp morning when I wake, still half-entangled in the remnants of last night's bizarre episode. For a moment, I wonder if it was all just a strange dream. The vividness with which I recall the incident, however, isn't typical of my usual dreams, which tend to dissolve into the morning light like salt in water. I shake the thought away and decide not to dwell on it —until later.

As I'm about to head out, I reach for the door, and suddenly, a mechanical catastrophe: the entire inner mechanism of the doorknob clatters to the floor in a mess of metal and mystery. My heart leaps into my throat. Was someone actually trying to break in last night? The pieces lie accusingly at my feet, and a chill runs through me. But then, the serenity from the night before washes over me once more.

Driven by a mix of newfound courage and lingering fear, I check the security cameras, only to find they've been disconnected. The last recorded footage? December 15th. That was the night of the Christmas parade when Bella was terrified by noises outside. It all clicks into place now, terrifying and bizarre in equal measure.

Even as my mind races with the implications, that unearthly peace clings to me stubbornly, a shield against the chaos. It's as if last night's guardian angel, left behind a residue of calm that insists, despite the evidence, that I am under some mighty wing. With my door knob in ruins and my security system sabotaged, I've never felt safer. Life, as usual, continues to be a paradox, and here I am, living right at the heart of it.

CHAPTER 53 JUST SURVIVE IT

As Christmas approaches, casting long shadows with its festive glow, Annie confronts not just the ghostly echoes of her past but also the fresh fear of a potential stalker. Yet, in a manner so characteristically hers, Annie refuses to dwell on these looming threats. Instead, she clings to the mysterious, comforting touch she felt that one restless night—a hand on her head and a soft kiss on her forehead, experiences too vivid to dismiss as mere figments of imagination.

To Annie, these moments, resonate with profound reality and significance. Perhaps God has chosen this harrowing ordeal as an opportunity to affirm His presence. It's a crucial reminder that even in her most isolated moments, when the past tugs at her heartstrings and the shadows of uncertainty creep in, she is far from alone. There exists a force, transcendent and potent, ready to safeguard her against the darkest tides, imbuing her with the strength to not only endure but perhaps to find a semblance of peace amid the chaos.

On Christmas morning, as the dawn unfurls its gentle light, Annie and her daughters gather around the tree, their faces lit by the soft glow of the tree. They unwrap presents, each expression a mix of happiness and gratitude, a bittersweet undercurrent weaving through their joy. Despite the festive cheer, the room is thick with unspoken memories, the ghosts of past Christmases hanging in the air, almost tangible as the date draws near.

Seizing the moment to confront the palpable sense of loss, Annie initiates a heartfelt conversation about the emotional weight this season carries. They sit together, surrounded by the remnants of opened gifts, acknowledging the shared ache that this time of year resurrects. Annie prays over the girls asking for peace and joy and that God would continue to comfort them. There's a silent agreement to continue the day with renewed spirit, delving into family dinners and the new toys and gadgets that have joined their household. Yet, the light that once filled Christmas with unadulterated wonder now seems to accentuate the darkness lurking at its edges. The joy of the present can't fully mask the pain of the past, and no matter how much they try to immerse themselves in celebration, the shadow of what was lost looms larger, stubbornly resistant to the efforts to cast it aside.

CHAPTER 54 PAIN DOESN'T STAY IN THE PAST

The day after Christmas unfolded with laughter and creativity as Annie and her daughters built an elaborate fort in the living room. The holiday's warmth lingered in the air, punctuated by the joyful challenge of assembling a palace from hundreds of colorful tubes and connectors—a gift that had captivated Eliana's imagination. Their joy was a bright bubble in the winter chill, a moment of pure, undiluted happiness.

That bubble burst abruptly when Annie's phone rang, cutting through the gaiety like a sharp winter wind. Steven, who had been pottering around in the kitchen, looked up as Annie answered the call, her face alight with the residual joy of their playful construction. However, the light drained away as she listened to her mother's voice, not with the expected pleasantries of a post-Christmas catch-up but with urgent, breathless words that made Annie's heart sink into her stomach.

"You need to go to Jeana's now, your sister needs you!" her mother's voice crackled through the phone with an intensity that sent chills down Annie's spine.

"What's going on?!" Annie pressed, her voice thick with sudden fear.

"It's Jeremiah... he just shot himself. We're driving back from Arkansas but we're still an hour away," her mother explained, her voice a mixture of panic and command.

The words struck Annie like a physical blow, "Oh God no! Is he okay? I'm leaving now!" she blurted out, though even as she asked, she felt the weight of the answer she already suspected.

Her daughters, sensing the shift in the atmosphere, watched her with wide, scared eyes. Annie tried to gather her composure as she explained to them in as calm a voice she could muster, "Something has happened with Uncle Jeremiah. I need to go to your aunt Jeana right now. Please stay here. I'll call you as soon as I can."

Steven, sensing the gravity of the situation, quickly offered to accompany her. As they raced to the car, Annie filled him in on the dire news. They drove through the back roads, they made the short journey to Jeana's house in half the expected time, each minute stretching and compressing with the urgency of their mission.

The usually short drive felt interminable, each turn bringing them closer to a reality Annie wished could be different.

As they pulled up to Jeana's house, the scene was grimly marked by the flashing lights of police cars. Jeana stood alone behind her car, a figure of utter desolation against the bleak winter backdrop, her face ashen and her posture stiff with shock. Without hesitation, Annie shut off the car and rushed to her sister, enveloping her in a forced embrace that Jeana hardly seemed to feel.

"Are you okay?" Annie implored, searching Jeana's face for any sign of the sister she knew.

Jeana's eyes were distant, her voice hollow as she recounted the nightmare unfolding around them. "I don't know. We were fighting, he was acting crazy, and I was on the phone with 911. He picked up the .22, and when he did, I turned to leave the room... then I heard the shot." She paused, her voice trailing off as if she were speaking from a far-off place. "I ran out."

Her expression was eerily calm, a stark contrast to the chaos that surely churned beneath. She seemed detached, almost an observer in her own tragedy, struggling to tether herself to a reality that had shifted irrevocably beneath her feet.

A police officer stepped out from the house, his expression grave. He shook his head slightly as he approached them, his gesture a silent herald of the finality of the situation. Jeremiah was gone. There was no need for ambulances or attempts at revival. The finality of the act was absolute, leaving a void that the cold, bright day seemed to echo.

The news settled over them like a heavy shroud, and Annie, despite her own shock, tightened her grip on Jeana. The police officer offered a gentle, "I'm very sorry for your loss," which seemed to hang in the air, too frail to bear the weight of such sorrow. As the reality set in, Annie knew that their lives had been altered in the most profound and irrevocable way.

Annie knew all too well the unbearable weight of imparting the news of a father's death to his children. The agony of telling her own daughters about their father's passing still haunted her, a pain upon pain that seemed insurmountable. Now, as she drove to fetch Mason, she was enveloped in that familiar grief, intensified by the echo of her past. Leaving Jeana alone in the raw aftermath was a necessity that stung bitterly. Annie's parents were headed on a similar mission to collect Isaiah and Jadyn. Soon they would all be back together.

The roads to Olivia's house, where Mason was spending his post-Christmas evening, were hauntingly empty, mirroring the emptiness Annie felt inside. With each mile, she rehearsed the words she would say, knowing no rehearsal could ease the burden of the message she carried.

Her heart pounded with dread not just for the act of delivering the news, but for the indelible mark it would leave on Mason. At 19, he was no longer the little boy who had made her a "Best Annie Ever" book, but in her eyes, he remained that sweet, innocent child. The thought of her face and voice becoming intertwined with the memory of his father's death was almost too much to bear.

The muted atmosphere in the car felt stifling as Annie struggled with the weight of her words. The journey back seemed both interminable and fleeting, as if each moment were at once dragging and slipping through her fingers. Mason sat silently next to her, his earlier casual demeanor shattered by the gravity of the news. His stoic facade, a mask worn too soon by someone so young, broke Annie's heart anew.

They arrived as twilight bled into night, casting long shadows across Jeana's home that seemed to mirror the darkening pall over their lives. The house, usually a sanctuary, now loomed like a monument to their collective sorrow. Jeana, still standing where Annie had left her, appeared frozen in place—a statue of despair, her face etched with the agony of irreversible loss.

Annie and Mason walked up the drive, their steps hesitant. As they approached, Jeana's eyes flicked between them, searching her son's face for signs of how deeply the cruel truth had cut. The reunion was a silent one, with hugs that were tight and desperate. There was comfort in the closeness, yet the air was thick with unspoken fear and pain.

Together, they waited for the rest of the family to arrive, each lost in their own tumult of grief and shock. The normalcy of their earlier Christmas celebrations seemed like a distant memory, now replaced by the harsh reality of their new, unwanted reality. Annie stood beside her sister, offering silent support, the bonds of sisterhood both a lifeline and a reminder of their shared burdens.

As the lights of her parents' car appeared, turning into the driveway, Annie braced herself. The night was far from over, and the process of grieving was just beginning. But in this moment of profound despair, the family's unity was the one beacon of hope flickering in the encroaching darkness.

The air was thick with grief as the family stood motionless, their eyes locked on the house that once echoed with laughter but now resonated with an unbearable silence. Each family member seemed caught in their own personal nightmare, frozen by the magnitude of the tragedy that had unfolded so suddenly, so irrevocably.

Isaiah's usually vibrant eyes were now dull, his youthful resilience shrouded by a veil of stoicism he wore like armor. Jadyn, once so bubbly and animated, stood numb, her innocence overshadowed by a cruel reality that no child should ever have to face. Mason, attempting to muster a facade of strength, bore the weight of premature adulthood. His shoulders seemed to sag under the burden of expectations to be the man of the family now.

Annie's own heart ached as she recalled the last glimpses of Jeremiah during the Christmas celebrations. His features, normally full of life, had been etched with an unspoken sorrow that she had failed to probe. The memory of his haunted eyes now played over in her mind, each recollection a stinging reminder of what she perceived as her failure to act, to inquire, to help.

The guilt was crushing, tightening around her chest like a vice. She felt responsible, somehow complicit in his despair for not having noticed the signs that, in hindsight, seemed glaringly obvious. This self-reproach was a familiar torment, a ghost that had haunted her many times before, whispering of failures real and imagined.

As the coroner's van finally arrived, breaking the oppressive silence, it seemed to herald the finality of Jeremiah's decision. The stark reality that there would be no more opportunities to alter the course of events, to reach out, to heal the wounds that had been too deep to see, was overwhelming.

The family remained together, a tableau of shared sorrow, as the coroner prepared to enter the house. Each step they took seemed to echo in the quiet night, a grim march towards an ending that none of them could have predicted. The scene was a stark reminder of the fragility of life and the profound impact of each moment, a lesson engraved in their hearts forever.

Annie replayed the scenes of Christmas Eve in her mind, the images tinged with a haunting prescience she could hardly bear. Jeremiah, a specter at the feast, watched the family from the fringes, his presence more absence than participation. As she busied herself with the festive activities, his solitary figure lingered in her periphery—a poignant reminder of a man adrift in his own despair.

The thought nagged at her: had Jeremiah looked at her, seen her seemingly content life with Steven, and drawn a bleak comparison with his own tumultuous existence? Did he believe, in those final, desperate moments, that his family might flourish in his absence? It was a sinister echo of the lie that had shadowed her own life with Mark—the lie that absence could somehow mean improvement, that vanishing could be an act of love.

Annie wished she had reached out that night, taken the

moment to affirm Jeremiah's worth, to dispel the darkness that clouded his vision. She could have told him how vital he was, not just to Jeana and the children, but to the entire fabric of their family. That no matter the trials, his life was a thread interwoven with theirs, impossible to extricate without unraveling everything.

She imagined what she would have said: that he was cherished beyond his own comprehension, that his presence was a gift of immeasurable worth. She would have reminded him of his intrinsic value, that he was beloved by God and needed by them all.

Now, reflecting on the tragedy, Annie felt a deep, searing pain —the realization that Jeremiah might have felt compelled to sacrifice himself out of a misguided sense of protection, a distorted act of love. He had seen himself as the problem, not part of the solution. How tragic, that in trying to shield his family from pain, he had immersed them in an abyss of grief.

The devil's whispers, or perhaps his own tormented thoughts, had convinced him that his absence was a solution. He had indeed died for his family, but not in the way a hero dies in a noble cause; he had succumbed to a devastating illusion that his death would be their salvation. Annie's heart ached for the opportunity lost, for the words unspoken, and the reassurances never given. .

CHAPTER 55 HAPPY NEW YEAR

The echo of the past hovered heavily over Annie as New Year's approached, turning what used to be a night of revelry into one of reflection, perhaps even dread. Her once cherished traditions had faded, now overshadowed by a timeline marked by loss rather than by milestones of joy. It was easier, she found, to let the holiday slip by unnoticed if she could just cocoon herself in her bedroom, away from the fanfare that seemed more and more disconnected from her reality.

Her daughters, now growing into their own lives and rituals, had made plans to celebrate elsewhere. This was a relief to Annie; their absence meant she didn't have to feign enthusiasm or cobble together some semblance of festivity. They were free to seek their joys in the company of friends, unburdened by the somber air that tended to settle around their mother as the calendar's page turned.

Yet, the brief respite the New Year's isolation afforded her was fleeting. The passing of Jeremiah still cast a long shadow, its second anniversary just receding, and now another somber date loomed ominously—a marker not just of time passed, but of pain endured and not quite forgotten. It was these anniversaries that made each new year not a fresh start but a reminder of the relentless march of days, each one a step further from moments and people past, yet somehow never quite moving forward.

In this cycle, Annie felt not just the weight of her own grief, but the inescapable pull of history repeating itself, each joyous occasion tinged with the residue of old sorrows. As the world celebrated renewal and promise, Annie braced herself, feeling less like a participant in her life and more like a bystander watching the years roll by—one grim anniversary at a time.

Annie, once an unyielding beacon of optimism, now felt like a grim shadow of her former self. Each year's relentless difficulties had battered her resilience, leaving her feeling more akin to a beleaguered boxer at the end of a brutal bout. Bloodied and nearly broken, her hope dwindled to a faint glimmer. The vibrant force of positivity that once defined her seemed like a distant memory, obscured by the harsh realities that had relentlessly pummeled her spirit. Yet, in the dim recesses of her heart, a fragile hope persisted. It was not the robust hope of earlier days, but a thin, wavering light in the darkness—a quiet whisper suggesting that perhaps, despite everything, there might still be a chance to rise again, to mend what had been shattered, and to find a way back to herself.

Annie was caught in the throes of desperation, a weariness so profound it echoed through her very bones. Day in and day out, she mastered the minutiae of survival—working, managing home, caring for her girls—but the grand tapestry of life remained frayed and colorless. She was tired, not just from the relentless march of daily responsibilities, but from a deeper, more insidious kind of fatigue: the exhaustion of the soul.

Each morning, she awoke with the remnants of dreams where salvation came not from her own actions but from an external savior, someone who could rescue her from the relentless cycle of errors that she seemed powerless to escape. These were not dreams of a damsel in distress; they were the desperate hopes of a woman who had fought valiantly and was tired of being her only hero.

Big picture change—that elusive, transformative shift in her life—seemed like a mirage on the horizon, always visible yet forever out of reach. She knew how to push through each day, how to smile for her daughters, how to keep the shadows at bay, but how to initiate a change of monumental scale? That was a map she didn't possess. The path to renewal, to redemption from her cascade of past mistakes, remained shrouded in mist, a puzzle whose pieces she couldn't seem to find, let alone assemble.

And so, trapped in the echo chamber of her own fraught thoughts, Annie faced each day with a shrinking reservoir of hope, wondering if perhaps the next sunrise might bring with it the catalyst for the change she so desperately sought.

CHAPTER 56 IN AN INSTANT

It was an unseasonably warm and sunny December day, the kind that made the heart lighter and the winter seem kinder. In the backyard, laughter and the hum of engines filled the air with vibrant life. Bella, clad in her new riding gear, was mastering the dirt bike she'd unwrapped just days earlier, her excitement palpable as she zoomed across the grass. Mark was by her side, cheering her on with wide grins, urging her to push the limits and jump over a makeshift hill they had set up.

Nearby, Eliana navigated her Power Wheels Barbie camper with the seriousness of a seasoned driver, her eyes focused and determined. Sophia, more relaxed, enjoyed the ride as her co-pilot, her new smartphone at the ready. She snapped photos, capturing the joyous chaos of their afternoon adventures.

From the kitchen window, Annie watched over them, occasionally stepping outside to feel the warmth of the sun and join in the fun. The laughter, the shouts of encouragement, and the roar of the engines brought a joyful noise that echoed warmly against the backdrop of a bright winter sky, reminding Annie of the simple pleasures that made life so precious.

The fun-filled day had dwindled into a quiet evening; the girls were nestled inside, winding down from the excitement, as Annie tidied up, the normalcy a comforting cloak around her shoulders. But then, her phone pierced the silence—it was Mark. His words were brief, "Hey, I'm coming home in a minute," but they sent a shiver down Annie's spine. The slurred speech, the heavy tone—signs she'd come to recognize all too well. He had been drinking, perhaps more.

Annie's voice was firm, tinged with a fear she'd worked hard to bury. "Don't come out here like that. You need to stay with a friend or go stay at your mom's again. I can hear it in your voice, I'm not going to have you out here like that." Silence stretched on the line, heavy and expectant. Mark knew she could tell; after so many years together, she was all too familiar with the precursor to his darker side.

His response was a plea, veiled in a softness that almost masked the impending danger. "I just wanna come home and be with you." The memories flooded back—furniture overturned, being shoved with nowhere to escape, shrinking into corners hoping to disappear. Nights held captive by tirades, her breaths shallow as she shielded their daughters from the horrors seeping through the walls.

It was too much. She had traversed this harrowing path too many times. Her resolve solidified, powered by the resolve to protect not just herself but their children from the storm that was Mark under the influence. "No, you can't come here like that. Go sober up," she insisted, her voice a mix of desperation and determination. It was a boundary drawn from scars too deep, a line she prayed he would not cross tonight.

Annie hung up the phone, and immediately, the atmosphere in her home thickened with an ominous weight. She felt the burden of her worry as if it were a physical shroud draped heavily over her shoulders. The uncertainty of whether Mark would heed her words and stay away gnawed at her. Each possibility played out like a dire warning in her mind: Would he arrive in a drunken fury, ready to unleash chaos? Or might he appear contrite and sorrowful, a temporary repentance that she knew all too well could pivot swiftly into violence as the night wore on?

Her heart raced with the all-too-familiar cocktail of fear and resignation. The evening had shifted from serene to fraught, a transformation she had experienced countless times but could never truly brace herself for. All she could do now was pray— pray that he was somewhere else, numbing himself into stasis, far from their doorstep. The dread of his potential arrival hung in the air, a silent specter in the dimming light of their home.

The next morning Annie awoke to a peaceful house and the guilt of pushing Mark away. Navigating the peaks of relief and valleys of worry, tried to press on with her daily routine, but the silence from Mark's end was unsettling. The morning stretched into afternoon without a single word. The void of his absence gnawed at her with increasing intensity, turning every unreturned message into a crescendo of concern.

Compelled by a mix of apprehension and duty, Annie reached out again, her messages a blend of hope and desperation. "Just give it to me straight what did you do? Where are you?" But again, only silence answered her. It was unlike Mark not to respond at all, even in the worst of times.

Finally, grasping for any thread of information, Annie messaged Mark's mother, her text messages tinged with anxiety. "Hey, did Mark come over there last night? He's not here and I can't get him to answer my texts." The reply was swift but disheartening: he hadn't been there either. A swell of concern rose in her throat as they agreed to keep each other posted.

The house felt quieter than usual, the silence amplifying her fears. As hours ticked by without a word, Annie's mind raced with possibilities, each more troubling than the last. She couldn't shake the feeling that something was profoundly wrong, the suspense twisting tighter around her heart.

As the sun set on a tense Sunday, the silence from Mark's end persisted, deepening the worry that gnawed at Annie's resolve. She clung to the hope that perhaps he had simply gone off on a bender, too ashamed or unable to face her just yet. The thought provided little comfort, but it was a scenario she could understand, one less frightening than others that flitted through her mind.

Monday loomed large with its routines and responsibilities. Mark, for all his faults, had been consistent in his commitments, especially work. He had never let a wild night derail his professional obligations, nor had he ever failed to ensure that she and the girls were provided for. With this in mind, Annie reassured herself that she would hear from him by morning. This semblance of normalcy, this thread of routine, she hoped, would bring him back to the surface, sobered and ready to face whatever needed facing.

As the early morning light crept through the windows, a chill settled over Annie that had nothing to do with the weather. Mark had neither shown up for work nor called in; his silence was deafening and out of character. Her panic escalated as the hours ticked by, each minute stretching into an eternity of worry and fear. Thoughts of Mark losing control or lying somewhere hurt haunted her every second.

Annie's attempts to contact his friends yielded nothing but more anxiety—none had seen him since he left their view. Despite the turmoil churning inside her, she maintained a veneer of normalcy for her daughters, her routine a fragile lifeline in the chaos.

She peppered Mark's phone with messages, each one a blend

of worry and reassurance. "Call me, whatever's going on we will figure this out and it will be ok," she texted, her phone feeling heavier with each word. "Call your mother or me; we need to know you are okay," she pressed, the desperation clear in her digital pleas. Finally, she warned, "We are going to file a missing person's report on you soon; we don't know what else to do."

But the silence that met her pleas was absolute, a void where Mark's reassuring voice should have been, leaving her to brace against the fear that something truly terrible had happened.

At 8:30 pm, Annie's phone vibrated, cutting through the background noise of giggles and games. She glanced at the screen to see Lynn's name, Mark's mother. Annie's heart skipped a beat, a mix of hope and dread knotting her stomach as she answered.

"Hey, I'm going to come by for a minute," Lynn's voice sounded strained, urgent.

"Okay," Annie replied, her voice tight with anxiety, trying to mask her concern from the girls. She assumed Lynn wanted to discuss Mark's disappearance, hoping for some news but fearing the worst.

It wasn't long until her doorbell rang. Annie approached the door, heart thumping with anticipation, her mind racing with possibilities. As she opened it, there stood Lynn and Brooke, their expressions grave, suggesting a severity that immediately sent a chill down Annie's spine. The cheerful chaos of the girls' play inside created a stark contrast to the somber scene at the doorstep.

Lynn, her eyes betraying a tumult of emotions, managed to speak, her voice faltering slightly, "Annie, can we talk outside for a moment?"

The urgency and seriousness in her tone alarmed Annie. Nodding, she stepped outside, closing the door behind her to muffle the sounds of laughter and play. The cool evening air felt sharp as she stood there, facing Lynn and Brooke, the weight of the moment pressing down on her, filling her with dread.

The words, "They found him," fell from Lynn's lips like lead, and the way she uttered them hit Annie like a freight train. A tortured "no" escaped her before she doubled over, the weight of the news folding her nearly in two. A sound so deep and primal erupted from her, it seemed her very soul was crying out in agony. Bent over, head nearly touching her knees as she gasped for air, another realization, just as harrowing as the first, struck her. Her girls—innocent, unknowing—were inside, their world about to shatter, and she had to be the one to break it to them.

The thought of her daughters was the only thing that kept her upright. Her head spun, breaths short and sharp, but she knew she had to compose herself, to be strong for them. Yet, she doubted her own strength to do so. She glanced at Lynn and Brooke, both looking just as shattered by the night's revelations. No one had explained what had happened to Mark, only that he was found dead at a house.

Gathering every ounce of courage, they all walked into the house. The girls, sensing something was wrong, looked up with worried eyes as they were guided to sit on the couch. Annie's voice broke as she delivered the crushing news, "Something has happened to your dad. He passed away. We aren't sure exactly what happened yet, but he's gone."

Sophia, just 12, oscillated between shock and despair, her young face crumpling under the weight of her grief. Bella, aged 9, began to whimper softly, while Eliana, only 5, sat in stunned silence, too young to fully grasp the magnitude of the moment.

Seeing Annie's lost expression, Lynn gently suggested, "Do you want to call your parents?" It snapped Annie back to reality, realizing she needed her own parents now more than ever. She nodded, retreating to the back bedroom for a semblance of privacy to make the call, not wanting to repeat those horrific words in front of her children.

When her mother answered, Annie's dam of composure finally broke. Sobbing uncontrollably, hyperventilating, she managed to choke out, "They found him... he's gone," between gasps. Her words were so choked with emotion, her mother could barely understand, but she caught enough to grasp the gravity of the situation. "Dad and I are on our way," her mother responded immediately, her voice a lifeline in the suffocating tide of grief that threatened to engulf Annie.

In the midst of Annie's darkest days, as she navigated the cruel aftermath of her greatest tragedy, it felt as though God was closer to her than ever before. She had cried out in anguish that chilling night on the porch, her soul raw and exposed, and she felt the presence of God beside her, a quiet strength amidst the storm of her grief.

The tasks that followed—choosing a casket, planning the funeral, enduring the somber atmosphere of the funeral home —were heavy with sorrow, yet a serene peace enveloped her, as if God were guiding her gently through each painful step.

The funeral was a powerful tribute to Mark's life, overflowing with love from friends and family. The church was packed, with people filling every space, some even standing on the stage, all united in their desire to honor his memory. This outpouring of support was a small consolation in her grief.

But the most piercing moment came as Annie stood before Mark's casket. Looking down at the lifeless form that once housed his vibrant spirit, she realized the profound finality of his absence. The man lying there was unrecognizable, a mere shell that no longer contained the soul she loved. This chilling realization made everything painfully real—Mark was truly gone. Even as she confronted the unbearable sight of what was left in the casket, God's nearness helped Annie bear the weight of her grief and start to navigate the path forward for herself and her daughters.

CHAPTER 57
EMBRACE THE PAIN

As the icy grip of January tightened, Annie faced the somber five-year anniversary of Mark's passing, each day a stark reminder of her tumultuous journey since. Reflecting on this period, she couldn't shake the feeling of failure that clung to her like a shadow. While God had been a beacon during her darkest hours, her moments of stability were often short-lived, quickly overtaken by her search for a companion to ease the loneliness.

This quest led her into the arms of Steven, whose initial fervor hid deep-seated insecurities and a pervasive victim mentality. Despite his passionate declarations, underlying issues soon came to light, revealing his inability to mature or change. Convinced she could help, Annie took on his burdens, including his two young sons and their complex custody battles, which not only drained her finances but left her emotionally spent.

The relentless stress and financial strain eventually proved too much for Steven, shattering the facade he had maintained. In a devastating outburst, he violently attacked Annie, leaving her to bear the scars of yet another broken relationship. Now, as she worked part-time from home to manage her debts, Annie still found herself looking for salvation in others rather than turning to the only One who could truly offer redemption. Amidst the ruins of her past choices, she continued to grapple with the profound lessons these experiences had imparted.

In the quiet of the evening, with her daughters asleep and the house finally silent, Annie felt the full burden of their past. The years of a strained marriage, the sudden death of their father, followed by the chaotic period with Steven that had ended so violently, had all taken a toll on her children. Annie knew something had to change fundamentally in her life, or they would continue spiraling into further chaos.

Haunted by the realization of all her daughters had endured —from witnessing volatile arguments to adapting to new, often disruptive family dynamics—Annie acknowledged her pattern of seeking comfort in relationships that often brought more turmoil than tranquility. However, giving up on finding companionship wasn't the answer she sought; instead, she recognized the need for a deeper personal change.

Resolved to break the destructive cycle, Annie committed to confronting her pain directly rather than numbing it with alcohol or temporary distractions. She resolved to face her haunting memories and deep-seated fears, believing that dealing with these directly would help her forge a new path not only of survival but of healing. This new commitment was daunting but necessary, as she aimed to show her daughters the strength and resilience needed to overcome life's hardest challenges. With this resolve, Annie took her first steps toward genuine healing, driven by a hope that this time, things would be different. As Annie let herself experience the raw emotions brought on by her memories, she found a small measure of solace in confronting them head-on. Sitting through songs that evoked pain and allowing herself to cry provided a touch of relief, a way to acknowledge her past rather than hastily pushing it aside. However, the specter of loneliness still haunted her, and her attempts at healing were punctuated by feelings of failure towards her daughters.

Amidst these steps toward facing her pain, Annie found herself slipping back into old habits. The quiet of the day often led her back to conversations with various men on Snapchat, a familiar distraction that filled the silence but did nothing to quell her deeper sense of isolation. While she hadn't abandoned all distractions, she recognized this as a flawed coping mechanism, a temporary salve on a wound that required more than just superficial attention.

This duality of progress and setback marked her days. Annie was painfully aware of her loneliness and the immense pressure she felt to somehow make things right, not just for herself but for her children. Each day, as she navigated the challenging terrain of recovery and personal growth, she grappled with the daunting realization that true healing might demand more than what she was currently giving.

CHAPTER 58
GIVING UP

Lying in bed, each ping from my phone feels less like an opportunity and more like a taunt. Every notification seems to promise a connection, yet each conversation only underscores a stark reality: the endless digital sea is nothing more than a desert of superficial interactions. As my 44th birthday approaches, a somber acceptance settles in. Perhaps it's time to face the inevitable: I might end up living out my days alone, my life a series of tasks without companionship.

This realization cracks the once sturdy armor of optimism that I've carried all my life. That shield, which protected me from harsh truths, now seems to crumble, exposing me to a cold reality I've long denied. The loneliness feels overwhelming, and as I contemplate this bleak prospect, my heart breaks a bit more with each thought.

Yet, in this moment of despair, I'm reminded of a constant presence that's been there all along—God. The realization brings a twinge of guilt; have I been ignoring the one who has always been there in pursuit of fleeting distractions? Tonight, my approach to God is different. It's not just about seeking relief or making half-hearted promises. Tonight, I'm truly open, vulnerable in a way I've never been before. With my defenses down and my heart open, I reach out, hoping to truly engage and find the deep, enduring connection that has eluded me in the noise of life.

Lying in the semi-darkness of my bedroom, I feel the corners of my mouth sag and a familiar lump forming in my throat. Tears, uninvited guests as always, make their way down my cheeks. "Okay, God, here I am," I whisper into the stillness, the words feeling heavy in the air. "I really wanted someone to share my life with, someone to help me navigate this mess, but I realize now—you're what truly matters."

As I sob, more from the fear of enduring loneliness than from my admission of misplaced priorities, I sense God's presence —not in words, but as a comforting reassurance washing over me. He is the essence of creation and pure love. If I am to be 'alone', having Him by my side should be considered an utmost blessing, not a sentence to solitude.

This revelation isn't close to the life I envisioned, but in a flash of unexpected clarity, I recognize that no partner could fill the space meant for divine companionship. With a sniffle, I muster whatever strength is left in me, "God, I'm going to try to keep my eyes fixed on you from here on out. But let's be honest, keeping track isn't exactly my strong suit, so I'm going to need your help to stay the course."

I don't hear a booming voice from the heavens or get a miraculous sign, but in that moment of raw surrender—of hopes, dreams, and the broken pieces of me—I feel a profound weight lift from my shoulders. For the first time in what feels like forever, sleep doesn't play hard to get. I drift off, comforted by the thought that perhaps, just perhaps, I've finally done something right.

CHAPTER 59
STILL ANNIE

Annie kicked off her 44th year with a bang—or more accurately, a hobble. Waking up to a foot throbbing so dramatically it felt like her toes were reenacting the battle scenes from "300," she figured, "Well, happy freakin' birthday to me." Initially, she'd dismissed the discomfort as a minor annoyance, chalking it up to her shoe rubbing or a little too much zeal on her run the day before. But this morning's agony was like a Broadway spotlight announcing something far more sinister.

Annie decided to channel her inner WebMD before actually limping into a real medical office. Her self-diagnosis session pointed toward Achilles tendonitis. Armed with this internet-certified diagnosis, she unearthed a pair of crutches from the depths of her closet and managed to snag a same-day appointment with her doctor, who promptly confirmed her suspicions and prescribed a regimen of steroids and strict couch-potatoing.

Back in the comfort of her home fortress, Annie flopped back into bed, now medically excused to do absolutely nothing. "At least I've got a legit excuse to lounge around on my birthday," she thought, finding some humor in the situation. It wasn't every day you got to be a bed-bound birthday queen, after all.

Maybe she'd even get some sympathy chocolates out of it—if she played her cards right.

Laid up in bed with a battalion of steroids coursing through her system, Annie found herself once again diving into the digital rabbit hole of Snapchat. Bedridden, she turned to her trusty stable of virtual admirers for some distraction and, admittedly, a good dose of sympathy. Her phone screen flickered with messages of pity and well-wishes, turning her temporary disablement into an odd sort of social gala.

As her birthday dawned, any plans for adventure were firmly tethered by the reality of her rebellious Achilles. Yet, her daughters, ever the spirited trio, orchestrated a celebration right there in the dining room. They decked the halls with streamers and laid out a modest spread of cake and gifts, making sure mom didn't feel neglected on her special day. It was a sweet, if stationary, affair, and Annie couldn't help but appreciate the effort. They laughed and shared cake, and for a moment, the throbbing in her foot seemed a little less insistent.

Despite the festivities, the nagging throb in her leg served as a grim reminder that her years were catching up with her more quickly than she'd like. But with each ping from her phone, Annie was reminded that, immobilized or not, she wasn't going through this alone—even if her companions were just pixels on a screen.

CHAPTER 60 EROS

Laid up with my rebellious foot and a battalion of steroids, I find myself wading through roughly 1,400 unopened Snapchat messages one quiet evening. Spinning the wheel of messages like i'm on The Price is Right, I tap into one that just says "hi." Let's see what I landed on. "Hey," I shoot back.

Quick as a flash, he replies, "What's up? I've been trying to get your attention on here for a while." His promptness suggests a vigil by the phone. "Well, you have it now! Can I see you?" I type back, intrigued.

"Just a sec," he responds, and soon enough, a selfie pops up. He's ruggedly handsome—name's CJ, from Tennessee. He sports a ball cap and broad shoulders that fill out his T-shirt nicely. A mounted deer head in the background confirms my guess: he's in a cabin. "Well hey, aren't you cute!! Where have you been hiding?" I flirt back.

"I've been here, trying to get you to notice me. You seem cool," CJ reiterates, painting himself with a shade of earnestness.

Charmed, I send back a quick video. His reply comes with a thick southern drawl, sweet as Tennessee whiskey, and his voice—a deep, soothing baritone—feels like a warm blanket on a chilly night. We exchange messages back and forth, each one melting a bit more ice from around my heart—or maybe just my foot. The night unfolds, woven with delightful chatter, until sleep nudges us both to part ways.

The next day, my digital escapade with CJ, or rather Chet as he later confesses, continues. Turns out, he's not in Tennessee but Alabama. A slight geographic tweak in his backstory— apparently, he was just being cautious with his real info on Snapchat, a sentiment I can appreciate given my recent brush with the broken lock.

As my rapport with Chet deepens, he reveals more about his life in Alabama, which seems to fit perfectly with an outdoor magazine spread. He's not just a rancher but also an avid hunter and fisherman, passions that go beyond hobby— he actually owns a hunting and fishing store. This revelation comes with a sprinkle of charm and a dash of intrigue.

Chet casually slips me his phone number with a nonchalant, "Now you've got my number, you can get a hold of me whenever you want." I must admit, the offer is quite appealing. Over the ensuing days, our chats lengthen, and the connection is palpable. I find myself increasingly drawn to him; he's not only genuinely smart and funny but seems to have his life together.

Living on a sprawling ranch with a few hundred cows, he spends his days amid nature. His pond isn't just stocked with fish; it also hosts an alligator named Lewis, adding an exotic twist to his already fascinating life. And as if to seal this budding relationship with a perfect note, we discover our music tastes are eerily similar, further entwining our unexpected connection.

Our conversations have evolved from playful banter to discussing our shared longing for a permanent, heartache-free relationship. Each morning, we exchange greetings that soon spiral into deep, meaningful exchanges about our lives, hopes, and the gnawing desire to finally meet in person.

Chet paints a vivid picture of his Alabama town, his close-knit family dynamics, and the life he's built around his passion for the outdoors. He speaks earnestly about wanting to take care of me, to introduce me to the places and people that mean so much to him. It's a promise of something more, something substantial and lasting, and I can't help but feel a surge of hope.

Im making my morning drink and as the tangy aroma of lemons lingers, I pause, knife in hand, overwhelmed by a profound sense of gratitude. Here is someone, after all the turmoil, who is offering exactly what I've yearned for —a genuine connection, a haven, a potential forever. The sensation is almost surreal, washing over me like a gentle wave, soothing yet invigorating my soul as I contemplate the possibilities that lie ahead with Chet.

As I stand in the kitchen, phone pressed to my ear, Chet's words resonate with an unexpected weight, "I want to come see you, meet your family, and your kids one day. I want to show them I'm going to take care of you all." His voice, rich with a Southern drawl, fills the space around me.

"You want all of that? You're sure? You want to take care of me, and I come with three girls?" I ask, half-amused and half-dazed by the gravity of his declaration.

"Yes, I want this to be my last stop," he replies firmly.

A wave of gratitude hits me again, overwhelming in its intensity. Here I was, slipping back into my old patterns after breaking down and asking God to steer my life, yet instead of a lesson or a punishment for my wayward focus, it felt like God had sent me Chet. A man who embodied not just what I had hoped for, but also what I hadn't even known I needed until he voiced it.

The trick now is to not let myself become so obsessed with

what God has given me that I push God out of the picture altogether. This has definitely been a problem for me in the past. When I get in a relationship, when Eros digs his claws into my heart, I give it fully. Even the part that should be reserved for God starts to slip away into his clutches.

I stop for a moment to question is this just another distraction? Is it a carrot on a stick from the devil or from my deceitful heart. Is Chet just something meant to distract me from my real purpose? In an instant, a wave of peace and gratitude hits me out of nowhere. This time instead of a peaceful and mysterious kiss on the forehead lulling me to sleep, it is a wave of excitement and assurance propelling me forward. Not only does God see me, but that he has been working on things all along. He's still here and his goodness is something I will likely never fully be able to comprehend.

As his assurance washes over me, a quiet voice echoes in my mind, reinforcing a message of divine benevolence: "God is so good and He loves you. He will never give up on you." It's a reminder of a presence much larger than any human connection, a cosmic embrace in which I find myself floating. This isn't just another romantic whimsy; it's a profound, almost celestial affirmation that maybe, just maybe, the pieces are falling into place not by my hand, but by a greater one.

Sinking into the comfort of that thought, the notion of God's vast ocean of goodness, I feel a peace I haven't known in ages. While I've often idealized relationships in the past, nothing has quite felt like this—so profound, so beyond myself. It's a new chapter, perhaps even a new beginning, and for the first time in a long while, I'm not just hopeful but certain that I'm exactly where I need to be.

A thought again drifts into my head trying to puncture my joyous bubble: "You are insane. You are concocting all this in your head. Or worse, the devil is weaving these fantasies to pull you away from God."

My heart momentarily sinks with the intrusion of doubt. But then, another part of my brain kicks in. Wait a minute—the devil doesn't operate that way. He doesn't affirm the goodness of God or the mercy found in Jesus. A scripture pops into my mind, sharp and clear, "We take captive every thought to make it obedient to Christ." Do these feelings and revelations deepen my faith in Jesus and His goodness? Absolutely. What I'm feeling now, even more than my excitement about the prospect of love and a new life on the horizon, is the absolute assurance that not only is God merciful and good beyond reason, but that he is here invested in me personally.

Reassured, I'm back to feeling buoyant, my spirit effervescent with joy. As I text Chet, sharing these waves of gratitude and insights about God's hand in our meeting, he throws in a proposal that sends my heart racing: "Why don't you just grab a plane ticket, and come see me? I'll take care of the cost; you just need to get here."

The immediacy of his invitation stirs a mix of excitement and nerves. Am I ready to leap into something this real, this quickly? The thought whirls in my mind, but the overarching sense of divine timing and rightness about this connection with Chet convinces me. Maybe, just maybe, this isn't about distraction but about alignment—aligning with someone who enhances my understanding of God's blessings.

"Okay, let me look at flights," I type back, my fingers trembling slightly over the keys. As I send the message, a smile spreads across my face, the kind that feels like it's lighting up the room. I'm embarking on a new adventure, and for once, it feels divinely appointed.

Well, there I was, phone in hand, flights unbookable due to ridiculous spring break prices and absurd layovers. But as I texted back and forth with Chet, feeling our excitement build, a wild, maybe even reckless, idea struck me. It's just an 11-hour drive. I've made nearly as long a trek countless times to see Misty with a carload of chatter and child chaos. Why not now, solo, to see him?

This could be lunacy—I've only known him a week. Yet, I can't shake this magnetic pull, this almost cosmic drawing together that's screaming inside me, saying, "Just go!"

So I floated the idea to him, half-joking but also half-serious, "I'm really thinking about just throwing a suitcase in the car and driving to see you. I don't want to wait." His response came back so fast it made my phone buzz harder, "DO IT! Just get in the car. I will pay for everything—just get here! I'll even take off work Monday, and if you want to stay Tuesday, you can hang out at the cabin and fish or whatever. JUST COME!"

The immediacy of his reply seals it for me. The thrill of the spontaneous adventure overtakes any lingering hesitations. This is the sort of thing that stories are made of, or at least the kind that makes life worth giggling about when you're old and grey.

With a mix of exhilaration and a dash of 'am I really doing this?', I begin to pack. Clothes flying into the suitcase, essentials grabbed without thought—shampoo, probably; toothbrush, definitely. My mind is racing but focused, my heart thumping with the promise of something new, something potentially wonderful or disastrously hilarious.

As I tossed the idea around in my head, the more it seemed not just doable, but almost necessary. "Alright, Chet," I finally texted, "I'm going to talk to my kids and my mom to make sure they can stay with her, but as long as all that works out, I'm coming your way soon." His reply buzzed through almost instantly, lighting up my screen and my mood: "Ok, keep me posted!"

First, the strategist in me kicked in. I showed Sophia his pictures, both the ones he'd sent and the ones that I'd found online—he was well-known locally due to his store, often featured in the hometown paper. "Look, he's a real person, and reputable," I explained, trying to coat my impulsive plan with a sheen of responsibility. Misty would be tracking me, and I'd check in constantly. Sophia raised her eyebrows in that 'Mom, you're crazy, but I love you' way, but eventually, she gave her blessing.

Next was Bella, and I braced for her to be the tough sell. However, her only question cut right to the heart: "Does he know Jesus?" I assured her he did. "Okay, that's all I ever wanted—for you to have someone who loves Jesus," she said. Her old soul shining through once again, she added, "You're amazing, Mom, and I'm happy for you." My heart swelled— Bella's approval felt like a warm hug.

Eliana was a breeze, hardly batting an eye as I explained. With the kids on board, it was time to face the final boss: Mom. My call went unanswered, so I shot over a text: "Hey, got invited to Alabama for a few days—can the girls come hang with you while I'm gone?" Her response was swift and supportive: "Of course!"

With family logistics locked down, I shared the good news with Chet, who was as thrilled as I was. Bella accompanied me to the store to stock up on supplies for the girls. We navigated the aisles with a mix of excitement and a tinge of nervous energy. After that, it was a flurry of preparation: showering, packing, and prepping the car.

Finally, with everything set, I hit the road, my heart racing with the possibility of what awaited. The highway stretched before me, a ribbon of opportunity leading towards what I hoped would be not just an adventure, but maybe, just maybe, a new chapter. As the miles ticked away, I couldn't help but smile, feeling both utterly insane and incredibly alive.

CHAPTER 61
ALABAMA

As I barreled down the highway with the landscape blurring past, the thrill of this spontaneous road trip infused me with excitement. Chet had sweetened the deal by sending me some cash for the journey. His message had a warm, caring tone: "Listen baby, I don't want you to pay for anything on this trip—not even a stick of gum. So if you need more money, you just let me know." This kind of pampering was new to me, but it was certainly something I could get used to.

Armed with Red Bull, a massive bottle of water, and enough gum to last the entire drive, I sang along to my favorite tunes, making the miles disappear more enjoyably. I had turned on my location sharing on my phone indefinitely, allowing Chet to keep an eye on my progress. It was a small gesture that should have comforted me, but a part of my brain toggled between exhilaration and worry.

"What if you drive all this way and he goes MIA?" a little nagging voice in my head would chime in. I didn't even have his exact address, after all. He planned to meet me in town and guide me to his remote home from there—so safe, I sarcastically assured myself.

Yet, every so often, my excitement would quash the doubts. "This is it, I can feel it. It's going to be amazing, I just know it," I'd reassure myself, my mood swinging wildly. His regular calls and his generosity in covering my expenses bolstered my confidence. This constant attention made it easier to push aside my fears and paint my adventure with colors of hope and potential. "It's all going to be amazing," I murmured to myself, focusing on the road ahead and the promising end to my journey.

As the evening wore on and the sun dipped below the horizon, Chet wrapped up his workday with an eagerness that was palpable even through the phone. He called me, his voice bubbling with excitement, to quiz me on my culinary likes and dislikes. "What should I stock up on for your visit? What do you like to drink? I want everything to be perfect for you," he rattled off, the anxiousness clear in his tone.

I reassured him with a light laugh, "Honestly, I'm easy to please —just no shrimp, okay? But I love fruits, veggies, meats, nuts, cheese... really, don't stress about it."

He was stressing, though. Amid our conversation, he confessed he'd spilled the beans to his brother and father about my impending arrival, admitting he felt butterflies cartwheeling in his stomach. "I'm so nervous," he confessed, a vulnerability in his voice that I found utterly charming.

"Hey, we're in the same boat," I reassured him, feeling my own stomach do flips. We kept the phone lines hot, chatting intermittently as I continued my drive and he scurried around prepping for my visit.

Around 10 PM, fatigue nibbled at my edges, and I decided it was time to hunt down a hotel. Chet, ever the gentleman, arranged a room for me at a Hampton Inn in Oxford, handling all the details. By the time I checked in, courtesy of his thoughtful planning, my excitement was at a fever pitch.

After settling into my room, I went through my nighttime routine—washing my face, brushing my teeth, popping in my retainer—and then crawled into the invitingly crisp hotel bed. But as the room darkened and the sheets warmed with my body heat, sleep coyly evaded me. My mind buzzed with anticipation for what the next day would bring, leaving me wide-eyed and restless, waiting for dawn.

Dragging myself out of the too-comfortable hotel bed at 4:30 AM, I gave up on the elusive dream of sleep. Might as well be productive, I figured, flicking on the lights with a resigned sigh. A morning ritual of coffee and some meticulous grooming—shaving legs, plucking stray eyebrow hairs—awaited. After all, I wanted to make a good impression on Chet, who wouldn't be off work until noon.

With hours to kill, I indulged in the hotel's breakfast buffet, munching on whatever I could find and downing cups of coffee, hoping the caffeine might mask my lack of sleep. By the time I checked out, I was buzzing—part caffeine, part nerves.

The drive to his town passed in a blur, fueled by a cocktail of excitement and more Red Bull than was probably advisable. Chet had texted that he was picking up some last-minute essentials—beer for him and vodka sodas for me. I had decided that this weekend was a fine time to break my nearly unblemished record of abstaining from alcohol; some occasions, after all, called for a toast.

As I neared the gas station where we'd agreed to meet, the reality of my state hit me. I was a jittery, slightly disheveled mess, brimming with caffeine and nerves, desperately needing a bathroom after all the liquids I'd consumed. The AC was blasted to full, directed at my armpits in a futile attempt to cool my stress-induced sweat.

Pulling into the gas station, I couldn't help but laugh at the absurdity: my first impression, about to be made on the brink of a bathroom emergency, powered by a sleepless night and too much caffeine. Well, if Chet was the one, he'd have to embrace all of this, I thought, as I parked and prepared to meet him, hoping my nerves didn't show as much as they felt.

CHAPTER 62 ALPHA

There I was, parked right in front of his truck he fondly called "Black Betty." Hopping out, I was on a mission not to embarrass myself with an urgent bathroom dash. Chet stood there, grinning from ear to ear, looking a mix of nervous and thrilled. Our greeting was a clumsy but genuine hug, and he immediately told me I smelled good—thank goodness for small victories, considering my battle with nervous sweats.

"Why thank you," I replied, instantly regretting my next words, "I've been blasting my armpits with the AC because of my nerves." Why I admitted that, I'll never know. But Chet just laughed and reassured me, "You smell great."

He gave me a quick peck, which felt a bit awkward. I quickly excused myself, "I have to pee so bad. Be right back!" Relief washed over me once I was out of the restroom, and I felt human again.

We headed out, me following closely behind him. I was pondering the awkward peck and hug at the gas station and wondering when we would be able to get past the nervousness that was palpable. Then, as if reading my mind, Chet abruptly stopped his truck in the middle of the road and walked towards me. Curious, I rolled down my window, and without a word, he leaned in, his hand cradling my head, and delivered a kiss so passionate it left me breathless.

"Sorry, I just couldn't wait any longer," he said, his eyes twinkling with mischief.

"I think... ummmm oh my Gaawd..... I love you... that was a power move and maybe the hottest thing anyone has ever done," I managed to stammer out, still reeling from the kiss.

With a wink, he grabbed a drink from the cooler in the back of his truck, and we continued down the road. The rest of the drive was a blur of excitement and anticipation, punctuated by the thrill of that kiss.

Chet had orchestrated a quick detour to one of his favorite local gems—a quaint little store packed from wall to wall with an assortment of delectable goods. The moment we stepped inside, the aroma of seasoned meats and freshly prepared sides filled the air, a promising prelude to a memorable weekend.

"Pick out what you want," Chet suggested, gesturing towards the seemingly endless options of pre-packaged meals and gourmet treats. My eyes darted around, finally settling on a bowl of chicken salad that looked just about perfect. "Oooooh, okay," I chimed, feeling a bit like a kid in a candy store.

"What else?" he prodded, eager to introduce me to the store's specialties.

I shrugged, overwhelmed by the choices. "I don't know, what's good here?"

He didn't hesitate. "You gotta try the chicken swirls; this place is famous for them." He grabbed a couple from the shelf, his familiarity with the fare reassuring.

"Anything else?" he asked.

"Nope, this looks great," I replied, content with the selections.

With our treasures in tow, we headed back to his truck, ready to continue our journey to his place. The promise of good food and good company had me buzzing with anticipation.

As we pulled through the gate, Chet pointed out his creek flowing under a quaint bridge with evident pride. He offered to take my suitcase inside, a gesture that immediately made me feel welcome. His property was expansive, with lush green fields stretching to a horizon dotted with cattle. His cabin, cozy and inviting, boasted an impressive porch decked out with every imaginable cooking device—a haven for any culinary enthusiast.

"I like to cook outside so the house doesn't smell like food," he explained, showing off an array of outdoor cooking gear, including a fryer, a Big Green Egg smoker, various grills, and a Blackstone. Then, with a chuckle, he introduced me to Meow Meow, the resident cat. "I'm not really a cat person and I'm allergic, but I love this guy," he admitted, which made me laugh because I felt the same way about cats and shared the allergy. It was just one more thing we surprisingly had in common.

Inside, after we navigated around the suitcase temporarily separating us, Chet moved in for another kiss, this one deep and thrilling, that sent my heart racing. He cracked open a cold beer for himself and handed me a vodka soda. "Here, looks like you could use this," he joked, and he wasn't wrong.

I took a sip, feeling the day's tension ease slightly, then another. With a glance, I closed the distance for another kiss. Chet was magnetic; utterly compelling, and I found myself irresistibly drawn to him.

The passion that ensued was a whirlwind, leaving us both breathless. Eventually, we found ourselves back in the kitchen, leaning against the counter with our drinks, cooling off and catching up. He then suggested a tour of the house, which led seamlessly into an invitation to see his pond. "Yes, please," I agreed without hesitation, eager to continue exploring both his world and the palpable connection between us.

As Chet revved up the ATV, he tossed a cooler of drinks in the back and flicked on the Bluetooth speaker, setting a lively soundtrack for our short journey to the pond. The landscape stretched wide around us, vibrant and lush, and the pond itself sparkled under the afternoon sun, a peaceful expanse nestled amidst the greenery.

Pointing toward a log half-submerged at the water's edge, Chet introduced me to Lewis, the resident alligator he'd brought in to manage the local beaver population. His nonchalance about having a predatory reptile as a pond cleaner amused me—only Chet could make ecological management sound like a casual hobby.

With a twinkle in his eye, Chet grabbed his fishing rod, an extension of his confident, outdoorsy persona. "Watch this," he declared, casting the line with a fluid, expert flick. The lure barely touched the water before he was reeling in a hefty bass, his movements smooth and assured. I've always had a soft spot for fishing, the patience and quiet it usually required, but Chet's method was electrifying in its efficiency.

After releasing the first bass, he immediately cast again. Like magic, another large bass took the bait. My astonishment must have been palpable because I blurted out, "How did you do that?! That's incredible!"

Grinning, Chet reeled in the second bass and replied with effortless charm, "Baby, this is what I do. I used to do this for money." His words, simple yet laden with the ease of true skill, sent a thrill through me.

There he was, the quintessential outdoorsman, casting and reeling as if born to it, each move more impressive than the last. It wasn't just his skill that captivated me—it was the passionate way he engaged with his environment. In that moment, with the late sun glinting off the water and Chet beside me, life felt suddenly exhilarating.

As we ambled around the pond with our fishing poles in tow, I managed not to catch a single fish. Instead, I somehow caught myself slipping right into the water. There was Chet, ever the proficient outdoorsman, and then there was me—clumsy, a bit tipsy, and now thoroughly soaked in pond water.

He looked over with a playful grin. "Did you just fall in the pond?"

Attempting to salvage some dignity, I responded with feigned surprise, "Ummm, noooo..." But my soaked appearance gave me away, and I caved, laughing at myself. "Okay, yeah, I fell in. I thought the ground was firmer, got too close, and well, I'm a dork. Sorry about that."

Chet's laughter was warm and inviting, not mocking, as he closed the distance between us. He pinned me gently against the tailgate of the ATV, his presence towering yet comforting. Then came another one of those deep, intoxicating kisses that made my head spin more than the alcohol ever could. His strong arms wrapped around my chilly, damp frame, pulling me into his warmth.

As dusk began to blanket the sky, he suggested, "Let's head back so I can get started on dinner, and you can get cleaned up." The prospect of a warm shower was inviting, but the thrill of his company was even more so. I nodded, eager for more of this unexpected adventure.

After freshening up, I stepped out to find Chet buzzing with an infectious energy on his porch, surrounded by an array of dishes he was enthusiastically preparing. The air was charged with his boundless vigor as he danced between the grill and the table, his speaker blaring tunes that matched his lively spirit. He greeted me with a beaming smile and a playful proposition, "How about we just graze on a bunch of stuff?"

The table was laden with culinary delights: smoked cream cheese with pepper jelly, bacon-wrapped green beans stuffed with cheese, loaded potatoes, and the mouthwatering chicken swirls, each bursting with flavor. Just when I thought the feast couldn't get any richer, Chet brought over ribeye steaks, seared to perfection, their aroma mingling with the crisp outdoor air.

Under the starlit sky, Chet's vibrant charm was as delectable as the food. He darted over for quick kisses, each one sweeter than the last, adding a personal touch to the evening that was as endearing as his chaotic energy. Dining al fresco with Chet, surrounded by his ceaseless animation and the rustic elegance of his porch, felt like a slice of paradise—an unforgettable night where every moment was infused with his boundless, bouncing charm.

After indulging in the feast and relishing each other's company along with a few too many drinks, the evening turned into a blur. Somewhere amidst that delightful chaos, fatigue from my sleepless journey caught up with me, and I woke in the middle of the night with a start, lying next to Chet. My mind raced, trying to piece together the cascade of events that led me here. Was this reality truly unfolding as wonderfully as it seemed? Chet was even more perfect in person than he had appeared in our conversations—his presence amplifying the sense that something extraordinary was happening.

I couldn't shake the conviction that had propelled me into my car, driven by a profound sense that God was orchestrating this grand adventure, signaling a promising chapter ahead. Lying there, I reflected on the undeniable confirmation of those feelings.

Sure, waking up beside him, slightly hungover, might not align perfectly with every biblical teaching, but in my heart, I felt a deep commitment to him. It might sound insane, but guilt was absent, replaced by a deep-seated happiness I hadn't felt in ages.

Gently, I rolled over and drew close to him, wrapping my arms around him. He stirred just enough to embrace me, planting a tender kiss on my forehead. Comforted and secure, we drifted back into a peaceful sleep, wrapped in the warmth of new beginnings and mutual affection.

CHAPTER 63
TOO FAST

On Sunday morning, Chet transformed our little kitchen into a scene straight out of a feel-good movie. Dressed in fish-patterned boxers and snug outdoor booties, with his hair tousled perfectly, he danced to tunes blaring from his Bluetooth speaker. He called it preparing a "brunch buffet," but it felt more like a performance. The counter was laden with fresh fruit, the chicken salad I'd admired at the store, and a smorgasbord of heated leftovers, not to mention queso and chips. To top it off, he handed me a morning vodka soda designed to ward off any potential hangovers.

As he moved about, buzzing with energy—grinding pepper onto my dish with a flourish and a mock French accent, making me laugh out loud. It was all so endearing, so perfectly him, that the joy of the moment was tinged only by the knowledge that Tuesday morning—and my departure—was just around the corner.

We still had the full luxury of two days and nights together, and I was determined not to let a second of it go to waste. After indulging in a leisurely brunch complete with tender moments of affection, Chet announced it was time to head into town. His cooking agenda was ambitious and relentless, a reflection of his boundless energy. He needed peppers and onions to perfect the beans he was planning to make and was running low on beer. Outside, a soft drizzle fell, adding a cozy layer to our small-town adventure, quite a contrast from the torrential downpour that had serenaded us through the night.

We dressed quickly, Chet in his usual casual flair and I, still feeling a bit out of my element but excited all the same. Climbing into his truck, affectionately known as Black Betty, we set off. The rain had transformed the usual dusty roads into reflective paths that shimmered with the promise of the day ahead.

As we meandered through the small town, Chet's energy was contagious, sparking laughter and lightness as we hopped from one quaint shop to another. His familiarity with each locale added a personal touch to every stop. Our final destination was a nondescript gas station, which Chet claimed housed the best burger you'll ever put in your mouth. Skeptical but intrigued, I followed him inside. The place was buzzing, a hidden gem among the ordinary. Indeed, the burger and fries we shared were unexpectedly delicious—a delightful surprise in such a humble setting. Chet's charm seemed to animate the entire store, leaving smiles in our wake as we departed.

Back at his ranch, with dinner preparations well in hand, Chet proposed a comprehensive tour of his land. He piloted the ATV with ease, navigating through trails that had transformed into small rivers from the previous night's downpour. We passed numerous deer stands, so many that I lost count, each marking a favorite haunt of his on the extensive grounds. The tour culminated in a vast forest of meticulously arranged rows of trees—his own creation from two decades earlier. Witnessing the fruits of his labor and the scope of his commitment to this land, I couldn't help but feel profoundly impressed. Chet wasn't just a man who lived on the land; he shaped it, cherished it, and thrived within it. I was utterly smitten, caught up in the wonder of his world and the easy charm of his presence.

As the afternoon rolled into evening, Chet and I decided to reel in our lines and head back to the cabin, with the sky hinting at more rain. Chet, a whirlwind of activity, didn't let the looming weather dampen his spirits or slow him down. He danced around the kitchen, setting out an array of delicious dishes, his Bluetooth speaker blasting tunes that became the unofficial soundtrack of our weekend. Every bite was a delight, every song a memory in the making.

The perfection of it all was overwhelming. It felt almost too good to be true, and the thought of leaving this idyllic setting in a couple of days cast a shadow over me. As if reading my mind, Chet suggested we take advantage of a break in the rain to visit Heaven Hill, an open field he'd shown me earlier where he dreamed of building a future home. We drove out and found ourselves under a vast, starry sky, sitting atop a giant hay bale, the universe sprawling above us. The music continued to play, a soft backdrop to the vastness above.

But nature had other plans, and soon a gentle drizzle urged us back to the warmth of the cabin. We showered, the sound of rain a soft accompaniment to the end of our day, and eventually drifted off to sleep, side by side.

Monday dawned, wrapping us in the soft light of our final day together. Chet murmured a sleepy "good morning," his eyes barely fluttering open. "It went too fast, didn't it? I don't want this to end," I confessed, a lump forming in my throat. Chet exhaled deeply, his arms tightening around me. "I know, baby, I don't want you to leave either," he said, voice thick with emotion.

Determined not to dwell on the inevitable goodbye, I pushed myself up and brewed us some strong coffee. "Let's not think about tomorrow," Chet proposed as we sipped our morning cups, "let's just enjoy today." Energized by caffeine and his boundless optimism, we dove into another of Chet's legendary breakfast spreads.

The morning slipped away as we tackled a clogged ditch near his creek. What Chet saw as a chore, I saw as an opportunity to play in the mud—laughing, splashing, and eventually solving the problem together. We wandered the property, and Chet's endless energy never waned as he fertilized fruit trees and tinkered in his barn. His vitality was infectious, his presence a constant source of amazement.

As the sun began its descent, Chet suddenly seized upon a new idea. "Quick, hop on the Ranger—and hold on tight!" he commanded, with a mischievous glint in his eye. I clambered aboard, clinging to the frame as he floored the accelerator, racing toward Heaven Hill. We arrived just in time to watch the sun spill its golden light over the horizon—a perfect end to our whirlwind adventure.

The evening blurred into a delightful haze of food, laughter, and drinks. We lingered over each moment, trying to stretch the time. But, like the beautiful sunset, our weekend had to end. Eventually, exhaustion claimed us, and we fell asleep side by side, wrapped in the satisfaction of a weekend neither of us would soon forget.

The shrill of Chet's alarm at 5 am sliced through the stillness, announcing it was time for him to head to work and for me to face the long drive back to Oklahoma. He rolled over, pulling me close, his voice thick with sleep and regret. "Baby, don't leave," he murmured.

"I don't want to, but I have to," I replied, the weight of the inevitable departure pressing down on us.

"I know," he sighed, releasing me reluctantly. "You can go back to sleep, you know. You don't have to rush. Just pull the gate shut behind you when you do leave." His words were gentle, trying to ease the sting of goodbye.

But I was resolved to face the pain head-on. "No, I just wanna go ahead and get this over with. Rip the band-aid off fast." We both scurried around, him getting ready for work and me stuffing my belongings into my suitcase, gathering items from around his cabin. He even had some of my clothes freshly laundered in the dryer, a thoughtful gesture that made leaving that much harder.

With my suitcase loaded and a bottle of water in hand, we shared a few last kisses at the doorstep—each one heavy with the sadness of parting and the uncertainty of when we'd see each other again. After a few more lingering moments, I climbed into my car, setting the GPS for home. As I started the engine, "Fooled Around and Fell in Love" began to play on the stereo—an almost painfully apt soundtrack for our whirlwind romance.

With a final wave, I pulled away, Chet's silhouette framed in the faint dawn light. He stood there in the darkness, watching as I drove off, every fiber of my being screaming to turn back. But forward was the only way now, as I navigated the quiet roads with a heart full of memories and eyes blurred with unshed tears.

CHAPTER 64 HOME

As Annie navigated the long road home, her mind churned with the weekend's memories and possibilities. Despite Chet's overt expressions of affection and the undeniable connection they shared, doubts still nagged at her. Could someone as incredible as Chet truly be interested in her? Was his interest genuine, or was she reading too much into a whirlwind romance?

Every hour, Chet checked in, his voice a comforting presence over the phone, reinforcing his earlier declaration by sending more money to cover her expenses, insisting she shouldn't have to pay for anything on her trip. His consistent care helped to quell the flutter of uncertainty that danced in her stomach.

Around 1 pm, as the landscape scrolled by, her phone rang. It was Misty, bursting with curiosity. "Ok, I've been waiting all day for you to call me and tell me about your weekend!"

Annie laughed, the sound mingling with the hum of the highway. "I wasn't sure if you were still feeling bad; I knew you weren't feeling well last I talked to you. But yeah, I have lots to tell! Firstly, I am in love with this man. And I will be so sad if I don't marry him one day. He is amazing!"

Misty's laughter filtered through the speaker. "You sound Twitterpated, Annie. It's spring, after all, and you're acting like one of those animals from Bambi!"

Annie couldn't help but agree, a smile spreading across her

face as she recounted the magical moments: that powerful kiss beside the road, the culinary delights that seemed endless, and the awe-inspiring forest Chet had nurtured from scratch. Each memory painted a picture of a weekend that was as perfect as it was surreal.

As she drove, Annie realized that no matter the outcome, this journey marked a significant chapter in her life. Whether or not the future held Chet, this experience had changed her, filled her with a hope that was both thrilling and terrifying. She was indeed twitterpated, thoroughly smitten, and for now, that was more than enough.

Annie's car crunched onto the gravel driveway of her home. The warm glow from the windows promised the comfort of familiarity and the eager embrace of her daughters. Despite the thrill of her romantic adventure, a part of her had missed these familiar walls and the chaotic warmth of family life.

Her girls swarmed her as soon as she stepped inside, their voices a cascade of excitement and curiosity, each one clamoring to hear about her trip. Annie, although weary from the road and the bittersweet departure from Chet, couldn't help but smile broadly as she recounted the high points of her weekend—the laughter, the food, and the stunning Alabama landscape that Chet had introduced her to.

Despite the joy in their faces and the comfort of being surrounded by her loved ones, a part of Annie felt oddly detached, as if a piece of her was still miles away, meandering through the lush fields of Chet's farm. The magic of the weekend hung around her like a sweet perfume, making the return to the routine a stark contrast.

Realizing her fatigue was starting to weigh heavily on her eyelids and the road's toll on her body demanded attention, Annie excused herself. "I had the most amazing time," she told them with a final hug for each daughter, "but right now, I need a hot shower and some time to unwind."

With that, she retreated to the sanctuary of her bathroom, letting the hot water wash over her, hoping it might also wash away the melancholy of departure. As the steam filled the room, blurring the edges of her reflection, Annie allowed herself to daydream just a bit longer about the sweet possibilities that might await with Chet, before finally settling into the reality of her everyday life.

CHAPTER 65 A SHIFT

Under the constant buzz of her new relationship with Chet, Annie found herself navigating the mundane elements of her daily life with a renewed vigor and optimism. Her mornings began with the gentle chime of text notifications, each one a sweet note from Chet echoing through her quiet kitchen as she prepared breakfast for the girls. Every "good morning" text, every call during lunch breaks, and each evening catch-up session served as reminders of the exciting possibilities that lay ahead.

Yet, with this excitement came the challenge of patience. Distance was a tough hurdle, and the excitement of their weekend together made the miles between them seem even more daunting. Annie found herself daydreaming often, envisioning a life on Chet's expansive farm, under the wide Alabama sky. She imagined the laughter and warmth that would fill their home, her girls adapting to the rhythms of rural life, and the peace she felt would surely come with leaving behind her past struggles.

However, Annie was mindful not to let her daydreams cloud her judgment. She reminded herself to take things slow, to build on the foundation they had started rather than rushing ahead. The distance, though challenging, was a good buffer, giving her time to think and pray about her next steps.

Chet had expressed concern that Annie's girls would forever

resent him if they had to leave Oklahoma and their friends and family. His doubts about ever making dreams a reality weighed heavy on not just himself but on Annie. In usual Annie fashion, she clung to her hope and faith that whatever God had in store for them was going to be wildly better than anything they could imagine themselves.

Her conversations with God became more frequent and heartfelt. She felt a deep gratitude for the sense of renewal Chet had sparked in her, and she prayed for guidance and clarity. Was this rapid heartbeat she felt for Chet a sign of God's hand at work, or simply her own desires pushing her forward? She sought answers in her faith, hoping that her renewed commitment to prayer and reflection would steer her towards what was truly meant for her.

In this new chapter of her life, Annie found herself at a crossroads, looking to balance the excitement of a potential new beginning with the responsibilities and realities of her current life. Each day, as she navigated this complex emotional landscape, she held onto the hope that, with patience and faith, the path forward would become clear.

As the nights grew longer and the quiet moments stretched, Annie found herself wrestling with thoughts of financial uncertainty. The reality of her dwindling savings loomed large, a constant reminder that the status quo was unsustainable. She knew something had to change, but the path forward was shrouded in fog, unclear and intimidating.

Lying in bed, Annie turned her worries over in her mind, grappling with the fear of re-entering a workforce that had evolved without her. What skills could she offer? What jobs were even available to someone who had prioritized family over career for so long? The questions multiplied, each one feeding her anxiety.

In the depths of uncertainty, Annie did what had always brought her solace—she prayed. She prayed not just casually, but with a fervor born from desperation. "Lord, guide me," she whispered into the darkness, her voice a mix of hope and fear. "Show me where to go, what to do. I need Your wisdom more than ever."

Each prayer was a plea for clarity, a request for a sign or direction. She knew she needed a practical plan, a way to support her family that didn't sacrifice the close-knit home life she'd fought so hard to maintain.

The idea of turning back to God not just in moments of crisis but as a regular practice began to take root. Maybe, Annie thought, this was about more than just finding a job. Perhaps this was a call to realign her entire life's path with her faith, to integrate her daily decisions and long-term planning with the wisdom she sought through prayer.

As the dawn light began to filter through the curtains, Annie felt a gentle calm settle over her. The answers were not yet clear, but the peace that came with surrendering her worries to a higher power gave her hope. With renewed resolve, she decided to start each day with prayer, not only asking for guidance but also opening her heart to the possibilities that faith might bring. It was a small step, perhaps, but for Annie, it was the start of a new journey.

CHAPTER 66 A PLAN

Amid the usual chaos of everyday life, Annie found herself at a crossroads, grappling with the frustration of her unwritten book. Pages of notes and a mind teeming with ideas, yet every attempt to formalize her thoughts into a manuscript felt clumsy and disjointed. That was until an epiphany struck one quiet afternoon. As she toiled away on feedback for AI responses in her part-time job, it dawned on her—why not harness this technology to refine her own writing?

With a spark of innovation, Annie began feeding her rough paragraphs into ChatGPT, instructing the AI to mold her words with precision and in various styles that resonated with her voice. The transformation was immediate and thrilling. What once felt like an insurmountable task now flowed effortlessly, page after page lining up like dominoes.

Reflecting on this breakthrough, Annie's thoughts turned to her prayers—the deep conversations she'd had with God about her life's direction, her finances, and her relationship with Chet. This book, she realized, could potentially be an answer to all those prayers. She envisioned it as a beacon that might guide others towards faith, a project that could stabilize her finances, and a testament to Chet that she was not merely seeking rescue but partnership.

Annie's faith had always been a cornerstone of her existence, but now it seemed to weave through her aspirations with even greater significance. She prayed fervently, "Lord, if this is the path You've laid out for me, use me as Your instrument. Let this book not only speak to those seeking guidance but also stand as a celebration of Your grace."

Emboldened by this prayer, Annie dedicated herself to her writing with newfound purpose, each chapter a step closer to a future where she stood independently yet open to the possibilities of love and companionship with Chet. This wasn't just a book; it was a mission, a tangible manifestation of her faith and her journey towards a life woven tightly with the threads of divine intention.

Annie, with a sense of clarity, knew that the journey she was embarking on would not be one of mere words on a page. It was a path of transformation, a divine crafting of her very being. As she committed herself to writing, she understood this process would shape her, chisel away at her imperfections, and perhaps even lead her through valleys of challenges and mountains of personal victories.

With each day spent in reflection and writing, Annie felt a resurgence of purpose that had long been dormant. Her faith, always a silent anchor, now became the sails catching the winds of change. She was no longer the woman who had meandered through life's trials with a passive hope; now, she actively sought transformation, embraced it.

The excitement of growth, even with its inherent pains and trials, brought a vibrant new energy to Annie's life. It was as if she was awakening from a long slumber, where survival had been her only goal, to a dawn where she actively participated in her own redemption story.

Her relationship with God deepened, becoming a dialogue filled with real surrender and earnest seeking. Each morning, as she set words to her experiences and insights, she wasn't just crafting chapters; she was penning her testament of faith, each paragraph a step closer to the woman she aspired to be.

This was not just about leaving a rut—it was about sculpting a new legacy, a narrative interwoven with divine threads, where each twist of fate and each turn of page was guided by a hand greater than her own. In this renewed walk with God, Annie found not just the thrill of personal evolution but the peace of being utterly, profoundly held within His grace.

CHAPTER 67 LISTEN

Evenings at home had transformed for me. The glow of the television, once a beacon of mindless relaxation, now felt like an intrusion. There was a whole world of experiences I was missing out on while sitting in its dull blue light. Instead of succumbing to the sofa's siren call, I found myself sprawled across my bed in the dark, pondering life's big questions and chatting with Chet, my heart's current occupant.

Chet, with his easy Alabama drawl, had become my favorite evening ritual. It was a sweet torment being so far from him, and yet, he felt so close when his voice filled the space around me.

When I wasn't tethered to my phone, absorbing every detail of Chet's day, I was actively seeking self-improvement. Not in a narcissistic way but in a genuine "I need to be better" kind of way. What could I change about myself? How could I grow not just for my own benefit but for the sake of everyone around me? These questions haunted the quieter moments of my nights.

As I lay there in the darkness, asking God for guidance or simply soaking in the silence, I realized how my relationship with Chet was inadvertently leading me on a path of personal evolution. It wasn't just about romance; it was about becoming someone who could love and be loved more profoundly. The desire to improve wasn't just for my own fulfillment—it was about crafting a life that felt worthy of the kind of love I was beginning to think I might actually deserve

As I sat in my dimly lit bedroom, thumbing through Instagram while waiting for Chet's call, I stumbled across a clip of Jordan Peterson. His voice crackled through the speaker of my phone, discussing an approach to prayer that wasn't your typical Sunday morning fare. "If you want an effective prayer, this one works every time," he asserted. "Sit up and ask yourself what bloody stupid thing you're doing that you could stop doing. What would make your life better if you stopped? The answer that comes to you is the right one if it's something you really don't want to give up."

I paused the video. There was something about the bluntness of that advice that struck a chord. So, there in the soft glow of my bedside lamp, I sat up straight and posed the question to myself. The answer hit me faster than a hiccup during a hangover—my AirPods.

Those tiny, inconspicuous earpieces were practically glued into my ears all day. They piped in everything from my favorite workout tunes to podcasts, and they helped me maintain a bubble of personal space while blocking out the world. They were my constant companions from morning runs to evening chores. But had they also become a crutch, a way to tune out more than just background noise? Maybe the perpetual soundtrack was keeping me from really engaging, from sitting in silence once in a while to hear what life, or God, or just the wind had to say.

The thought of parting with them—even temporarily—was as appealing as a cold shower in December. But there it was, the uncomfortable answer I knew I had to face. I reached up, took the AirPods out, and placed them on my nightstand.

In the stillness of my newly quiet world, a thought hovered

like a well-dressed mosquito at a nudist colony—just how long should this AirPods fast last? I remembered skimming an article once, probably while procrastinating something important, that claimed habits could be reshaped or dismantled in about two weeks. It seemed both a short enough time to endure and long enough to test my resolve.

"Two weeks," I declared to the empty room, feeling a mix of resolve and impending doom. No podcasts, no playlists, no discreet background noise to shield me from the raw acoustics of everyday life. After those two weeks, I would negotiate terms with myself, set some boundaries—like only during workouts or cleaning sprees, times when I could argue their utility over their distraction.

It sounded reasonable, yet as I lay there considering the silence that would stretch out before me, it felt like agreeing to walk through a familiar neighborhood but blindfolded. What would I hear in their absence? The creaks of my house settling, or the more unnerving creaks of my thoughts needing attention? Only one way to find out. With a sigh, I mentally braced myself for the first morning of this experiment, wondering if the sound of my coffee brewing would be as comforting without Rogan or Vaughn chattering in my ears.

CHAPTER 68 A LIL HELP HERE PLEASE

Over the past few weeks, it seems my possessions have developed a rather vindictive streak, launching a coordinated strike against my sanity and bank account. First, the back door deadbolt gave up the ghost. Then, as if on cue, the dishwasher sputtered and died, a mechanical flatline right in the middle of the rinse cycle. And the front door? Well, with my recent stalker-ish entertainment, you'd think it would have the decency to function properly, but no, it barely clings to its frame, locking and unlocking with all the enthusiasm of a teenager asked to clean their room.

As if on a roll, Sophia's radiator began its weepy rebellion next, followed by a front porch board that snapped underfoot, revealing a festering pit of rot underneath that demands a complete overhaul. Oh, to top it all off, my mower has started blowing white smoke like an old man puffing on a cigar, guzzling gas as it coughs its way across the lawn.

Strapped for cash? That's an understatement. It's dance competition season for Eliana, a triple birthday fiesta looms on the horizon, not to mention summer camps and a Disney World invite that might as well be a summons to climb Everest. With the lingering aftershocks of surgeries and legal skirmishes still nibbling at my finances, I am, frankly, drowning. Yet, in a small mercy, I managed to coax Brian, an old friend, to peek at the mower. That rusted guardian is all that stands between me and a backyard jungle. A new one? Out of the question. Sometimes, all you can do is laugh—or perhaps, start a bonfire with the repair bills.

Lately, my prayers have taken on a rather specific tone, namely, "Help!" If there's a job out there that doesn't feel like slow-motion soul extraction, I'm all ears. Or, if the divine plan is for me to buckle down on this book, then some celestial navigation would be appreciated because, frankly, I'm as lost as a sock in a laundromat.

This morning, as I schlepped out breakfast to our ensemble of squalling goats and a chicken that acts like it's forgotten it's a bird, I noticed the thick patches of clover carpeting my yard. It struck me—how miraculous it would be to find a four-leaf clover. I've never spotted one. Not one. And you'd think with my luck running as it has, the odds might tip in my favor for a change.

So there I was, muttering to the heavens for a tiny green anomaly in a sea of sameness. "Just one four-leaf clover, that's all I'm asking for. Point it out, make it glow, do whatever you do, but let it be a sign." A sign that everything might just turn out okay. Because sometimes, you need a bit more than faith; you need a sign that's hand-picked and foolproof, or at least something that won't die on you or require fixing with tools you can't afford.

Just as I'm negotiating terms with the universe, Brian's car grumbles into the driveway, a promising interruption to my plea for divine intervention on the mower front. "Dear God, please let this be an easy fix," I whisper, not quite ready to face another financial debacle. I scoot the golf cart aside—my trusty chariot—and coax the mower to life. It responds with a backfire, belching a plume of white smoke, as if to spite me. I wince, rolling it out as Brian's expression morphs into a visual 'uh oh'.

"Please don't make that face," I say, though I'm well aware that white smoke in mower language is about as good as a black spot on a pirate's palm.

"Um, yeah," Brian mutters, squinting at the mechanical beast. "But let me take a look."

He dives into the belly of the beast, wrestling with spark plugs and oil levels, as Chet rings in, perhaps sensing that another man is encroaching on his long-distance turf. He's 700 miles away, which in terms of home repair, might as well be the moon. We chat, navigating a maze of jokes and jabs, the laughter a welcome respite from the day's stresses.

Eventually, I let him go and settle myself on the concrete steps, a makeshift spectator's seat, watching Brian tinker away. It's one of those moments where hope hinges on a wrench and a prayer, and all you can do is sit there and root for a miracle, disguised as an ordinary Tuesday fix.

As Brian pokes around, his diagnosis drops like a bad punchline: the mower is hemorrhaging oil—a rather grim symptom in the world of outdoor machinery. In my mind, a stubborn chorus rises up, "No, I refuse to accept this is bad news." But denial is a tricky beast, especially when Brian starts muttering about needing a new motor.

It's not just any mower, after all. This is a $15,000 commercial zero-turn beast that can pirouette on a dime. We both nod solemnly at the unspoken verdict—repairing it, even at the cost of a few grand, would be a bargain. Except, my wallet is currently on a diet of cobwebs and old receipts.

So there I am, standing in my yard, silently broadcasting my SOS to the heavens. "Please, just make this work," I plea internally, envisioning a divine mechanic swooping down to patch things up with celestial duct tape. It's moments like these when financial reality bites you right in the aspirations, and all you can do is hope for a miracle—or at least a very generous error in Brian's initial assessment.

Brian, practical as ever, suggests we add some oil and clean the spark plugs as a first step—basic mower first aid. "Sure, spark plugs and oil are as easy as it gets, right?" I agree, clutching at any straw of simplicity in this whole debacle. While he tinkers, I meander around the yard, my gaze snagging on a tiny splash of green.

Is that—could it be? A four-leaf clover! My heart does a little jig of excitement. It's a sign; it has to be. Everything is going to be just fine. Eagerly, I bend down to pluck it, and what do you know? There's another, and another, and then another. Soon, I'm squealing, the sound probably reaching decibels only dogs can truly appreciate.

Brian ambles over, drawn by my commotion. "Wow," he says, peering at the clutch of luck in my hands. "Yeah, once you find one, you can usually find a couple in the patch." Four clovers now press against my palm, each leaf a little green benediction.

I excitedly recount my earlier prayer, my request for a sign. Holding these, I feel a swell of reassurance, as if each leaf is whispering, "It'll all work out." I snap a quick photo to send to Chet, then dash inside to share my find with the girls, the clovers resting like treasures on the counter.

In that moment, with Brian covered in oil and grime, working on a mower that represents so many of my troubles, these little plants feel like an unexpected answer to my calls for help, a small, perfect miracle in the grass.

When I return outside, Brian is still giving the mower a skeptical once-over, as if it's a puzzle meant for brighter minds than ours. Meanwhile, I'm buzzing with an unprecedented level of optimism, fueled by my recent discovery. "These four-leaf clovers are a divine signal," I proclaim with a flourish, holding them up like tiny, victorious banners. "This mower's going to come through just fine, definitely just a minor hiccup."

Brian, ever the pragmatist, suggests a workaround: "Well, even if it's leaking oil, you could keep topping it off. Might get another season or two out of it." Normally, I'm quite the optimist, but with the clovers in hand, my usual hopefulness has skyrocketed into realms that some might indeed call delusional. But today, with such a palpable sign, I'm utterly convinced of our good fortune.

As Brian digs deeper into the mechanical innards, I scan the grass again and—what do you know—more clovers. One, two, six, ten... I keep picking until, in less than ten minutes, I have 23 additional four-leaf clovers in my grasp. Added to the four I already found, I'm now wielding a grand total of 27 symbols of good luck.

Even Brian has to stop and stare, taken aback by the sheer number I've amassed. "Wow, okay, that is a lot of four-leaf clovers," he says, his voice tinged with amazement.

I can't contain my excitement as I parade back inside, laying my newfound treasures on the counter and squealing to the girls, who seem amused though not quite as enraptured as I am. I quickly snap a picture to send to Chet, who becomes genuinely impressed once I recount my prayerful request from earlier and my lifelong clover-less streak. The sudden shift from never having found a single one to holding 27 is more than luck—it's almost a celestial nod, an emerald endorsement of my hopes and prayers.

After Brian reassembles the mower, his expression is a

textbook case of skepticism. But he gives me the nod, "Go ahead, take her for a spin around the yard." So, I fire up the old girl, and she roars to life like a seasoned warrior fresh out of the spa—no backfiring, no smoke, just purring perfection as I swirl around the yard.

Brian stands there, scratching his head as I make my rounds. He signals for me to cut the engine. "Well," he says, watching the mower with a mix of surprise and reluctance, "it seems just fine, no white smoke." He had opted for thicker oil and new spark plugs, though he'd seemed convinced that wouldn't entirely solve our problems. But now, witnessing the mower's flawless performance, his certainty wavers.

Looking puzzled, he finally admits, "I think you might be good. Just change the oil and the spark plugs, and then keep an eye on the oil level." My grin stretches wide across my face—well, that I can definitely do. I've never changed oil or spark plugs myself, but I'd watched him closely, and I'm fairly confident in my newfound mechanical aptitude. An easy fix, maybe $40 total.

Snapping pics of the exact plugs I need before he reinserts them, I feel equipped and ready to handle this on my own. Parking everything back in the garage, I'm enveloped by a renewed sense of hope. Sure, I still have a laundry list of things needing attention, but finding those 27 four-leaf clovers and witnessing this minor miracle with the mower—it's like a clear signal from above. Despite the occasional chaos of life, everything is indeed going to be just fine.

Later that evening, as I settle in to watch an Alabama basketball game with Chet on the other end of the phone, I have to admit I have zero intrinsic interest in basketball. But Chet bleeds crimson and white, and "Roll Tide" is practically a reflex for him. I tune in because they've made history this year, landing in the Final Four, and Chet's enthusiasm is contagious —even through text.

As we exchange messages, Chet brings up how his mother used to press her four-leaf clovers in her Bible. "What a great idea," I think, momentarily envisioning my trove of clovers neatly tucked between the sacred pages. But there's a hitch—I've got quite a collection, and I've recently taken to reading my Bible daily again. I can just see the mess of clovers tumbling out mid-Psalm.

So, I pivot to plan B. I pull out one of the old encyclopedias I inherited from my grandmother—a hefty tome perfect for pressing. As I carefully place each clover within its pages, it feels like I'm embedding a little bit of today's luck and miracles into a slice of family history.

Chatting with Chet and securing my clovers in my grandmother's encyclopedia, even with the cloud of uncertainties that typically loom over my daily existence, everything, in this moment, just feels right. The simple acts of preservation, both of the clovers and our shared moments, seem to anchor me. In a life often marked by chaos, these small rituals and connections provide a much-needed sense of peace and continuity.

CHAPTER 69 THE GOOD PART

As life bumps along, Annie manages to change the oil and spark plugs in her mower, a task that requires several calls to Chet for guidance, and three separate trips to AutoZone. She figures it's good to let Chet feel needed—because, well, he is. With the mower now purring like a kitten in a sunbeam, life proceeds with minimal hiccups. But the ache of missing Chet gnaws at her; she yearns for his cuddles, his kisses, and the electric thrill of his presence. The uncertainty of their next reunion twitches at her nerves. Annie, perpetually over-eager even on her calmest days, finds herself wrestling with the routine of her life: reading, workouts, work, schooling the girls, writing her book, chauffeuring the kids. She longs for more, for the next chapter, for something to propel her forward.

One day, while tackling a mountain of dishes by hand—because, yes, her dishwasher is still a casualty of appliance warfare—she daydreams of better days. It's then that a familiar voice whispers in her mind, "These are the good times too." Struck by the simplicity and truth of it, she realizes that this era of change and growth, rife with uncertainty and hard work, also bristles with its own brand of excitement and wonder.

"Okay, God," she thinks, a newfound resolve steadying her voice, "I will try to appreciate the present too, not treating it as anything less than the miraculous gift that it is." While she looks forward to the future, she also understands that, much like a child reveling in the anticipation of Christmas, much of the joy and fun lies in the buildup to the actual day.

As Annie furthers her efforts toward sculpting her novel, the intricacies of her long-distance romance with Chet stir a symphony of emotions. Yet, beneath these orchestrations, a sinister whisper of doubt and self-deprecation begins to intrude, echoing the seductive hiss of the serpent in the Garden of Eden. This little voice taunts her relentlessly: "Who do you think you are? You're wasting all your time on this stupid book that no one will ever want to read. Meanwhile, you're marching straight to the poor house. You and your children will struggle and have nothing. You are insane if you think you can accomplish anything noteworthy."

These thoughts, venomous and suffocating, threaten to unravel her. Yet, Annie turns to prayer in her moments of greatest doubt, over and over again she lays her vulnerabilities bare before God: "Am I doing the right thing, God? I am nothing without You, and I know I'm not good enough on my own, but I believe You can make something beautiful of my life. Here I am, use me. My life is Yours."

With these words, the shadows of inadequacy that cloud her mind are scattered. She concedes that she might indeed not be "good enough" on her own—a realization that doesn't depress but liberates her. Annie understands that she doesn't have to be the paragon of perfection. Her task isn't to conquer the world on her own but to let God guide her steps. By relinquishing control and allowing faith to lead, she finds that the path, though not devoid of obstacles, becomes clearer. This submission to a higher plan doesn't just dispel her doubts;

it transforms them into stepping stones towards a greater, divinely orchestrated destiny. Through this surrender, Annie learns that by not being "good enough" alone, she is perfectly poised to be used for something far beyond her individual capabilities.

Despite the regular cadence of Chet's calls at lunch, after work, and the texts fluttering between them throughout the day, Annie harbored a creeping fear that somehow he was drifting away, that she was losing him. This wasn't rational —she knew it. Her past entanglements had been with men who clung too tightly, who controlled too much, making this current normality with Chet feel unsettlingly unfamiliar and frighteningly loose.

Even with this awareness, the specter of anxiety clung stubbornly, weaving through her thoughts and coloring her emotions with worry. In these moments, she found solace in a higher dialogue, hearing the reassurance of God's voice cutting through the fog of her fears: "What is meant for you will not pass you by."

When the shadows of losing Chet loomed, she would catch herself, consciously halting the spiraling thoughts. Sometimes, she'd even speak aloud, a mantra to anchor her drifting worries: "Annie, what is meant for you will not pass you by." This became her shield against the barrage of insecurity, reminding her that if Chet was truly meant for her, no force on earth could sever their bond. And if he wasn't —if their paths were meant to diverge—it was only because something greater, something even more right for her, lay ahead.

With this faith, Annie learned to let go of the reins of control she so desperately wanted to grip. She had already entrusted her path to God, casting her lot not in the fickle hands of fate but in the assured promise of divine oversight. This realization didn't just ease her mind; it fundamentally shifted her perspective. The future, whether with Chet or not, held good things—because what was meant for her would surely find its way, just as anything not meant would drift past, leaving her poised for the next blessing on her journey.

Thus, Annie honed her skill in mastering these invasive fears and anxious thoughts, identifying each as it surfaced like unwelcome intruders in the calm of her mind. With each recognition, she employed her armor—scripture or the keen blade of rational thought—to parry these assaults. Every successful deflection, every time she silenced the anxiety with a verse or a logical reassessment, counted as a personal victory.

These were not just mere moments of triumph, but building blocks, fortifying her resilience, strengthening her resolve. With each battle waged against fear and won by faith or reason, she grew sturdier, more steadfast in her journey. This process, repetitive and enduring, was not merely about overcoming but about transformation. Annie was not just moving through life; she was evolving, each victory a step further in her profound journey of self-discovery and spiritual trust. In learning to confront and conquer her fears, Annie was not only surviving; she was thriving, each step forward an echo of progress on a path laid out by a higher power.

CHAPTER 70
BE BRAVE

I had come to the decision that God had more in store for me than merely scraping by, miserably tethered to a job I loathed until retirement or death, whichever came first. This was gearing up to be big, headline-making divine intervention. And I understood that if I was going to be a vessel for such a purpose, it would require a complete annihilation of the ego. I had to let go of everything I clung to, diving headfirst into whatever cosmic plan was in store.

The thing about me is, I often leap before I look. Like the time A1 convinced me to test out her dad's dog's new shock collars. With the reckless abandon that only a fairly drunk person can muster, I strapped one around my neck and took off running, only to be jolted by an electric shock so fierce when I crossed the invisible line, it launched me straight up and flat on my back. A normal person might have paused to consider the consequences. Me? I saw a dare and a chance to be the evening's entertainment—not permanently harmful, but definitely a shock.

Well, the path I was now committed to was lined with its own set of shocks—spiritual, emotional, existential. Some were painful, others delightfully surprising, but all were undeniably exciting. Like navigating a field rigged with invisible fences, each step was a pulse of new life, a jolt to the system, pushing me toward an unknown boundary that, once crossed, promised to redefine everything I thought I knew about life's limits.

One evening, as I'm lying in bed, the phone's glow casting shadows across the room, I'm texting Chet and missing him something fierce. And if I'm completely honest, I recognize that my eyes—and maybe too much of my focus—have been glued to him. Inadvertently, or perhaps conveniently, I've slipped into placing him above everything else, romanticizing to a degree that might even make a seasoned poet cringe.

As much as I hate to admit it, I'm doing it again—putting a man before God, letting my earthly desires shadow my spiritual needs. It's not something I consciously think about, possibly because deep down, I'm terrified of what it implies.

That night, amidst a tangle of sheets and emotions, I send him a message that's all too revealing of my innermost wishes: "I wanna hang out with you every day... and go to sleep snuggled up and wake up with you every morning." The response comes back swift, a little too swift for my liking, "Me too and it's probably never gonna happen but I'm being optimistic. Just saying!"

His words, meant to be lighthearted, I guess, hit like a truck. My heart, a fragile thing on the best of days, feels like it's shattered into a thousand irretrievable pieces. It's as though he's nonchalantly scooped it out with a spoon. He probably didn't mean to come off so blunt, but the sting is sharp and deep. He really doesn't think we'll ever truly be together? Then what are we even doing? Am I just a placeholder, a convenient voice on the other end of the line until something more geographically and logistically feasible comes along for him?

Now, broken-hearted and a touch angry, I put the phone down sharply and roll over. Tears carve wet trails down my cheeks as I turn my heart upwards. "Okay, God," I choke out, my voice a tremble of betrayal and hurt, "you gave me Chet and instead of staying grateful, I started to ignore you, putting him above everything else."

I don't know why I always end up this way, but I admit, through tears, that I need help to do better. "If he's another lesson, and my heart needs to break again, then let's just do it. I'm ready." The words are barely a whisper, my sobbing loud in the quiet of the room, because the thought of losing Chet and the future I'd envisioned with him feels like watching a cherished dream swirl down the drain.

"God, I trust you, and I know whatever you have in store for me is for the best, even if it doesn't feel like it right now. I know you can see what I can't." Gratitude mixes with my grief as I add, "Thank you for sending Chet, for as long as I had him, and for leading me through this."

Then, summoning a courage I didn't know I had, I offered up everything: "God, my life, my heart, my soul—whatever I have, it's all yours. Do whatever you will with it." I've said similar things before, and really meant them...but this time it was different. It came from a place deep and raw, a cry from the very guts of me.

As the words left my mouth, that slithering, serpent-like voice tried to invade, hissing catastrophes into my ear, "God will put you through pain and trials, that's how he teaches. He might give you cancer; he might even take your children." It painted every horrific scenario one could imagine.

But God had been preparing me for this battle, and I knew now how to fend off these assaults. The terrifying thoughts were strong, yes, but I countered them with reminders of

God's inherent goodness. Scriptures like Jeremiah 29:11 came to mind, "For I know the plans I have for you, plans to prosper you and not to harm you, to give you hope and a future."

Yes, God allows us to face trials, but He never wastes our pain. Suffering with God at my side is infinitely better than any pleasure experienced in His absence. This night, with its tears and prayers, wasn't just another low point; it was a turning point, a profound surrender that reshaped my faith, stronger and more resilient than ever before.

CHAPTER 71
SILENCE, SORT OF

The next morning, I woke up to sweet messages from Chet, a comforting reminder that he was indeed still there, and that perhaps my heartbreak from the night before had a purpose that had nothing to do with him giving up on me. So, I returned the usual "Good morning," and got up to start my daily routine, now noticeably quieter without my AirPods for the past few days.

Living without them was getting easier, though I wouldn't go as far as saying it was easy yet. The hardest part? Working out without music. I mean, seriously, who does that? But something unexpected had happened in the silence: thoughts and ideas seemed to flow through me more freely, and my kids appeared to appreciate my increased presence. I hadn't realized how unapproachable I had been, effectively wearing a 'Do Not Disturb' sign on my head with those AirPods in all the time.

Now, the house was slightly more harmonious without them. I was still adjusting to the incessant chatter and background noise I'd been drowning out—turns out, my family had a lot to say, and I was just starting to listen.

But aside from the voices of my girls, which had become more prevalent in the absence of my usual soundtrack, there was another voice speaking to me—and no, it's not the kind that would prompt someone to gently suggest psychiatric care. It was a whisper in the stillness, a quiet guide imparting wisdom and lessons through everyday thoughts and actions, finding purpose in parts of life that usually felt stuck in the day-to-day rut.

Without my AirPods, it was as if I had removed a barrier I hadn't even realized was there, making me rawer, more open. I was ready to listen, truly listen, and accept whatever might come my way. I was still recognizing that this adventure was in full swing, and while to the outward observer it might look like my life was at a standstill, inside, I was moving toward something at light speed.

It was a curious feeling, knowing that beneath the surface calm, I was undergoing profound shifts, barreling down a path of personal enlightenment—or at least stumbling along it— with an unexpected clarity that came from simply tuning into the quieter, often overlooked whispers of life.

Being someone who could easily get lost in the Instagram scroll—reels upon reels of motivational and inspirational videos, along with tips on how to biohack and lifehack your way to greatness—I was all too familiar with the mantra: get out of your comfort zone, work hard, do the hard things if you want to achieve greatness. I'd heard it more times than I cared to count. But doing hard things had never been my problem. My challenge was in knowing what to do. I could easily accomplish the task in front of me; my misery lay in floating aimlessly, feeling lost, not knowing where to direct my energy.

However, it seemed I had finally stumbled upon the hard things those videos talked about. And it wasn't really as hard as they made it seem; in fact, it was a heck of a lot easier than floating around lost. Step 1: give up and ask God for help. Step 2: listen to what He says. Step 3: do it, and its ok to ask for help to get it done. Really, not that hard.

Sure, there were tears shed off and on as I let go of some things and realized some hurts I didn't even know I was still carrying. But even that felt good, at least more than it felt bad. It was like cleaning out a closet you'd been afraid to open: daunting at first, but refreshingly liberating once done. It turned out that the true challenge wasn't finding new mountains to climb or oceans to cross but rather, simply surrendering to the journey already laid out before me, and finding the courage to listen closely, not just to the noise of the world, but to the quiet guiding whispers of a more divine direction.

And something else was working for me, in its own quirky way. I found myself constantly ping-ponging mentally about my book. One minute, I'd think, "Wow, this is going to be great, it's going to help people," and, perhaps to my detriment, visions of fame and fortune would dance in my head—which I know I shouldn't want or covet, but hey, I'm only human.

Then I'd pong over to the other side with thoughts like, "Okay, this book is probably just for you. God is having you write it because, let's face it, the level of self-examination happening when you write your story is something I can't imagine achieving any other way." And while the first thought was vastly more appealing, filled with accolades and acknowledgments, the second thought, this worst-case scenario, was still good.

It was a grounding realization, a reminder that even if my book didn't turn out to be the blockbuster I daydreamed about, it was serving a profound purpose. It was therapy, an introspective journey that forced me to look deeply at who I was and who I was becoming. Either I'd write something that resonated widely, or I'd write something that resonated deeply —with me.

CHAPTER 72 EASTER

For a while now, Annie had known she needed to return to church, but the mere thought spiked her anxiety to new heights. She recognized the irrationality of her fear, yet it continued to hold her back. Firstly, her mother would undoubtedly be overjoyed at her return and would likely make a grand spectacle of it, parading her around like the prodigal son come home. Annie cringed at the thought; maybe she was that lost child in some metaphorical sense, but she certainly didn't want to be cast as the loser making a grand, shameful return.

Secondly, there was the palpable fear that church—like no other place—had the potential to unlock an emotional floodgate. The thought of crying, of breaking down in a torrent of tears in front of a whole congregation was something Annie absolutely could not abide. The vulnerability of it was terrifying.

Yet, she also recalled a quote she had heard that nagged at her with inconvenient truth: "What you want most will be found where you least want to look." Ugh, she thought, recognizing with a mix of dread and clarity that church, for whatever reasons, was precisely the place she least wanted to look. It seemed that her path to whatever she was searching for—forgiveness, acceptance, peace—might just run right through the very place she was most reluctant to revisit. The irony wasn't lost on her, and with a heavy sigh, she began to consider facing her fears, wondering if perhaps what lay beyond them could indeed be worth the emotional upheaval it threatened to unleash.

The previous Sunday, Chet had casually dropped into conversation, "Well, I'm going to church. I haven't been in a while, but I feel like I've got a lot to pray about, and I need to go back." Holy moly, he did it again—just when Annie thought he couldn't get any better. He was mature, loved God, and was actively seeking guidance, presumably about their relationship and his future. And, once again, he set an example for Annie, sparking in her a desire to be a better person.

Annie wanted to be worthy of this relationship and of him. She felt like, finally, she was in a place and had found a person who actually did what a partner should do: made her feel loved and good. And while he never asked her to change, his goodness, his own striving for improvement, made her want to strive to be better. It was a testament to the kind of influence he had on her—subtle yet profound, leading by example rather than demand.

This revelation, coming from Chet's simple declaration about returning to church, struck a chord with Annie. It nudged her towards confronting her own hesitations about church. His actions reminded her that growth often comes from facing the things we avoid, and that sometimes, being part of a couple means being inspired by the other's actions to reexamine and better our own.

Annie's phone rang—it was her mother. The invitation to church on Easter was delivered in a tone that seemed to expect the usual polite decline. This time, however, Annie surprised not only her mother but herself as well by accepting.

Sure, it was Easter, and everyone and their dog showed up on Easter, even those who avoided church like a tedious chore for the rest of the year. But who cares? Annie was taking her first step back to church. It was a significant step, a public re-entry into a place she had avoided, filled with personal trepidations and echoes of past discomforts.

This return wasn't just about showing up; it was about challenging her own apprehensions, about stepping into a space that, despite its familiarity, now felt like uncharted territory. It was a decision that felt both monumental and trivial, typical of the complex contradictions that so often colored her life. Easter, with all its symbols of renewal and resurrection, seemed an apt time for such a beginning. After all, if there was any day to make a comeback, why not on a day celebrated for its story of miraculous comeback?

Eliana was away on a mini vacation with her friend, and Sophia had work commitments, so that left Bella and Annie to attend church together. They both got dressed up and made their way. And to no one's surprise, Annie's mom was overjoyed when they arrived. True to form, she launched Annie into a sort of prodigal son publicity tour around the congregation. Annie survived—after all, she had definitely been through worse.

The good news is that nothing broke Annie down that morning; there was no crying, no emotional breakdown. She survived the service just fine. While she felt no miraculous difference and hadn't felt the need to rededicate her life or anything dramatic, she was glad she went. She felt like she and Jesus were on great terms, church or no church, but if there was a possibility that attending church could be beneficial to her personal growth, then she resolved to start showing up, whether it felt like it instigated a big change or not.

After church, the Easter celebrations were to be simple for Annie and Bella. There were no grand dinner plans, no festive gatherings; it was just the two of them, and Annie's wallet was light—just a few dollars, but enough for a couple of roast beef sandwiches from Arby's. They stopped, picked up their modest Easter meal, and headed home.

This year, the financial tightrope Annie was walking on had been too strained to allow for the luxury of Easter baskets, something that gnawed at her. She felt a pang of guilt over it, but her girls had been angels about the situation—always sweet, never complaining or even hinting at disappointment about not receiving anything. Their understanding was a small, comforting grace in the sting of financial hardship.

Driving home, sandwich bags in hand, Annie's mind wandered to prayers and hopes that soon God would help guide her out of the financial mire she'd found herself in. She prayed for the wisdom and opportunity to claw her way back to a place of stability, to someday make it up to her sweet girls. In her heart, she carried both the weight of her current troubles and the flickering light of hope that things would get better, that she could give Bella and her sisters the kind of carefree joy that every parent wishes to provide. With each mile home, these thoughts mixed with a quiet gratitude for the day's simple blessings and the steady presence of her daughters.

As meager as this Easter was, it still stood in stark contrast to the previous year, a grim season when Annie had been left bloodied and beaten by Steven, her children traumatized in the wake of violence. That dark chapter was still vivid in her memory, a reminder of how far they had come. So, while this Easter might not have boasted the festivities or abundance of others, it marked a significant step forward from the depths they had once known.

Sitting in their modest living room, with Arby's roast beef sandwiches in hand instead of a lavish feast, Annie could not help but feel a surge of relief mixed with a quiet determination. It was a humble celebration, yes, but it underscored a vital truth: they were moving in the right direction, slowly but surely climbing out of the shadows of the past.

The simplicity of this Easter, devoid of baskets and grandeur, carried its own message of resilience and hope. For Annie and her children, this Easter was not just a holiday; it was a milestone, a quiet affirmation that they were on a path to recovery and renewal.

CHAPTER 73
REMEMBER THE
DANG CLOVERS

As Annie continues her journey of self-discovery, with Chet's voice a constant reassurance on the other end of the phone, she takes one step at a time. Doubt, however, is an uninvited guest that tries to make a home within her thoughts. With money tighter than ever and no clear remedy in sight, her prayers become a steadfast ritual. "Lord, I'm not afraid of work, and I'm not lazy," she prays, "so if I'm supposed to be doing something other than what I'm currently doing, if I need to find another job, please show me what and where. Otherwise, I'm going to keep on this path and believe this is where you want me for now."

When doubts creep in, as they invariably do, she combats them with scripture and a deep-seated knowledge that she has placed her life entirely in God's hands. She is walking in faith more than she ever thought possible. The longer she stays on this path, the more she finds she must trust.

It's not just a matter of believing in the unseen but a daily, sometimes hourly, reaffirmation of her commitment to follow through with this faith-driven life, despite the financial insecurities and emotional turbulence it sometimes brings. Her journey is less about finding quick solutions and more about learning to endure, to sustain faith through the storm, trusting that her steadfastness will lead to growth and understanding that can come no other way.

When the relentless surge of doubts threatened to overwhelm her, Annie would recall the 27 four-leaf clovers—her tangible tokens of luck and divine reassurance. This small memory served as a bulwark against her fears, enough to fortify her faith and propel her forward.

One day, inspired to keep this symbol of hope always in sight, Annie ventured into the clutter of her garage and retrieved an old picture frame. She carefully removed the now dried four-leaf clovers from the pages of the encyclopedia where they had been carefully pressed and preserved. Methodically, she arranged them within the frame, creating a mosaic of green, each leaf a testament to serendipity and divine attention.

She hung the frame above her lamp next to her bed, positioning it so it would be one of the first things she saw each morning and the last each night. All 27 reminders that not only is God listening, but He cares even about the little things. There they were, just staring at her, a daily affirmation that the minutiae of her life were under divine surveillance, that her journey was noted, her struggles seen, and her faith acknowledged. Each clover was a small whisper from the universe, an echo in her room, reaffirming that she was never truly alone in her doubts or her dreams.

One day, as Annie was texting Chet, he lamented another long day at work. Trying to offer some comfort, she texted, "I sure wish I could be there when you get off to make you dinner and take care of you, you do too much and we could have so much fun." His response was less than hopeful, "That's the dream but I'm afraid it's just fantasy."

This time, instead of succumbing to heartbreak, Annie chose a different tack. With a mix of wry determination, she replied, "Ok, I would just like to remind you that I found 27 four-leaf clovers in the yard the other day, and that's kind of a big deal. So from now on, when you text me crap like 'it's probably never gonna happen,' or 'this is the dream but probably never gonna be more than our fantasy,' I'm just gonna send this." She then sent him a picture of her framed four-leaf clovers.

Chet's immediate reply came with a laugh, "Ha! Ok ok, point taken, you're right."

Annie's response with the clovers wasn't just about countering his pessimism with her optimism; it was about challenging the notion of what's possible, grounding their dreams in a tangible symbol of luck and hope. Her creative rebuttal served not only to lift their spirits but also to keep the flame of possibility alive in their relationship. It was her way of saying that sometimes, reality can be bent towards our dreams, and occasionally, a little faith might just turn the so-called "fantasy" into something real.

CHAPTER 74 YOU ARE LOVED

So, I hadn't exactly announced my plans to make my return to church a regular engagement, and I'm pretty sure my parents thought my appearance on Easter was just a one-off miracle. But I wanted to keep going, quietly, without turning it into some big production. However, knowing my mother, the slightest whiff of regular church attendance and she'd likely organize a parade in my honor.

Her birthday was approaching this Sunday, though, and I figured, what better birthday gift for her than my continued presence in the pews, followed by a celebration? I shared my plan with her: the girls and I would join her at church for her birthday, then we could all enjoy a lunch afterward. She was delighted, quickly agreeing to a barbecue celebration afterward.

With my newfound clarity—thanks, in part, to the absence of my AirPods—I noticed an emerging desire to work on my relationships with family and friends, something I hadn't felt in a long time. I had been quite the hermit, really—closed off, attending family gatherings out of obligation rather than desire, always looking forward to the moment I could retreat back to my solitude. But something had shifted. I was no longer just showing up; I was present, actively seeking to mend and deepen these relationships that had frayed over time.

Part of this renewed focus, I think, was inspired by Chet. Listening to him talk about the love he has for his family, friends, and community, and how vital they are to one another, sparked something in me. It was just another way he was nudging me to be better, to do better.

And, of course, I felt God's gentle push in this direction too. It wasn't just about attending church; it was about what I carried out of those church doors each Sunday. It was about reconnecting, rebuilding, and perhaps, forgiving—not just others, but myself too.

Lately, something else had been nudging at my thoughts: A1, my dear friend who passed away unexpectedly a couple of years ago. She was more precious to me than words can convey. She was that person who truly got me. She'd listen to any bit of craziness I was cooking up and, without making me feel guilty or judged, would tell it to me straight. She was also a free spirit —I'm pretty sure we had more fun together than most people have in their entire lives. A real kindred spirit, something special.

I think one reason I've grown so fond of Chet is that he reminds me a bit of her—outdoorsy, adventurous, and funny in the strangest way, brimming with energy and perpetually on the move. Anyway, for whatever reason, she had been heavily on my mind.

And it wasn't just her that had been important to me; her whole family had become like my own. I truly love them, and they seemed to love and accept me right back. There's something special about people who aren't your family by blood, and who love you just as you are. That's a kind of love that feels above a lot of others—it's not romantic, it's not obligatory because you were born into it; they choose just sort of love you for you.

It's a deep and unconditional acceptance that, once you've tasted it, leaves a mark. And now, missing her and feeling her absence, I found myself cherishing not just the memories of our wild escapades and heart-to-hearts, but also the profound sense of belonging her family provided. It was a reminder of the different textures of love and connection that weave through our lives, shaping who we are and how we see the world.

A1's sister, Kat, had once extended an invitation to come out to her place to fish, an offer I had tucked away like a coupon I might never remember to use. But now, emboldened by my new life and a burgeoning sense of self, I thought, Why not?

So, I texted Kat to ask if the offer still stood for us to come fish sometime. "We would love to," I added, "and maybe little Isabella, Kat's daughter—not to be confused with my Isabella—would like to show us the ropes." Kat's response was immediate and brimming with enthusiasm: "We would love that!!" We settled on the following Saturday afternoon, and she mentioned she wanted to get pizza for us all first.

With that, the weekend was shaping up to be full—church and birthdays and fishing and lunch with lots of people. Normally, the thought of such a packed schedule would have made me cringe and filled me with dread. But now, I find myself actually kind of looking forward to it.

It's funny how change creeps up on you. I used to view social gatherings as a sort of chore, a series of events to endure rather than enjoy. But here I was, genuinely excited about spending time with Kat and our respective Isabellas, about reconnecting with a part of my past that was linked to someone who meant the world to me. It felt like a step toward not just moving on, but moving forward with a full heart and an eagerness for whatever lay ahead.

Thinking about it, I suppose I've always harbored this nagging feeling that I wasn't quite good enough, that I wasn't really wanted, which is why I often shied away from going out around people. When I did brave the social scene, I somehow always managed to have a good time, to enjoy the people around me—and they seemed to enjoy me, too. I've been called the life of the party more than once, which should count for something.

But once I'd leave, that insidious hissing serpent of doubt would slither into my ear, twisting memories to make me feel as though I must've been annoying or awful. It would then craft a future based on those reframed past events, convincing me that I would just be a nuisance, unwanted at the next gathering. Yet, all the evidence, if I were honest, pointed starkly to the contrary.

Letting God lead the way and embracing the personal growth I was undergoing helped me to see things differently. If God loves me enough to work on me the way He has, then surely I must be something pretty special. And if that's the case, I surely wouldn't want to deprive the people I love of whatever it is that makes me, well, me.

This new realization was liberating. It allowed me to shed that old, unfounded belief of not being enough and embrace the fact that not only am I enough, but I am also a beloved, integral part of my circle.

The weekend went smashingly. It kicked off with pizza and fishing, where little Isabella and I had a blast. She really reminded me so much of A1—it was almost like getting to spend time with my dear friend again. Without even realizing it, I had picked the two-year anniversary of A1's death for our fishing expedition. Maybe somewhere deep inside, some part of me remembered it was this day, or perhaps God knew it would be good for all of us to be together then and nudged the idea into my mind. Either way, the day was perfect, and had A1 been there, she would have absolutely loved it.

The sun was shining, the fish were biting, and laughter filled the air, almost as if she were right there with us, cracking jokes and making the kind of silly comments that only she could make. It was one of those days that felt both ordinary and extraordinary at the same time, stitched together with moments of joy that seemed to defy the very concept of loss.

I hope God gave her a peek at us from heaven. I like to think that she was watching and laughing along with us, delighted to see us all together, living and enjoying the moment.

Then church on Sunday was good, and I managed to avoid another emotional breakdown in public, so I chalked that up as a win. This was followed by a lunch with my family; it was very nice—pleasantly uneventful, with just the right amount of family banter that didn't veer into the territories that typically required a therapist's intervention afterward.

Somehow, God was pulling things, people, and all the little parts of my life back together just right, and it really was miraculous to watch. It was like observing a masterful technician working on a complex, beautiful machine, fitting all the intricate gears and springs into place until it hummed with life. I was both a component and an observer, amazed by the unfolding coherence where there was once disjointed chaos. Watching it all come together gave me a sense of being part of something larger, something profoundly intentional.

CHAPTER 75
WHAT ARE YOU LOOKING FOR

Annie completed her two weeks of no AirPods, and when the self-imposed exile was over, she popped them back in. Surprisingly, being without them for so long had made the music resonate more deeply than before, its rhythms and melodies now even more of a powerful motivator rather than just background noise. After a week of intense workouts, trying to keep herself from slipping back into the habit of wearing them all day, Annie found herself in a comfortable, seemingly healthy groove.

As life continued, the main source of difficulty in life was the little voice of anxiety that incessantly tried to creep in, reminding her of how inadequate she was and how terrible things were bound to be just over the next hill. However, she had armed herself with a nice little collection of scriptures, sayings, and reminders to fire back when that voice spoke up. "What is meant for me will not pass me by," "God's love is good and merciful," and the knowledge that she was truly giving everything she had to following Jesus and His plan for her life were enough to keep her steadfast and on the path laid out.

At one point, the little voice of anxiety spoke up for about the millionth time that day, and something in Annie snapped back, "Wow, you've really got that devil worked up today; you must be doing something right." Suddenly, the voice of anxiety, meant to bring her down and stop her in her tracks, instead of making her freeze, now emboldened her. Every time it spoke up, she would remind herself of her motives, her work, and the reasons she knew she was following God's will. Then, that anxious voice became just more proof that she was headed toward something big, and the forces of darkness really wanted to put out the light that was now burning brightly within her.

This new perspective transformed her anxiety from a hindrance into a sign of progress, a paradoxical encouragement that she was moving in the right direction, disturbing the peace of whatever opposed her growth. Each challenge to her spirit reinforced her resolve, turning her fears into fuel for her faith-driven journey.

Some days, Annie wasn't sure if she was in a dream now, or she was still trying to wake up from the dream she'd been living her whole life. Like every time she rubbed her eyes, things got a little clearer. Realizations were coming faster than ever, so many that she wanted to share, impart, and remember, but often they would come so fast she would just pray she could hold on to them all and not forget. They felt like the most precious gifts, peppered throughout each day.

She began to realize what it meant to live intentionally. Being intentional wasn't just about making huge plans for the future and setting big goals. If that had been the case, Annie would have been in trouble, because she knew she was no good at big decisions. But instead, for her, it meant being intentional in every single little detail of her day, down to the very last thought.

As thoughts came to her mind, she would, just like the verse said, hold each thought captive to Christ and see whether or not it belonged in her mind, which now felt like a precious temple, not just a rattling claptrap full of angry wasps. This new approach transformed her inner life, turning every moment into an opportunity for reflection and choice, fostering a sense of sacredness in her daily experiences that she had never felt so acutely before.

Indeed, it often felt as though her mind was a battleground. Armed with God's word, the Holy Spirit, and her superpower of boundless optimism, Annie fought tirelessly. Her heart ached for the day when the changes she felt brewing in her mind and spirit would begin to manifest physically around her, bringing to life the transformations she sensed internally.

In the last couple of weeks, Annie had taken to praying incessantly; she prayed out loud, she prayed in her heart and mind, she prayed in the Holy Spirit every chance she got. Each prayer felt like a missile launched against the encroaching forces of despair, each verse recited a shield raised against the onslaught of negativity. She found herself speaking to God, not just in moments of quiet solitude but amid the hustle and bustle of daily life, her prayers weaving through the fabric of her everyday activities, turning routine into ritual.

This constant communication with the divine wasn't merely a way to seek divine intervention, but a transformative practice that reshaped her outlook, fortified her spirit, and prepared her for whatever lay ahead. She clung to her faith as a soldier clings to their weapons in the heat of battle, knowing that her arsenal of prayers and positivity was crucial not just for winning the skirmish of the moment, but for securing ultimate victory in the war waging within.

As Annie grew to understand the importance of her thoughts, she also began to scrutinize the music she was listening to. Songs that once pulled at certain emotional strings or motivated her with their beats now often carried messages that clashed with the truths she had come to know in her soul. She began the meticulous process of filtering out any music that conflicted with what she now knew was right and good.

It became clear to her that every element of her environment, including the lyrics that filled her ears, influenced her mental and spiritual state. If all the progress she had made so far had been achieved through small, deliberate steps forward, then it stood to reason that small steps backward could just as easily lead her right back to where she started—a prospect that was utterly unacceptable.

With this realization, her approach to consuming music transformed. It wasn't just about what sounded good anymore; it was about what felt right, what resonated with the new paths she was forging in her life. Each song she chose to listen to now had to pass a sort of spiritual litmus test, aligning with her values and the direction she was determined to continue moving in. This was yet another battleground, albeit a quieter one, where the stakes were her continued growth and steadfast adherence to a life lived with intention and truth.

Even though the circumstances of her life had not physically changed—the same job, the same home, the same daily routines—the way Annie experienced them had changed drastically. She had a realization one night, as she found herself eager to go to sleep. Initially, she wondered if this eagerness was a sign of depression, a desire to escape the waking world. But she quickly dismissed this thought, recognizing instead that she looked forward to the quiet of the night, to laying down in the dark with her thoughts, reviewing her day and her inner self.

Annie also realized something profound: she had developed a new obsession, something that now occupied her thoughts even more than Chet, or romance, or the physical love for which she had so yearned. She had developed an ever-growing hunger for the voice of God, for the voice of correction and guidance that she had been tuning into, and she wanted more and more.

She found herself frequently singing and praying along with one of her favorite songs, pleading for God to "set a fire down in my soul, that I can't contain and I can't control. I want more of you, God." It seemed her prayers were being answered. Her desire for divine connection had become insatiable, outstripping all her other longings. This craving wasn't born out of a need to escape her daily realities but rather to engage with them more deeply, more spiritually.

Equally, she was excited for each morning, eager to start her day, read, and work on her book. For the first time in a long time, she wasn't looking to escape her evenings with television, alcohol, or random internet interactions. Instead, she was enthusiastic about actively working on her own life and embracing God's promises for her future.

This shift in perspective transformed her daily experiences. What had once felt like an endless loop of monotonous obligations now seemed filled with moments of opportunity and reflection. Each day, though outwardly similar to the last, was internally met with a new perspective, a heightened sense of awareness that she hadn't possessed before.

Annie found meaning in the mundane, significance in the subtle shifts of her heart and mind. This internal revolution was a testament to the idea that while external change is often slow to come, internal change can redefine the world in which one lives.

CHAPTER 76
PATIENCE

Sometimes I know I can be a bit of an impatient toddler. God has been giving me continued nudges, speaking to me throughout the day to reassure me that He is indeed involved in my life and things are headed in the right direction. Yet, despite this divine reassurance, I find myself plagued by impatience, always rushing towards the next milestone. I try to pull myself outside of time, reassuring myself, "All these good things and all the changes I'm looking for are as good as done. I'm on the path, I'm not turning back, and there's no stopping what God has put in motion." But then, my toddler brain chimes in with a petulant, "But I want it now!"

This impatience extends to my relationship with Chet. He texts me every morning, calls during his lunch break, rings me on his way home from work, and then again in the evening once he's finished with his chores. Despite this steady stream of contact, my impatient brain tries to convince me that if he really liked me, we would already be together—this is obviously absurd considering we've only known each other for just over a month.

Apparently, God still has quite a bit of work to do with me when it comes to patience. Ugh, that probably means I'm going to be forced to practice it for a while. Can I reframe my brain to see this waiting as a lesson from God and make it positive? Maybe. If I can manage to see each day not as a delay in getting what I want but as an opportunity to grow into what I need to be, for when I finally get it, perhaps I can transform this frustrating waiting game into a constructive part of my spiritual journey.

One thing I'm certainly not missing is any opportunities to obey God and move forward. I'm chomping at the bit like a racehorse in the stall, practically begging God to give me the next step, the next bit of direction. It's as if I'm poised at the starting gate, every muscle tensed, every nerve fired up, waiting for that bell to ring.

You could say I'm a bit eager, or as some might gently suggest, bordering on neurotic. There I am, daily, pacing back and forth in my mental stall, peeking out, asking, "Is it time yet? How about now?" It's a wonder I haven't worn a path in the carpet.

But it's not just about the big, grandiose leaps; it's those small, seemingly mundane steps that I crave. Each little nudge from God, every subtle hint of divine will, feels like a secret map being unrolled a square inch at a time. And here I am, squinting at it under the dim light, trying to make out the next turn, the next marker, ready to sprint ahead the moment the path clears.

God isn't just helping me to move forward in time, he's also helping me go back in time, he's showing me how to step outside of time and heal my past as well. Somehow the light that is now shining on my life isn't just illuminating my present and my future; it's also casting its rays backward, shedding light on my past. I can see the road I've traveled more clearly, each twist and turn, each rut, and pain now vividly illuminated. The mistakes I've made stand out, not to induce guilt but to clarify their true nature and intent in the narrative of my life.

Reflecting on my recent dip into the Snapchat sea, I recognize how I felt lost and lonely, desperately searching for companionship, a lifeline, really. Back then, I was exhausted and adrift. Now, when I peer into the realms of Snapchat, it resembles a stormy sea, more people than water, where everyone seems to be drowning, some already submerged, pulling others down with them.

This perspective shift reveals the double-edged sword of our digital age's interconnectedness. It is powerful and sharp, and if you're not careful and mindful of what you're seeking and doing, it can cut you down, stealing your time and thoughts, and spinning you into a whirlpool of destruction. However, if wielded with intention, it transforms into a tool of immense value. There's no bit of wisdom, scripture, philosophy, or science that can't be accessed in an instant. Just as one can dive into a sea of lost souls, it's equally possible to find like-minded ones who are in search of something more.

Over the past few days, fasting has been cropping up everywhere for me—in my reading, thoughts, even in the endless scrolls on Instagram, where I still occasionally find myself ensnared. Then, one night, around 2 a.m., my bladder rudely interrupts my sleep. After dealing with that, as I lay back down trying to reclaim the warmth of sleep, a little voice in my head murmurs, "You should do another fast. Give God a few days. You're dying to do something, dying for change. Do this; it will be good for your body, mind, and spirit."

"Why not?" I think to myself. I just completed one not too long ago with Paul. It was hardly a party, but it wasn't the worst experience either. And this one will be different; this time, it's just going to be me and Jesus.

So with that thought, my fast has begun. I'm not entirely sure what I'm hoping to find at the end of this—enlightenment, a new sense of purpose, or maybe just the ability to say no to a second slice of cake. Whatever it is, I'm on this path now, a path that promises nothing but demands quite a bit, guided only by the belief that sometimes, to find what you're really hungry for, you have to let yourself feel a little starvation.

CHAPTER 77 HUNGRY

The first morning of the fast would've been a breeze had I not developed quite the addiction to caffeine, and since I've decided to allow myself only water, it takes an agonizingly long time to sort of wake up. It's not long before the withdrawal headache starts to set in, throbbing at the temples like it's trying to hammer out Morse code.

Somehow, despite the grogginess and the pounding in my head, ideas are flowing through my brain like Niagara Falls—a torrent of revelations, one after another. Sometimes, amid this rush, I wonder if I'm just a little bipolar and this is what mania feels like. I don't know, but it's a strangely exhilarating feeling.

I think back to how I've been physically and mentally training for years, not sure what I was training for but I trained anyway, just knowing that having a sharp mind and body is best even if they're just used to homeschool and weed eat. But what if all along, God had been nudging me in a direction long before I even realized it? And my wakeup call with Chet was only the sounding bell for the next level.

It's almost as if all those years of preparation were not just random acts of health or boredom, but a prelude to something bigger, a foundation for whatever is coming next. As I navigate the fog of caffeine withdrawal and the clarity of fasting-induced insights, I can't help but think that maybe, just maybe, I'm on the verge of understanding something significant—not just about where I'm going, but why I've been brought here in the first place.

Something about being hungry and wanting that coffee—and then deliberately depriving myself—felt oddly satisfying. It was like being a little kid running laps around the playground, or meticulously cleaning my room just to stand back and ask God to take a look and see how good I'm doing. "Look, God, I'm here, ready to do anything, just say the word. I just wanna be put in the game, use me for something big."

Yes, I am aware that He is obviously using me for something; I'm not just idly sitting by. But again, my patience—or the lack thereof—is a bit of an issue. I'm eager to see things happening outside of my own head, in the tangible world where I can point and say, "See, something is indeed happening!"

At the same time, I'm realizing that the transformations happening inside my head are changing everything—past, present, and future. It's like rewiring an old house. Sure, the outside might look unchanged for a long time, but inside, the very ways in which power flows and lights flicker on and off are being fundamentally altered. And these internal changes, they're significant, even if they're invisible to everyone else. It's a profound realization that while I'm waiting for the external to catch up, the internal renovation is already well underway.

Working on my book just helps to shine a light on past events, like writing about my childhood and my sister, who, let's face it, definitely made some waves. But then I'm led to think, without that wild spirit of hers, who knows what we would've missed out on? My niece and nephews, knowing Jeremiah, and I think an experience that humbled the family in a way I'm not sure many other experiences could have. It was something to keep us all grounded.

Had I worked hard, gone to a good college, landed some

brilliant career, maybe I also would've had a giant ego and not been able to empathize with people. I also may have never had my girls. There are so many lessons and gifts I can now see from that incredibly rocky and difficult time.

It's strange how the act of writing it down, of sorting through the past like old photographs tucked away in a drawer, allows me to see the events not just as they happened, but in the context of their consequences.

And while I wouldn't say my head is clear from fasting on day one, my mind is definitely working at an unusually fast pace. So I keep writing. There are areas of my past that cry out for forgiveness, and I finally see that I need to forgive myself, perhaps even more than I need to forgive others. Starting with the rape in high school. I had always blamed myself for being naive and for somehow allowing it to happen.

But looking back, I also see how emotionally fragile I was leading up to that event, and I was just a kid. Through writing, through this intentional fasting and reflection, I'm finding a way to forgive myself, or maybe to let go of something that I should have never needed forgiveness for in the first place.

And as for Mark and Steven, who both hurt me in different ways, I think I'm beginning to see the part I played in both of those relationships, always trying to take on the job of fixing and saving. It was as though the only way anyone could ever love me was if I somehow rescued them. And maybe I did for a while. I saved them from themselves a little, helped work through problems, and made our own little lives. But in the end, I was trying to fix problems I had no ability to fix. Only God can heal some hurts, and the person with the hurt has to be willing to let Him fix it. I can't do that for them.

Mark had so many hurts and issues, and he did fight against them, but doing it alone, he would eventually tire out. He believed in Jesus, but I don't believe he ever fully figured out how to surrender his problems—not that I know anything for sure because that is really between him and God.

And with Steven, I think I did help him sort things out and gave him a good life with me, but in the end, he wasn't ready to have all of it. He didn't believe he deserved it or that he could handle what he now had with me and his kids, and he resented me for it. And then one day, that dam broke violently.

Reflecting on these experiences has brought a new level of understanding. I see now that my role as a rescuer was flawed from the start, more about my own need to be needed than about what was truly best for them. I was casting myself as the savior in my own story, trying to earn love through sacrifice and repair, without recognizing that some things, some people, just can't be fixed by human hands, only held by them.

My writing went so well the first day that I was starting to harbor grandiose dreams of finishing my book in days. Again with the patience—or the lack thereof—I know it's a real problem. Anyway, day 2 hit like a lead weight to the brain. I woke up so tired I didn't even feel like standing up, and the pounding in my head was now about 300 percent worse. "Ok, maybe today I give the writing and work a break, and I just survive," I thought. No TV, no scrolling on my phone for distraction, just me, my misery, and God.

So that's exactly what I did. I managed a very, very short workout, which did almost nothing because, well, it was almost nothing. I sort of felt like falling over every time I stood up. But I told myself and God, "Ok, obviously I'm not going to be able to move mountains today, but I'm here being obedient, and my ears are open."

Not much happened that day, but I did survive. It was one

of those days where the victory wasn't in the productivity or breakthroughs; it was simply in enduring, in staying the course despite feeling like a human version of a deflated balloon. Sometimes, that's all you can ask for—a day where you manage to keep the faith, hang on by a thread, and tell yourself that this too shall pass, and perhaps tomorrow, the words and energy will flow again.

Day 3 of the fast and I woke up feeling a bit like a spirit who had forgotten to take his body with him. Still dizzy, and the headache was stubbornly playing the encore. I'd been leafing through some books and trawling the depths of the internet, trying to figure out why this fast felt more like a slow crawl through a field of molasses. Turns out, it could be a lack of sodium. And good news—salt doesn't break a fast.

So, after tossing back some Celtic salt like it was tequila on spring break and downing some water, I started to feel more human and less like a deflated parade balloon. I even managed to squeeze in a workout and a little bit of writing, but not much else. It wasn't the burst of divine inspiration I'd fantasized about during my more optimistic moments, but it was progress.

I rounded off the day with a bowl of chili and a modest feeling of accomplishment. The chili was hearty, my body was less rebellious, and my spirit was, if not exactly soaring, at least clearing the treetops. It's remarkable how a bit of salt can turn you from a tragic figure back into an active participant in your own life. Not exactly the revelations and life-altering visions one might hope for from a fast, but I'll take the ability to stand upright without seeing stars as the universe's lesser-known form of mercy.

CHAPTER 78 SPRING TIME IN OKLAHOMA

It's springtime in Oklahoma, which means along with wildly unpredictable temperatures and a through-the-roof pollen count, we also get our fair share of extreme thunderstorm activity—thunder, lightning, hail, 80 mile-an-hour winds, and the occasional tornado just to keep things interesting. Earlier in the week, the weather prophets had started their chorus of doom, predicting that the weekend was going to be a real doozy.

So, it wasn't a huge surprise when I woke up at 3 a.m. to a wind that sounded like it was about to rip the roof right off. It died down quickly only to whip up again around 4 a.m., and then again at 5 a.m. By 5:30 a.m., I figured I might as well get up. If the house was going to get carried off to Oz, I might as well be awake for the ride.

I shuffled into the kitchen to make my morning concoction— a ginger, cinnamon, and cayenne cocktail. I followed that with a protein shake and started the coffee while I was at it. The storm outside matched the storm in my head, a cacophony of swirling thoughts and brewing ideas, punctuated by the occasional lightning strike of clarity.

Standing there, mixing my drinks while the wind howled like a chorus of disgruntled ghosts, I couldn't help but appreciate the metaphor. Life's been a bit like an Oklahoma spring lately —unpredictable, a little threatening, and filled with moments that take your breath away, not always in a good way.

Just about the time I'm adding a dash of cayenne to my morning concoction, the familiar howl of the tornado siren starts up, followed promptly by every phone in the house screaming to life with an emergency alert. Juuuuust great. I glance at my phone: tornado warning for Creek County. I'm momentarily transported back to a couple of years ago when I woke up to about 17 missed calls and the same cacophony of alarms because three tornadoes were headed straight for my house. Luckily, those missed me.

So, in a somewhat less than graceful scramble, I run down the hallway to gather the girls and get them all together in my closet, which is the innermost part of the house. They're all semi-awake, their phones also shrieking at them. "Sorry, girls, we're under a tornado warning. Come down to my room while I try and pull up some radar," I say, trying to keep the edge of panic out of my voice.

They all shuffle down and plop on my bed. Eh, close enough, I guess. Tornadoes aren't exactly silent, usually you can hear what sounds like a freight train barreling towards you. I know this from more than one experience I've had in my life with the buggers.

The wind is whipping like it's trying to audition for a lead role in "The Wizard of Oz," and I manage to pull up the local weather station's live stream on my phone. Well, it looks like we've got rotations all up and down the eastern part of the state, and yep, one is headed straight for us. After about 20 minutes, which felt more like a couple of lifetimes, the storm passes us. I tell the girls they can go back to bed, their faces a mix of sleepiness and adrenaline. "Well, guess they were right —it's gonna be a doozy," I say, mostly to myself. Friday wasn't even supposed to be that bad. It's Saturday night everyone has been freaking out over.

As I shuffle back to the kitchen to check on my abandoned ginger-cinnamon-cayenne cocktail, I think about how living in Oklahoma requires a peculiar blend of resignation and resilience.

We sail through Friday night with just a few small scattered storms, nothing to write home about here in Oklahoma, but elsewhere, the story unfolds differently. Up in Nebraska, an absolute monster wreaks havoc, the likes of which hadn't been seen since the big one in Moore back in 2013. Watching that 2013 tornado unfold on television was more than horrific; it was a visceral punch to the gut. A tornado so terrible and wide it utterly decimated a town, claiming lives and leaving a path of destruction that was hard to comprehend.

Later that afternoon, the surreal aftermath of the disaster manifested in a bizarre way: debris from that tornado rained down all over the eastern part of our state. I found pictures and baseball cards scattered in my backyard, over 100 miles away from where the tornado had touched down. Picking up a faded photograph from my lawn, a snapshot of strangers smiling for a moment forever gone, was an eerie reminder of the storm's ferocity.

In Oklahoma, we may be used to tornadoes, but we also know never to underestimate their potential. They can be capricious, unexpected, and unyieldingly destructive. The sight of remnants from someone else's life deposited in my backyard serves as a stark reminder of this power, a note from the universe that while we may predict and prepare, we are ultimately at the mercy of nature's whims.

By Saturday afternoon, the storms were firing up in a big way just west of us. Oddly, instead of moving east as they invariably do, they just sort of stalled out there, leaving a long line of storms across several states, all spawning tornadoes and strong rotations. Some areas found themselves under tornado warnings that lasted, off and on, for more than six hours. Travis Meyer, a local weatherman who is something of a patron saint of weather in these parts, was live, dissecting tornados and tornado warnings for well over 12 hours continuously by the time the night was over.

Feeling the onset of what I feared might be a cold, I took some NyQuil and managed to fall asleep around 9 p.m., as the storms still hadn't made their way to us. But at 11 p.m., I was jolted awake by the howling sirens and the incessant bleating of phone alarms. So, once again, I gathered the girls. This time, the threat was more immediate: we had rotations headed for us and one tornado already on the ground south of us and moving in our direction.

The attitude of someone native to Tornado Alley might be a bit perplexing for outsiders. Having lived through 44 years of weather here in Oklahoma, I've not only seen my fair share of carnage but also grown accustomed to the ever-present threat that looms over each day. Moreover, it's not just my experiences that shape this attitude; it's also the myriad harrowing tornado tales imparted by family and friends. Whatever I haven't witnessed with my own eyes, I've experienced through a hundred different firsthand stories.

Tornadoes, with their unpredictable nature, can materialize quickly, demolishing one house while skipping the next. Perhaps that's one of the reasons this area is also known as the Bible Belt—nothing nudges you closer to God faster than the ever-present awareness that any moment might be your last.

Living here, you develop a certain philosophy: if it's my time, it's my time. This doesn't mean you should be careless or stand out in the yard gawking at the sky, although you'll find plenty of Okies who do just that. But really, there's only so much you can do to stay safe without completely losing your mind. And let's face it, worry has never done much for anyone.

So now, with my girls lounging in my closet, eyes glued to their phones, I'm poised outside the closet door on my bed, watching the radar. The NyQuil is still in full effect, and while the threat of a tornado has my hackles up a bit, I'm mostly just irritated that I'm not snoozing in my warm bed right now. As has been its annoying habit all day, this storm is moving very, very slowly. Half of me just wants to leave the girls in my closet; they're lounging on a mattress and blankets, fairly comfy and as safe as I can make them at this point. So maybe I should just go to sleep and hope for the best. No, I can't do that. I'd have to go lay in the closet too because being a mom also means my life has more value than just being me, so I've got to keep me safe as well.

Now I'm just irritated, watching poor Travis Meyer trying to talk for what must be his ninth consecutive hour or something. "Yeah, they've got debris; it's definitely a tornado south of us and heading our direction." I mutter to myself, "Alright, God, we really don't need this, and I'm tired and over it, so could you just stop this stinking thing so I can go back to bed?" And yes, maybe this isn't my most empathetic and Christian moment, and my prayer could not be more selfish. I realize that later, of course—there are real people actually in the wake of that tornado right now.

But my toddler brain was again being a toddler. There I was, internally throwing a small fit because the universe wasn't aligning with my preferred schedule of events. Despite the seriousness of the situation, my immediate concerns revolved around sleep and the inconvenient timing of nature's fury. It's these moments that remind me that no matter how mature and composed we try to be, there's always a part of us that just wants to throw a blanket over our heads and wish away the storm.

Eliana pops her head around the closet door and gives me that look—the one that only she masters. Then she glances at the TV. "How long is this show anyway?" she asks, with an irritated gesture and a deadpan look back at me. I can't help but cackle out loud. Satisfied with the delivery of her joke, she plops back down in the closet and dives back into her game on her phone, a grin spreading across her face.

A few minutes later, while Travis Meyer is passionately detailing the 7 millionth rotation popping up somewhere in the viewing area, another voice cuts through the cacophony of storm chatter. "We've got something else happening now down by Beggs!" she announces. Oh, great—that's exactly where the tornado is that's headed our way. Travis Meyer shifts his attention immediately.

"It's another rotation but... yes, the National Weather Service just confirmed it's anticyclonic," the voice continues. Travis Meyer looks utterly dumbfounded. He does a double take. "Anticyclonic?" he echoes, his voice a mix of confusion and surprise. The voice repeats herself to confirm.

Now, Travis stands semi-frozen for a minute, his face a picture of bewilderment before he shakes his head. "Ok, well, that is highly unusual. I expect they will be calling off the tornado warning for that location soon then," he concludes, looking like he's been thrust into some bizarre dream. Regaining his composure, he moves on to the next threat on a screen that's absolutely blinking and screaming with them.

True to Trav's word, the tornado warning for our area lifted, and with the leading edge of the storm now past us, we're left with only the usual suspects of lightning, thunder, and torrential rain. I send the girls back to bed, and I climb into my own bed as well. Of course, once I lay down, my mind is wide awake and not at all ready to sleep. I start to wonder, What does anticyclonic mean, anyway? It's a term that, in all my 44 years, I've never heard—just as I've never seen tornado warnings that last so long. Curiosity getting the better of me, I decide to Google it.

According to the all-knowing internet, which I consult with the desperation of a man trying to assemble Ikea furniture without instructions, anticyclones are just rotations that spin clockwise here in the northern hemisphere, which is the opposite direction that a cyclone or tornado would spin. And they usually mean fair, nice weather. I don't see any instance of anticyclones occurring alongside regular ones, although I don't delve too deep into it because, let's face it, I'm sleepy and not a meteorologist. So my normal-person understanding will have to suffice for tonight.

Navigating through the explanations and diagrams with bleary eyes, I try to piece together a coherent understanding from fragments of scientific jargon, feeling a bit like I'm deciphering an ancient text rather than reading a weather explanation. I think about how this little bit of late-night research might just be another one of those unnecessary life skills, like knowing how to fold a fitted sheet or understanding the tax code.

So around 1 a.m., after digesting a modest helping of meteorological minutiae and feeling the first genuine yawns of the night tug at the corners of my mouth, I turn off my phone. The screen goes dark, and the room is suddenly silent but for the residual drumming of rain against the window—a natural lullaby in the wake of chaos. Not long after I drift off to sleep, my thoughts unspooling along with the calming patter of raindrops and the distant rumble of thunder, carrying away the last remnants of the evening's adrenaline and leaving in their wake a tranquil, if temporary, peace.

CHAPTER 79
ANTERIOR MID
CINGULATE CORTEX

The morning comes quickly, far too quickly for my taste. My 7:30 alarm goes off, and I really don't want to get up—it feels like I've just managed to close my eyes. I'm sure most of the state is still asleep after last night's meteorological theatrics. But I've recently committed to going back to church, and I'd need to leave in a little under two hours if I intend to make it on time.

I lay in bed negotiating with myself and maybe a bit with God for a few minutes. I doubt my parents will even be there—let's face it, with tornado warnings and sirens blaring well after midnight, everyone is likely still tucked in bed. And I could just watch the service online, from the comfort of my bed, wrapped in my comforter, which seems far more appealing at the moment.

After debating it a little longer, I decide to compromise: I'll get up and start my usual morning routine and then see how I feel. Maybe the act of getting moving will invigorate me, or perhaps it'll solidify my desire to attend church virtually today. Either way, I'm up now, and the day has begun, albeit reluctantly.

After my ginger-cayenne drink and protein shake, I move on to coffee, and my mind is still trying to weave its way out of going to church this morning. Something in me says, "You know how when you least want to work out, that's when you need it most? Church might be the same way. The days you least want to go might be the days you need to go most." Ugh, that has an annoying ring of truth.

Ok, so I go down the hallway to see if Eliana wants to wake up and go with me still. Sophia has to work, so she can't. Eliana, however, is passed smooth out and wakes up only enough to assure me that she will be getting her beauty rest today, which I understand and let her. I meander back to my room.

I text Bella, who spent the night with her grandparents, "You guys going to church this morning?" But after ten minutes and still no response, I'm assuming they are all still asleep and not going.

It looks like it's just me then, grappling with my own excuses and the echo of my earlier revelation.

I'm really struggling here. There is no rational reason why going to church alone should feel so terrifying and intimidating. I sit and reason it out: What's the worst that could happen? I have an emotional breakdown in a pew by myself—which, honestly, seems almost preferable to doing it in front of my family. So that's not it. Am I afraid that the church people will chase me out without the shield of my parents or children? I mean, if that happened, it would certainly be a story worth telling, and also not really that bad.

Still, I've got this tightness in my chest and my stomach is in knots. Something inside of me reminds me of the very big, very bold prayers I've been praying lately, asking God to use me in a big way and take my life and make it into something amazing for Him. And then a little voice inside me says, "If you can't even make yourself walk through the church doors alone, how are you going to be able to obey God when there's a lot more in play and the stakes feel much, much higher?"

And there it is again, that bell of truth dinging loudly in my ears. It's a jarring sound, not the gentle peal of a Sunday morning bell calling to the faithful, but a sharp clang, a clarion call that demands attention and action. It makes the decision for me. Fear or no fear, breakdown or not, story or no story, the next step seems clear, dictated not by comfort but by commitment.

And so I take my shower and get ready to face church alone. As my car pulls into town, there's almost no one out and about; everyone is still presumably asleep after last night's meteorological excitement. I make it to church and park in a lot that is usually full but not today. Feeling like a skydiver about to jump out of a plane, I exit my car and walk through the front door.

Navigating my way to a seat, I nervously smile and greet all the people waiting to welcome and chat on the way in, but I'm also hoping I don't have to actually stop and talk. I make it to my seat without too much pain. Okay, now all I have to do is make it through this service and back to my car—the hard part is over.

Again, I have the attitude of, "God, I hope you're watching this because I'm here doing this right now." It's an odd mix of defiance and devotion, a cocktail of nerves and faith. As I sit there, the church quieter than usual, the sense of individual presence is more pronounced.

Praise and worship feels a little different when it's just me on the row. My singing, usually lost in the chorus of congregational harmony, now feels starkly individual, like I'm giving a solo performance in an otherwise empty theater. It's just me and God, and my slightly off-key voice seems to carry more weight in the quiet. It's intimate, and honestly, not a bad thing.

Then the sermon starts, and true to form, God's got a surprise for me there too. The pastor begins speaking, and it's as if he's read the diary of my recent days, or has been eavesdropping on my prayers.

He begins by explaining that we are all called to be witnesses for Christ and that this is essentially our job here. Then he goes on to clarify what being a witness entails. We are not called to be judge or jury; we aren't attorneys here to argue legalities. We are witnesses. God wants us to share our testimony with the world. That's it. Let God do what God does, and then share that with other people.

My main struggle in life lately has been wondering if the writing of this book, the writing of my story, is something worthwhile. Could God actually use it, use me, or am I just being delusional? I've kept going, believing God can use even me to do great things, and even if His plan isn't to do something great with my book, that the writing of the book and of my story is allowing God to work on me in amazing ways.

But now here I sit on this church pew that I marched into almost at gunpoint, and the message is to tell my story. That's it. Tell my story and let God do the rest.

As the pastor's words sink in, they strike a chord, resonating with my own fears and aspirations. It's as if I've been circling around this very point without really seeing it, and now it's laid out clear as day. This isn't just about crafting a narrative or spinning a good yarn; it's about honesty, about vulnerability, about letting others see God's work in the mess and beauty of my own life.

Sitting there, I feel a mixture of relief and challenge. It's daunting to think that my story could mean something more, that it could touch someone else's life. Yet, there's also an incredible lightness in accepting that my part is simply to share, not to shape the outcome. The pressure shifts, the burden eases, and I find myself almost eager to put pen to paper again, not just to tell my story, but to see how God will use it, once I let it go.

And just like that, this message and this church service feel like another four-leaf clover I've just found to add to my frame. It's another reminder that God is indeed in charge and that as long as I'm walking with Him, I'm going to be better than good.

Made in the USA
Columbia, SC
01 October 2024

42741883R00190